10855100

LAND OF MOORS AND DALES

LAND OF MOORS AND DALES

Published by The Reader's Digest Association Limited

LONDON • NEW YORK • SYDNEY • MONTREAL

MOORS AND MONASTERIES, choral singing and cricket, brass bands and the Brontës, chalk cliffs and cheese-makers—the story of Yorkshire embraces all these elements and more. And who better to guide us through the many faces of this most beautiful region than that quintessential Yorkshireman, Fred Trueman?

Written in 1984, *Fred Trueman's Yorkshire*, the legendary cricketer's personal snapshot of the county he loves, is at once travelogue, history book and county diary.

Here, Trueman's work is reproduced in condensed form, though with none of his earthy Yorkshire wit and acute observation lost from the mix. His text is boosted by informative features that shed light on the area's history, local crafts, wildlife and more. Preceding *Fred Trueman's Yorkshire* is a specially commissioned introduction, and rounding things off is a helpful 'Highlights' section and map, pointing readers inspired to visit the region in the direction of its most outstanding sites and attractions.

LAND OF MOORS AND DALES was edited and designed by The Reader's Digest Association Limited, 11 Westferry Circus, Canary Wharf, London E14 4HE

Fred Trueman's Yorkshire Original full-length version by Fred Trueman and Don Mosey, first published in 1984 by Stanley Paul (now an imprint of Random House UK Ltd)
© Fred Trueman 1984
British condensed version © The Reader's Digest Association Limited, 1998
The author asserts the moral right to be identified as the author of this work.

© The Reader's Digest Association Limited, 1998, 1999. All rights reserved. No part of this book may be reproduced, stored in a retrieval system, or transmitted in any form or by any means, electronic or mechanical, photocopying, recording or otherwise, without prior permission in writing from the publishers.

® READER'S DIGEST, The Digest, and the Pegasus logo are registered trademarks of The Reader's Digest Association Inc. of Pleasantville, New York, USA.

CONTRIBUTORS

Series Editor Steve Savage

Volume Editor Elizabeth Tatham

Assistant Editor/Researcher Mark Lewis

Associate Editors David Blomfield, Hugo de Klee

Copy Editor Barbara Roby

Editorial and Administrative Assistant Rica Dearman

Art Editor Dilhan Attanayake

Designer Gary Evans

Picture Researchers Jane Lambert, Kay Rowley

Additional material by John Dyson, Mike Gerrard, James Harpur, Lawrence Joffe, John Kahn, Tim Locke, Keith Spence

Cartography Anthony Sidwell (page 9), Malcolm Porter (pages 136–7)

Index Brian Amos

FRONT COVER *Beneath a bruised sky, snakelike dry-stone walls curl sinuously across the untamed Farndale moors.*
BACK COVER (TOP) *Tapping into millennia-old skills, craftsmen slowly but unerringly sculpt a dry-stone wall from the Yorkshire landscape.*
BACK COVER (BOTTOM) *Castle Howard's lavish charms earnt it a starring role in the BBC's dramatisation of Brideshead Revisited.*
THIS PAGE *Tumbledown Whitby Abbey stands dramatically silhouetted against the sunset skyline of the Yorkshire coast.*

TITLE PAGE *The winds that whip across the North York Moors have left their mark on this heather-besieged marker stone signing the way from Blakey Ridge to Kirkbymoorside.*
PAGES 6–7 *Banks of daffodils add a splash of springtime yellow to the ochres and tans of picturesque Helmsley.*
PAGES 24–5 *A dot-to-dot of stone barns and homesteads stipples this grand Swaledale panorama.*
PAGES 134–5 *Viewed from street level, venerable York Minster represents a truly breathtaking sight— especially when it lies basking in mellow sunlight.*

CONTENTS

EXPLORING YORKSHIRE

with John Kahn

YORKSHIRE

with John Kahn

INCONSISTENT IN APPEARANCE, complex in personality, unpredictable in mood, sprawling Yorkshire scorns any simple portrait. It is a shambling giant of a place. Even the broadest and most time-honoured definition—'England's largest county'—misses the mark. Until 1974 there was a county of Yorkshire with one High Sheriff and York as the county town. Even then, however, the county was divided into three ridings (the word derives from the Old English *thriding*, which in turn came from an Old Norse word meaning a 'third'), each with its own county council. In the last few decades new boundaries have been drawn and redrawn, unitary authorities have taken over the reins of government in several areas, and now the only Yorkshire riding listed on official maps is the East Riding of Yorkshire.

Try thinking of Yorkshire in geographical terms, and you also run into trouble, for nature is no respecter of boundaries either. Each of the region's national parks straddles county borders. The Yorkshire Dales National Park in the northwest, for example, has one of its information centres at Sedbergh—well within Cumbria.

So, if Yorkshire is more than a matter of local government, and more than a matter of geography, what makes it so distinctive? What gives it such a strong identity? In short, what makes Yorkshire Yorkshire?

THE ESSENCE OF YORKSHIRE

Perhaps it is better to think of Yorkshire not as a place, but as a state of mind, as an attitude—even as an adjective.

'You can't get much more Yorkshire than that,' exclaims Fred Trueman at one point in the book that follows, and the place clearly does have an identifiable spirit, or character. You can always tell a Yorkshireman, goes the saying (though you can't tell him much, it continues).

It's Yorkshire to be economic, not just with your 'brass' but with your words as well—'nowt said needs no mending'—yet to be no-nonsense and blunt when speaking is called for. It's Yorkshire to be doggedly and enduringly stubborn. It's Yorkshire to be gruff and impatient, yet extremely kind (if ashamed to admit it).

And to be unashamedly proud of the region's sportsmen, its music-making, its dialects, its cooking and its beer—that's Yorkshire, too.

'You mustn't believe all these stereotypes,' warned a laconic Dalesman. 'They're all true, you see.' Oh, and it's Yorkshire to have a very dry sense of humour.

If these characterisations are at all accurate, and there really is such a thing as a typical Yorkshire personality, then it has probably been formed over the years, shaped by the region's traditional way of life, and the physical environment that sustained it. Only 'hard graft' earned a living here—toiling down the mines or 'up at mill', herding sheep on wintry hillsides, quarrying tons of stones and painstakingly hand-building miles of dry-stone boundary walls, or fishing from open sailing cobles on the stormy North Sea.

ABOVE *A silver-grey water hole and some vivid patches of purple heather add blushes of colour to this exposed moors landscape; find a sprig of white heather amid the purple, so they say, and good luck will be yours.*

The place itself is almost a country within a country—a land of wide-open moors, sheltered dales and grassy meadows where you'll find mountainous landscapes and intimate, picturesque valleys, great cities born of industry, and villages whose charms have survived the test of time.

A PLACE IN HISTORY

Although the city of York acted as England's administrative capital on several occasions between 1298 and 1392, violence and strife have proved commoner punctuations to the story of Yorkshire than the exercise of power. When the Norman invaders reached York in the 11th century, they marched where Romans, Saxons and Vikings had gone before. Provoked by local resistance in 1068–9, the new rulers devastated the Vale of York with cold-blooded thoroughness—a prototype scorched-earth policy referred to as the 'harrying of the North'—and civil peace remained fragile through the next six centuries. In 1190 the Jews of York lost their lives in a riot; Scottish invasions followed the 1314 Battle of Bannockburn; and a dynastic struggle for possession of the English Crown, fought between the supporters of the houses of York and Lancaster, raged during the 15th century. Subsequently named the Wars of the Roses, this conflict involved many Yorkshire families and included two significant battles in Yorkshire itself—Wakefield (in 1460) and

Towton (in 1461). The Tudor era that followed brought its own unrest: the ill-starred northern rebellion of the 1530s against Henry VIII's Dissolution of the Monasteries, known as the Pilgrimage of Grace; and the rising of the northern earls in 1569–70, unsuccessfully opposing the Reformation. Although many parts of the county became Puritan strongholds, the Civil War of 1642–9 caused divisions in Yorkshire as elsewhere. The city of Hull's decision to close its gates against the King, in 1642, is viewed by many as the start of the Civil War, and a decisive battle was fought on Marston Moor, not far from York, in 1644.

Naturally, these conflicts impinged upon trade and development, and there were times of recession. Nevertheless, the county's merchants and tradespeople prospered intermittently, and the 16th and 17th centuries saw the development of craft-based industries, particularly in the West Riding, where opportunities arose because the towns and manorial estates were less restrictively regulated than elsewhere in Yorkshire. Two examples of such industries were cutlery in Sheffield and Halifax's cloth trade. Textiles and other industries developed dramatically in the 18th century, as the Industrial Revolution took hold. The 19th century brought astonishing demographic changes, and by the middle of that century ancient York had been overtaken, in terms of population, by upstarts like Leeds and Bradford. New forms of rebellion emerged: the Luddites broke the machines that put people

ABOVE *The majesty of Yorkshire: a backpack, waterproofs, hiking boots and a keen sense of humility are important companions on a trip to this most breathtakingly beautiful of regions.*

TOP RIGHT *Liberated from the incessant rumble of car engines, these hardy mountain-bikers are able to revel in the peace and silence of the wilds of Yorkshire.*

out of work; and groups like the coal miners began trying to form unions. This traditional combination of enterprise and rebelliousness is part of Yorkshire's heritage, and no bad heritage to build on, as old industries decline and new ways of working emerge.

GETTING YOUR BEARINGS

Yorkshire is shaped rather like a diamond, and I find it helpful to visualise the county as though it were divided into four triangular segments. Where they all meet stands the city of York, once so dominant that the entire surrounding shire was named after it. The Pennines—a range of hills often called 'the backbone of England'—run down the western side of Yorkshire and stretch across the two left-hand segments. In the lower of these, we find the region's industrial heartland—notably Leeds, Bradford and Sheffield—and the upper skirts of the Peak District; while the hilly top-left segment is roughly the area covered by the Yorkshire Dales. One other major upland area, quite unconnected with the Pennines, lies in the top-right segment: the North York Moors. And one other minor upland area—the Yorkshire Wolds—lies between the top-right and bottom-right segments. The rest of the region is low-lying: the long, wide strip down the middle, including the Vale of York, and almost all the bottom-right segment: the hinterland of the North Sea coast and Humber Estuary. In that sector lies the port city of Kingston upon Hull, usually known as plain old Hull.

Each area has its charms—some more than others, it must be said. If the vast majority of Yorkshire residents live in the southern two segments, the vast majority of Yorkshire's tourists make for the northern two, and for venerable York itself.

The natural beauties of the Moors and Dales cast a spell over visitors, luring them back time and again to explore by bus or bicycle, on horseback or by rail; by car, of course, and, above all, on foot. The network of walking trails and bridlepaths far outstrips that of roadways in length and complexity.

With only a weekend to spend in Yorkshire, you could concentrate on the Dales without going far wrong. But if you have a week to explore the area, there are many other places worth visiting. If I had six days to spend on a whirlwind tour, here is what I would do, although I am all too conscious that I can merely hope to scratch the surface of this extraordinary region. As you can see, I would start in York.

A WALK AROUND YORK

If you are looking for a place with real old-world charm, York must rank very high. As you pass through one of the great stone gates in its medieval city wall, the sense of history is almost palpable. York dates back to AD 71 when, as Eboracum, it was founded by the Romans. It far exceeds larger cities such as Leeds and Sheffield in historical importance, having served as royal court and administrative capital, and as an economic and ecclesiastical centre, in the course of its long history.

York's compactness is a bonus: a leisurely stroll through the old town takes you past many fascinating sites and scenes. Much of the city's colourful history is recorded or even reconstructed in its cornucopia of museums, displays, plaques, heritage centres and exhibitions: among them the Archaeological Resource Centre, Yorkshire Museum, York Story, the Jorvik Viking Centre, even the celebrated National Railway Museum, just behind the station. Best of all, perhaps, is the award-winning Castle Museum, an Aladdin's cave of interest and information, and definitely worth including in any walking tour.

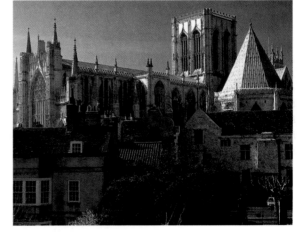

BELOW Like a benign giant, venerable York Minster towers over the rooftops of the historic northern city of York; though known universally as the Minster, its real name is the Cathedral and Metropolitical Church of St Peter in York.

You might start your walk outside the old city walls and on the banks of the Ouse, in the Museum Gardens—a ten-acre botanical park with three distinct sets of ruins. Or you could head straight for York Minster. Cleaned and repaired in recent years (after the fire of 1984—the latest of several disasters over the centuries), it stakes a convincing claim to be the most beautiful medieval cathedral in all England. Certainly it is the largest: 519 feet in length, with a central roof 197 feet high. Its construction took some two hundred and fifty years, from about 1220 to 1470, with intermittent alterations and extensions, and, while it may exude a seamless unity, it actually displays three distinct Gothic styles. Highlights include famous stained-glass windows such as the Great East Window, similar in size to a tennis court; the nave's breathtaking 15th-century screen; and exquisite carvings in the chapter house and its vestibule.

Don't tarry all day in the Minster, though—there's much more to see in York. Just south of it is a hive of ancient alleys, interspersed with elegant 18th-century

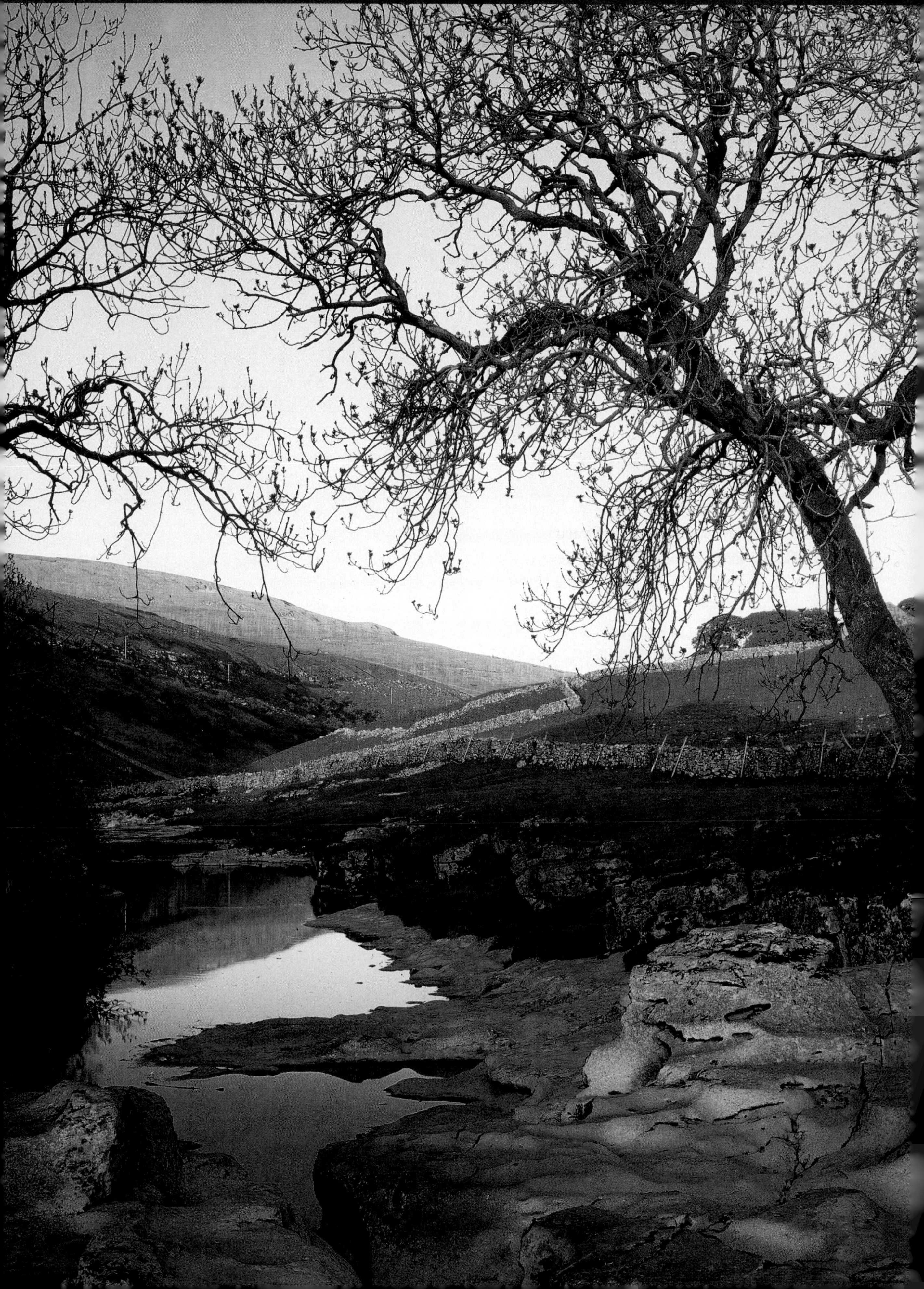

squares. You could stop first at Holy Trinity Church, rejoicing in a fine stained glass window that depicts St George slaying the dragon. Then, continuing south, you'll come across York's most famous street, the Shambles—so narrow that the roofs of its teetering Tudor houses seem almost to touch each other; hooks hanging above windows betray the street's origin, as a butchers' market.

Beyond the Shambles is the splendid medieval guildhall known as the Merchant Adventurers' Hall; and Fairfax House, a magnificently restored Georgian town house. Stroll on to Clifford's Tower, the 13th-century keep of the now-ruined York Castle, built by Henry III. The mound on which it stands was the site of the Normans' original wooden tower guarding the Ouse. From the top of the tower you can look back over your route, before moving on to the promised last stop, the Castle Museum, housed in the old prison building. Be warned: it is far larger than it looks, and you might end up covering the same distance inside as you did when walking to it. The museum concentrates on everyday Yorkshire life through the last 500 years. Its basis was the collection of household objects amassed by a Pickering doctor in the early 1900s on his daily rounds: old cooking equipment, craft tools and biscuit tins all feature. Prepare yourself for a nostalgic trip; it's quite possible that you might spot a vacuum cleaner or wireless familiar from your childhood. Extraordinarily lifelike reconstructions of Victorian and Edwardian street scenes take you even further back in time—cobblestones, gutters, lanterns, shop fronts and background noise, perfect in every detail.

Not that current-day York is in any way lacking in character. Ramble through its antique alleyways, and you'll feel as if you've wandered into a bygone age.

THE SPLENDOUR OF THE DALES

Our second day-trip takes us northwest to the Yorkshire Dales and into an area of stunning natural beauty. Here there is scenery indeed. Tourists from around the world are drawn by the varied beauty of the Dales and the characterful villages nestling in their valleys. Awaiting them are windswept fells; steep hayfields filled with wild flowers and bordered by stone walls; cottages and farmhouses seemingly as old as the rock itself. Viewed from on high, the terrain might resemble a green, crumpled parchment: five or six main furrows—narrow and steep-sided Swaledale, broad Wensleydale, long and sinuous Wharfedale, and so on—intersected by numerous lesser wrinkles, with evocative names like Langstrothdale and Arkengarthdale. (The dale in each case is a deep river valley, covered no longer with ancient forests but with farms of sheep and cattle, and dotted with old stone barns and stone villages.)

This abundance of varied rivers and valleys produces a ravishing counterpoint of the harsh and the lyrical: giant caves and crags in the southerly reaches—as at Ingleton, Kilnsey and Malham Cove—glower upon the kindly undulating hills in the east. There is a repeated rise-and-fall pattern, as weathered peaks and exposed fells descend through patchworks of sloping meadows to lush and restful lower valleys.

Not always restful, mind you. This is cascade country, too. Rivers and becks descend steeply and often unevenly from their high Pennine sources. For long

OPPOSITE Green buds sprouting from this overhanging tree in Langstrothdale herald the return of spring.

stretches, water tumbles rather than flows, especially along the rivers Swale and Ure; and at glacier-cut gorges and limestone ravines, dramatic waterfalls result. For all that, the abiding impression is less of rushing torrents and chasms than of amiable, gurgling brooks, fringed with wild flowers and crossed by ancient hump-back bridges of mossy stone.

If I had just one day in this wonderland, I would start by making my way to Ribblehead, out to the west. Three great scenic walking trails converge in the vicinity: the Ribble Way, the Dales Way, and most famous of all, the Pennine Way, snaking north from the Peak District in Derbyshire, right up to the Scottish border. The backdrop to my trip would be Yorkshire's famous Three Peaks, each rising boldly to approaching 2,500 feet: Whernside, Ingleborough and Pen-y-Ghent.

At Ribblehead itself is the spectacular twenty-four-arch viaduct of the Settle–Carlisle Railway. Over into the next dale now, to the Wensleydale town of Hawes, some ten miles northeast. If time allows or weather compels, you can visit the Dales Countryside Museum in Hawes, which illustrates traditional crafts and ways of life. Or you could drop in at the local ropemakers' craft centre, or visit the Wensleydale Creamery to watch the famous local cheese being made. The outdoors will beckon again soon enough, though.

Except during a long dry spell (not impossible, despite the region's rainy reputation), the Dales waterfalls are a dramatic delight. Taking the path behind Hardraw's Green Dragon Inn, you soon reach the natural rock amphitheatre containing thunderous Hardraw Force ('force' here being from an old Viking word for waterfall)—the highest unbroken above-ground falls in England, boasting a drop of some ninety-six feet from its projecting limestone lip. Marvellous! Another waterfall, Cotter Force, clamours just a mile or two away, but you might do better to visit the contrasting falls at Aysgarth. (Take the side road to get there, and you pass through the village of Askrigg, the 'Darrowby' of the much-loved television series *All Creatures Great and Small*.) At Aysgarth, a gentle riverside walk leads you along the River Ure as it rushes over several long ledges through its tree-lined gorge.

From here other sites are tantalisingly close, but that is probably as much you can do justice to in one day's exploring. No matter: you will return. The Dales have you in thrall.

YORKSHIRE'S LOW COUNTRY

Our third day-trip would explore the central lowlands, north of York and Leeds. And I rather think I'd begin at Harewood House. A regal 18th-century mansion set in grounds shaped by Capability Brown, the house has magnificent Robert Adam interiors, Chippendale furniture, a famous porcelain exhibition and a fine collection of paintings by the old masters. The spectacular Gallery, its inner wall covered with paintings, stretches the entire seventy-six-foot length of the house's west side.

But on a sunny day, the views from its windows may soon lure you outdoors. The restored rear terrace overlooks an elaborate formal garden, beyond which, in striking contrast, stretch fields of livestock and 1,000 acres of parkland. A Victorian-style pleasure boat plies the sparkling lake, and a series of specialised gardens and features beckon, among them a woodland garden, an artificial waterfall, a penguin pond and the famous bird garden. And if you are visiting Harewood in the late spring, its 100 species of rhododendron will overwhelm you.

The floral theme continues as you drive north into the vicinity of Harrogate (England's Floral District, some call it), reposing contentedly in the Vale of York. Harrogate itself contains such an expanse of parks and public gardens that its buildings seem almost an afterthought, especially now that their celebrated elegance is growing slightly faded. As a spa town and health resort, Harrogate enjoyed a long lease of life, from Shakespeare's time through to its Victorian heyday and beyond. But those days are gone. The source of its prosperity—a natural abundance of mineral springs—is no longer valued. The proud Victorian edifices have come down in the world: the Royal Baths and Assembly Rooms are now used as Turkish baths and exhibition halls; the Royal Pump Room, site of Europe's strongest sulphur well, has become the Royal Pump Room Museum. And the grand hotels are filled with conference visitors and craft-fair exhibitors rather than genteel hypochondriacs on a rest cure. The giant international conference centre that now stands on the edge of the Victorian district symbolises the town's uneasy transition to modern realities.

ABOVE *Harewood House has been owned by the Lascelles family for over two centuries. The foundation stone was laid in January 1759 and the building was then funded through the family involvement in Barbados sugar plantations.*

But the antique stores and teashops flourish. Rather than 'taking the waters', you can pay homage to a newer Harrogate tradition by taking tea—specifically at Betty's, the famous tearoom founded in 1919 by a Swiss pastry-chef. And the Valley Gardens still present their dazzling blend of formal and informal flower displays. If only all towns could boast such an inner-city idyll! The serious horticulturist will want to make a supplementary expedition to the nearby Harlow Carr Botanical Gardens—sixty-eight acres of landscaped paradise, complete with stream and tarn, woodland trails and a gardening museum.

Next stop: Knaresborough, just a few miles to the northeast. This quaint old market town is a maze of unspoilt alleys, with a ruined castle and England's oldest chemist's shop, dating back to 1720. But its particular glory is its location, right on the edge of the limestone gorge of the Nidd. If your first sight of this ravine is from a train window, as mine was long ago, it'll stay with you for ever. The ground seems to give way as the train from Harrogate rattles onto the stone viaduct straddling the river. For a moment you look upon emptiness, before lowering your gaze and staring spellbound at the chasm stretching away on either side. Just as suddenly the view is cut off, when the train reaches the far bank and draws into Knaresborough station.

ABOVE *Autumn leaves litter the Temple of Fame, one of a medley of charming follies within bucolic Studley Royal gardens.*

TOP *Post-Dissolution, Fountains Abbey sank into disrepair; its stones were used in the 17th-century construction of nearby Fountains Hall.*

After exploring the old town, you can clamber down into the gorge. The railway viaduct, built in 1851, towers magnificently overhead. Picturesque riverside walks extend for miles in either direction, passing such curiosities as The Chapel of Our Lady in the Crag and St Robert's Cave, an ancient hermitage and the third oldest shrine in England. Across the river is Mother Shipton's Petrifying Well, in which porous objects quickly acquire a mineral coating that seems to turn them to stone; and Mother Shipton's Cave, birthplace of the legendary Tudor prophetess.

A dozen or so miles to the northwest lies the highlight of the day: Fountains Abbey. Situated within the only UNESCO World Heritage Site in Yorkshire, it constitutes the fullest ruins of a medieval abbey house in Britain. The unadorned and austere architecture of the abbey matches well the simple and strict life promoted by the Cistercian monks who founded it in the 12th century. For over four hundred years, until Henry VIII ordered the Dissolution of the Monasteries, generations of monks and lay brothers extended and enriched the abbey's estates, first through wool production and later through dairy-farming.

After the abbey's closure in 1539, the buildings fell into private ownership. In 1768 they passed into the hands of one William Aislabie, owner of the adjoining Studley estate, who ingeniously incorporated the ruins—regarding them as a kind of ready-made Gothic folly, it seems—into the designs of his landscaped grounds, with tranquil ponds, temples, statues and deer park that can be visited today.

If you still have the stamina, there are attractions aplenty in the vicinity.

To the west, Brimham Rocks, a group of otherworldly weather-carved limestone outcrops, with a lordly view over Nidderdale. To east and south, Newby Hall and Ripley Castle, respectively—two highly contrasting houses with very different gardens. To the northeast, the city of Ripon, with its fine 12th-century cathedral, constructed over a Saxon crypt. But don't overdo things. Garner your energy for tomorrow's day-trip—the Moors!

THE MOORS AND THE COAST

Yorkshire's northeast corner resembles its northwest one in that it is rural and remote, and is conserved as a National Park. What's more, many of the valleys in the North York Moors, such as Rosedale and Farndale, are distinctly reminiscent of the Dales—richly pastured on the valley floor, dry-stone-walled on the slopes, and teeming with sheep. But there are marked differences, too. If the Dales seem to consist mainly of valleys divided by fells or ridges, the Moors seem to consist mainly of fells scored by occasional valleys. The Moors scenery is often more austere: a vast treeless plateau is crisscrossed by Roman roads and paths for monks and miners, but is otherwise featureless, save for the occasional Bronze Age burial mound, mining relic or medieval stone cross. And there are endless expanses of heather—a sea of purple in the early summer, but otherwise bleak and uninspiring. Yet for many visitors, hiking along the upland stretches of the various trails, this emptiness is precisely the appeal of the place. The unimpeded horizons, beneath the vaulting sky, inspire an uplifting sense of release.

Today's suggested itinerary covers a richer array of landscapes. A convenient starting point is ancient Pickering, source of the North Yorkshire Moors Railway. On this restored Victorian line, a steam train puffs along a captivating eighteen-mile route—one of the steepest in England—to Grosmont and back, passing through Pickering Castle deer park and the spectacular Newton Dale gorge. Take a walk at either end of the line, or at one of the stations in between—Levisham Station or Newton Dale Halt, perhaps—or else leave the train at Goathland (setting for the television series *Heartbeat*), and follow some of the woodland and moorland trails from there. Inspect Wade's Causeway, for example, the best-preserved stretch of Roman road in Britain.

Our next destination, Whitby, lies just a few miles from Grosmont station. No wonder Bram Stoker chose this dramatic cliffside town as the landing point for Count Dracula! Looking appropriately eerie in twilight or poor weather, the brooding ruins of Whitby Abbey loom over the port from a windswept clifftop. From the adjacent graveyard, and quaintly furnished St Mary's Church, a flight of 199 steps descends to the east side of town.

Whitby itself is full of reminders of its whaling and seafaring past. Twin stone piers still form a narrow entrance to the harbour. The fish docks still await the day's catch, although nowadays it is much reduced in quantity. The Captain Cook Memorial Museum commemorates the explorer Captain James Cook, who spent three years based here in the 1740s. And on a plinth above the town stands a striking memento—the huge jawbone of a whale. Other picturesque elements lend further texture: pier and cobbled alleys, fine Georgian houses, and the old swing bridge over the River Esk that bisects the town.

A few miles down the coast lies Robin Hood's Bay—both the fishing village and the bay of that name. The origin of the name may be a mystery, but there is no doubting the bay's underlying air of romance. This stretch of coastline developed a proud tradition of smuggling during the 18th century. The structure of the village itself—red-roofed houses snuggling tightly together in their cliffside cleft—must have foiled the excisemen often enough. To make things even harder for them tunnels, in which contraband could be conveyed or concealed, ran beneath some of the houses.

At Boggle Hole, a small stream has cut a gully into the cliffs, convenient for a scramble down to the sea and a walk across the rocks at low tide to Stoupe Beck Sands. Collect a fossil or two on your way as a souvenir. The coast offers sweeping views, such as that from the rugged Old Peak headland of Ravenscar, looking towards Robin Hood's Bay village. And to the north there are quaint hamlets and fishing villages above Whitby, such as Runswick Bay and Staithes. If you want a change of mood, head south instead, to Scarborough and Filey—holiday resorts with miles of sandy beaches. But it might be better to keep them for another visit, rather than break the spell of a day in the Moors.

THE SOUTHEAST OF YORKSHIRE

Now for the fifth day-trip—to the southeast section of Yorkshire. Heading south, down the coast from Filey, you detour eastwards along the Flamborough peninsula. The chalk cliffs near Bempton are the highest in Britain—400 feet at some points—and extend for some four miles. The RSPB reserve here stages a sea bird 'carnival' each summer, with the competing shrieks and acrobatics of guillemots, kittiwakes, puffins and gannets. Beyond lies the promontory, Flamborough Head, with its wave-sculpted caves and rock formations.

From Bridlington, just south of the Head, the Holderness coastline sweeps smoothly down for about forty miles—virtually one long beach, backed by crumbling clay cliffs—to Spurn Head, a long, narrow, shifting spit of sand and shingle, curving into the racing tides of the Humber Estuary. But you could also head inland into the Yorkshire Wolds, the rolling chalk ridge that stretches towards York. Here there is good walking country. To the south, you will find magnificent Beverley Minster, built between the 13th and 15th centuries, much as the one at York was. You will marvel at its graceful twin towers, and the exquisite carved figures between them, framing the west door. Among the other treasures to admire are a stone seat dating from Anglo-Saxon times and the ornate Percy Tomb.

And so to Hull at last, on the Humber Estuary—the largest estuary in England. It is sobering to think that this bustling port city, servicing oil tankers, international ferries, cargo ships and fishing fleets, began life as a remote and quiet Cistercian monastic settlement. One particularly impressive memento of those distant medieval times is 14th-century Holy Trinity, one of Britain's largest parish churches. Of the several fine museums in Hull, oldest and most famous is Wilberforce House,

ABOVE *Dazzling white gannets tend to nest in large colonies, on seaside ledges; chicks remain in the nest for two to three months before plunging into the sea and swimming off to fend for themselves.*

a venerable brick-built merchant's mansion in the middle of the old town, birthplace of William Wilberforce and a memorial to him. Displays recall the horror of slavery in the 18th and 19th centuries, and Wilberforce's heroic struggle to abolish it.

Just to the west of the city stretches a modern landmark—the Humber Bridge. Completed in 1980, the suspension bridge boasts a total anchorage-to-anchorage span of 7,284 feet, substantially more than a mile. Its twin towers are 510 feet high, and the suspension cables twenty-seven inches thick.

ABOVE *Some nine years in the making, the Humber Bridge is remarkable for the fact that its towers are made from reinforced concrete rather than steel.*

POST-INDUSTRIAL BRADFORD

I would spend the last day of my Yorkshire trip exploring the industrial towns and cities of southwest Yorkshire. This region also includes the elevated village of Haworth, lifelong home of the Brontë sisters, and now virtually a shrine to them. Lovingly converted into the Brontë Parsonage Museum, the house they occupied overlooks the church where their father was curate. Enjoy the museum, with its poignant memorabilia such as the sofa on which Emily died, and Anne's childhood collection of seaside pebbles. Then, for a further impression of the life led here by the brilliant Brontës, take a walk across the blustery moor beyond the village, and see the same expansive views they did.

Next, head down towards contrasting Bradford. The southwest of Yorkshire, despite a handsome Pennine setting, is dominated by the image of 'dark satanic mills': steelworks, coal mines, textile factories. As for Bradford itself, it came to prominence partly as a colliery, but mainly as a wool centre—in common with many Yorkshire towns. As early as the 14th century, it was active in the wool trade, and in the early 19th century it became the country's leading manufacturer of worsted. At its peak, it boasted more than fifty worsted mills, a cluster of dye-works and hundreds of warehouses. Here the full force of the Industrial Revolution left its mark on both people and place: if its effect upon the population of the time was often devastating, then at least the architectural legacy it left in its wake would prove a treasure trove for later generations. The wool barons' architects unashamedly imitated classical designs from Europe. The great Wool Exchange, which at one time handled a hefty percentage of Britain's wool trading, resembles the great cloth halls of Flanders. St George's Hall, a concert hall opened in 1853, resembles a Greek temple. Mill chimneys impersonated Venetian bell towers. The City Hall, its 220-foot-high clock tower crowned by a golden dolphin, is reputedly modelled on the Palazzo Vecchio, the town hall of Florence.

Once blackened by soot from the coal that powered the Industrial Revolution, these grand honey-coloured buildings have now been washed clean. They serve as apt emblems of the renewed business confidence and civic pride that have followed Bradford's valiant emergence from devastating industrial decline. Not that prosperity has suddenly replaced dereliction throughout the town. But you should at least sense the hopeful spirit of renewal as you stroll about the city centre and the 'Little Germany' district—the quarter developed by 19th-century German textile merchants (among them, the father of the Bradford-born composer Frederick Delius).

To the northwest of the city is Saltaire, where, in the 1850s, the industrialist Titus Salt built a showpiece mill, complete with mill workers' village. The front wing of the enormous mill is open to the public, now transformed into a multistorey mall of designer stores and a gallery dedicated to Bradford-born painter, David Hockney.

For all its pride in its Victorian past, Bradford is very much a city of the present, progressive and go-getting, exuberantly multicultural, crackling with energy. One modern feature that you really should try to see, particularly after its refurbishment in 1997–8, is the National Museum of Photography, Film and Television. Brilliantly

RIGHT *Yorkshire's multicultural melting pot conjures some arresting images, none more so than this carnival float taking part in the annual Bradford Festival.*

inventive, audiovisual, hands-on, it is one of the country's most visited museums outside London—and deservedly so. It symbolises, in several ways, the new face of Yorkshire: forward-looking and outward-looking.

A CORNUCOPIA OF ATTRACTIONS

Our six days have flown by. Yorkshire is a Cleopatra: 'she makes hungry where most she satisfies'. No matter how often you return, custom cannot stale the region's variety. Many of the highlights covered in these trips are matched or even surpassed by counterparts elsewhere.

If you were bewitched by the cascades of Wensleydale, try those of Swaledale to the north, near Keld, or those more to the southwest, around Ingleton. If you enjoyed the elegance of Harewood House and its gardens, you will want to visit the comparably lavish Castle Howard, star of the television series *Brideshead Revisited*. If you found York and Beverley minsters breathtaking, seek out some of their contemporaries—Ripon Cathedral, perhaps, or Wakefield, with its 247-foot spire, Yorkshire's tallest. If Bolton Castle stirred your imagination, there are castles at Richmond and Skipton, for instance, with attractive surroundings. And if your ramble through the ruins of Fountains Abbey and Studley Royal was a particular favourite, head for the romantic ruins of Rievaulx Abbey and its adjacent Terrace.

The region caters for many different tastes. Hence its appeal to such a catholic range of visitors. For birdwatchers, the often-overlooked southeast segment of Yorkshire comes into its own: apart from its reserve at Bempton Cliffs, the RSPB has sanctuaries at Hornsea Mere and Blacktoft Sands. For amateur archaeologists, there are several scattered sites of prehistoric standing stones, and numerous excavations from Roman times. In the village of Aldborough, for instance, you will find the extensive remains of a Roman town, including two mosaic pavements, while not far away stand three eerie prehistoric stone pillars—the famous Devil's Arrows, some twenty feet high and several millennia old. For theatre-lovers, the West Yorkshire Playhouse in Leeds and the Stephen Joseph Theatre in Scarborough (where Alan Ayckbourn premieres most of his own plays) are virtually places of pilgrimage, being widely cited as two of the most exciting provincial theatres in the country. For garden-lovers, and sports-lovers, and ramblers…the region offers an embarrassment of riches, all there for the taking.

INTRODUCING FRED TRUEMAN'S YORKSHIRE

But before you go, read the impressions of an insider—one of the great representatives of Yorkshire, and a considerable expert! Fred Trueman's zest for cricket, both as fearsome fast bowler and, subsequently, as commentator, is if anything excelled by his zest for his birthplace. He not only loves it and celebrates it—he typifies it. The book you are about to read is an abridgement of *Fred Trueman's Yorkshire*, his classic portrait dating from 1984, and in its pages this great Yorkshire personality has evoked the spell of the region with all the vividness of a real visit.

FRED TRUEMAN'S
YORKSHIRE

A condensation of the book by Fred Trueman and Don Mosey

CHAPTER ONE

THE NORTHERN DALES

ABOVE *The author, Fred Trueman, OBE, commentates on a Test match for BBC Radio. When his playing days came to an end in 1968, Trueman retained his passion for the game, forging a new career as a broadcaster and newspaper journalist.*

THERE ARE 'DALES' ALL OVER YORKSHIRE, in the northeast—Rye Dale, Farndale, Rosedale—and a little to the west, where streams cut deep into the Cleveland Hills, but it is in the extreme west, in the High Pennines, that the real Yorkshire Dales, as most of us know and accept them as a geographical area, begin. To my mind, five dales stand out. From north to south they read Swaledale, Wensleydale, Nidderdale, Wharfedale and Airedale. These five dales all have their own tale to tell and we shall look at each of them in turn. If favouritism filters through my travels in Wharfedale it is because it was there that my love affair with the Yorkshire Dales first began.

My knowledge of Yorkshire, as a young man, was largely confined to that part of the extreme south of the county where I was born, and the towns or cities where first-class cricket was played. The Dales were simply a mysterious area far away to the northwest, which I had vaguely heard of but never seen. Then I was called to a practice match in Settle, far away on the main road that took Yorkshire families to summer holidays in Morecambe or the Lake District. From the east coast, where my journey began, I took the most direct route according to the map (no motorways then) and found myself climbing over craggy hills and dropping down into one valley after another, until at length I topped just one more summit. Here I stopped, my breath caught by the beauty of the panoramic view. I had climbed past the workings of the old lead mines on Greenhow Hill out of Nidderdale, and now I was looking down on Wharfedale for the first time. There and then I promised myself that somehow I would have a home there, one day. It took twenty years for that day to arrive, but I finally achieved it and, since 1970, once in my home, I have been able to let the world pass me by.

Here, between still-rural Airedale and the limestone splendour of Wharfedale, is parkland that was at its noblest when the fine houses were the homes of families who had been there for centuries (the Currers, Wilsons, Hammertons, Carrs). Other residences were built in Victorian times with the new wealth accumulated in the mills of Airedale. The houses are now mostly private schools or homes for the elderly. Some have disappeared altogether, although their fine, dressed sandstone or gritstone is incorporated into a hundred smaller but newer buildings. Only the trees remain, solitary and magnificent, like sentries who know relief will never come—oak and elm, beech and sycamore. Simply to stand and look at one of these proud giants in the grounds of Flasby Hall or Eshton Hall gives me an indefinable pleasure. I can do it by walking William and Tara (my Old English sheepdog family) for two minutes down my country lane. Such immense pleasure from so simple an act!

All the dales have remarkably distinctive attractions and histories; all provide different kinds of scenery; all have their individual character, accent, and dialect words and phrases. Two of them have individual breeds of sheep named after them. Only one thing do they seem to have in common—their waters all end up mingled together in the River Ouse.

ABOVE *A stone barn nestles in a Swaledale valley skeined by dry-stone walls, and crowned with buttercups.*

THE ROMANS IN YORKSHIRE

LEGIONARIES OF THE ROMAN invasion force that waded ashore onto British soil in AD 43 found themselves in a land carved into a series of independent tribal territories. The largest of these lay in the North, where a tribal federation known as the Brigantes ruled a swath of land stretching from the Trent up to where Hadrian's Wall now stands. Tucked into their eastern flank were the Parisi, a smaller tribe whose sway extended roughly from the Humber Estuary to the North York Moors.

First-century Britons in Yorkshire lived, as elsewhere, in circular dwellings made of stone or timber and rising to conical roofs of thatch or turf. These 'round-houses' stood either in enclosed oval farmsteads or in grander hill-forts, whose lofty positions and defensive earthworks or ditches provided security in times of conflict. Granaries and animal bones discovered by archaeologists suggest that Brigantian life revolved around arable and pastoral agriculture.

The Romans found the southern tribes relatively easy to subjugate, but settled for a treaty with Cartimandua, Queen of Brigantia, which left her at the helm of a semiautonomous client state. The treaty provided Cartimandua with a strong ally during the internal struggles that punctuated her rule, and gave Rome a friendly buffer state on its northern frontier. Legionaries marched north to help quell tribal unrest three times, the third in AD 69, when Venutius, Cartimandua's ex-husband, rebelled. Whatever his motives (and his ex-wife's romantic involvement with his armourbearer was surely one), his offensive was successful, and Rome was forced to retaliate. In AD 71, Governor Petillius Cerialis led the Ninth Legion northwards and defeated Venutius, possibly at Stanwick hill-fort. With the region conquered, the Romans consolidated their rule in the following years by laying out a network of roads, and by stippling the terrain with forts.

For many Romano-Britons, life would have been altered little by the conquest. Yet tendrils of Roman influence spread throughout the country. Villas appeared on the landscape, and communities grew up beside forts to service their occupants. In Yorkshire, one such village evolved into Isurium Brigantum (modern-day Aldborough, where relics can still be seen), Brigantia's tribal capital.

ABOVE Coins existed in Iron Age Britain, but became far more widespread in Roman times; imperial currency comprised gold aurei, silver denarii and brass sestertii and asses.

ABOVE An artist's impression of a Romano-Brigantian settlement illustrates the central role that agriculture played in the society's existence.

BELOW An exquisite mosaic pavement from Aldborough. To decorate a 15 foot-by-9 foot floor, craftsmen would have laid as many as 120,000 individual pieces, or tesserae.

First, the Swale and Ure join together northwest of York, in the plain between the North York Moors and the Pennines, which admitted the Great North Road to connect the opposite ends of the country as the coaching roads were developed. Next, the Nidd twists its way past Harrogate and Knaresborough to join the Ouse, which is then the confluence of three rivers as it flows through York. Here it has been landscaped superbly to form yet one more attraction in this jewel of a city, which was a metropolis for the Romans, then for the Vikings, and a commercial and military centre in the Middle Ages. There was a beautiful Georgian York, and in the 19th century it became an important centre for the railway system, as well as for chocolate confectionery manufacture. To emerge from the station at York in springtime, leaving behind the high-speed trains and electronic signal boxes of the 20th century, and see the daffodils in bloom beneath the medieval city walls takes the breath away. And beyond the walls are the three towers of the sublime Minster—yes, York has a special place in the hearts of all Yorkshiremen.

As the Ouse flows on towards the North Sea it is joined next by the Wharfe, which has first threaded its way through some of England's loveliest scenery, levelling out into fertile farmland east of Otley and meeting the Ouse near Cawood, just south of York. That leaves only the Aire, with its own story—starting mysteriously in Malham Tarn and finding its way through the limestone honeycomb of the great Cove, then past Skipton, bidding farewell to its rural innocence as it heads for the once-great textile empire that began at Keighley. From this point, the Aire is tainted with industrialism, skirting Bradford but unable to avoid Leeds. It winds shamefacedly through the coalfields until, with a final shudder of relief, it collapses into the Ouse at Goole, and barely has time to recover its self-respect as a river before the Ouse becomes the Humber Estuary.

THE JOURNEY OF THE RIVER SWALE

The upper reaches of the Swale are so remote that the area seems to have undergone little change in something like two thousand years. There were three periods of major industrial activity and they all involved the mining of lead from those wild and lonely fellsides.

First, the Romans valued lead so highly that they laid their roads and marched their legions over these hills, and then had to rein in the warlike Brigantes, whose land this was. Incursions by Romans, Normans, Scots, Norsemen and Celts obviously mixed up the bloodstock considerably, but I like to think that there is something of the Brigantes' character remaining in most Yorkshiremen. The rest of the country seems to consider us awkward, stubborn, independent blighters, and certainly that is how the Romans must have found our ancestors.

The Normans were the next to mine the lead in great quantities and it was carted out of the valley to cover the roofs of castles and abbeys throughout the North and much further afield as well. The next 'boom' came in the 18th and 19th centuries, and went on right up to the 1880s, when it became cheaper to import lead into England than to dig it out ourselves, much as our wool and cotton textile industries came to be priced out of world markets after the Second World War.

The head of Swaledale is just beyond the village of Keld and, ironically, this has been opened up to the outside world as much by the establishment of the Pennine Way as by any form of mechanised transport. It is a land of bare moorlands and spectacular waterfalls with, here and there, more sheltered patches of farmland. Thwaite, the next village, with a purely Norse name (meaning 'clearing' or 'paddock'), is hemmed in by the High Pennines and, in particular, three individual peaks called Great Shunner, Kisdon and Lovely Seat; and the next Swaledale village of Muker also bears a Norse name, meaning 'cultivated enclosure'. The memories of those wild invaders who savaged their way inland, then settled peaceably to graze their stock in clearings they must have created themselves, are everywhere around us. In their day, the fells would have been covered with thick scrub and forest, and finding 'paddocks' and turning them into 'cultivated enclosures' must have been damned hard work.

ABOVE *The leading used to bind and craft this vibrant stained-glass window on display in a Haworth church was almost certainly fashioned from lead mined in Yorkshire.*

RIGHT *Swaledale was the hub of the Dales' thriving lead-mining industry for many centuries. But when cheap, imported lead triggered the industry's decline in the 1880s, buildings like the Blakethwaite Smelt Mill at Gunnerside Gill were abandoned.*

At Gunnerside, the water of the Swale gathers reinforcement from a beck that has carved out a course down the slopes of Rogan's Seat, which towers 2,203 feet above the valley. This was 'Gunner's pasture' to the Norsemen and a very extensive lead-mining area to the Normans. Today, it is as quiet and peaceful as it must have been a thousand years ago, though the forests have been cleared and the hillsides are scarred with the burrowings of the miners. It's a glorious area in summer sunlight, yet I can still enjoy it when the clouds sit low on the tops of the fells and the day is grey and forbidding. Somehow this seems to give Swaledale a character very much its own. There is an eerie quality about this part of the dale; it seems haunted by ghostly memories.

At Reeth, tucked away in the shelter of Fremington Edge, we begin to move into tourist country, with a charming village green surrounded by shops and hotels, and Arkengarthdale springs suddenly upon us from the northwest. This superb little valley leads out to Tan Hill where the highest inn in England stands hospitably firm against the bleak winters. For miles in all directions the moorlands stretch to the horizon, dotted with those curly-horned sheep that bear the name Swaledale.

ABOVE *A sheep of the Swaledale breed pauses to chew on a mouthful of grass. Its coarse, weatherproof fleece will in time be used in the manufacture of carpets.*

Back in the main valley we run into folklore at Swale Hall where, it is said, the great British institution of a pot of tea first arrived upon the social scene. James Raine and his wife are supposed to have been given a brass kettle, together with a supply of tea and (apparently) rather imprecise instructions, as a wedding present. They put the tea and water in the kettle, then mixed in cream and sugar before boiling up the whole concoction and serving it to their guests in bowls, with spoons to eat the mess. I wonder how many guests survived that wedding feast!

Marske has a fair claim to rival Burnsall, in Wharfedale, for its setting of exquisite natural beauty. It has so much natural charm, with its surround of thick woods and lush valley bottom, that the high moors do not dominate it as they do so many of the villages further upstream. The Huttons of Marske Hall were a remarkable family, producing two Archbishops of York—one of whom went on to Canterbury in the 18th century.

As the dale begins to open out onto the northern part of the Vale of York, the Swale finally reaches Richmond, one of the most interesting towns in the whole county and the Gateway to the Dales in the north, as Skipton is in the south. Everything is dominated by the magnificent red-sandstone castle on its cliff above the river. It is from a cavern under the castle that, according to legend, King Arthur and his Round Table knights will emerge in England's hour of need. Also for the romantics, what about that 'Sweet lass of Richmond Hill'? Don't let anyone try to kid you that she was anything to do with Richmond, Surrey. Absolutely not. She was Frances I'anson, born on October 17, 1766, at Leyburn in Wensleydale, and as a young girl she lived in Richmond (Yorks.). It was here that she was courted by Leonard McNally, a dashing Irishman, who was bound to win her after writing:

> *On Richmond Hill there lived a lass*
> *More bright than Mayday morn,*
> *Whose charms all other maids surpass,*
> *A rose without a thorn.*

They were married in 1787 and McNally's tribute to his love became top of the pops in Georgian London.

A less well-authenticated story—and one without a happy ending—is that of a drummerboy who was sent down a secret passage in Richmond Castle that was reputed to lead to Easby Abbey, a mile away. He was supposed to drum his way along the tunnel so that its route could be charted by people up above. It seems a remarkably ham-fisted way of going about things to me, and so it turned out for the little lad with the drum: he was never seen again. But they do say that by putting your ear to the ground between Richmond Castle and Easby Abbey you can still hear the drumbeat!

The Swale now leaves the high moorlands behind, but what is left of its course is just as fascinating as its upper reaches, if only for the fact that it takes in Catterick, which is known (possibly without any great affection) to thousands of ex-servicemen. Lord Baden-Powell (better known and probably much more warmly regarded as the founder of the Boy Scout movement) was asked, as an army commander in the North before the First World War, to find a suitable site for a military training centre, and his report was an important factor in the decision to build a camp near Catterick. It is really an army town now, spread over a vast area, and from being a dreary place, remote from any major centre of population and with few amenities beyond the NAAFI, Catterick Garrison has been developed to a remarkable extent since the war.

Long ago, Cataractonium was a Roman city, as the Romans had appreciated the strategic importance of the route between the Pennines in the west and the Hambleton and Cleveland Hills to the east. It still rated the title of 'town' in the Middle Ages. In the Second World War the area took on a new military significance as the whole Vale of York was dotted with airfields. From Catterick and Leeming Bar, Topcliffe and Dishforth, first the Wellingtons, Whitleys and Hampdens started out on their bombing raids in Europe, and later came the Stirlings, Halifaxes and Lancasters. It is between these airfields that the Swale now winds the last few miles of its course towards Boroughbridge and its meeting with the Ure. Swaledale meets Wensleydale and the River Ouse is born.

WENSLEYDALE

Wensleydale is one of the few dales that does not take its name from its river. Instead, the valley takes its name from the attractive village of Wensley, which was an important market town until a large percentage of its population was wiped out by the plague in the 16th century.

The altitude is something over two thousand feet where the valley's natural artery, the infant River Ure, begins to wind its way down the high fells, or rather its several ways, because there are half a dozen or more tributary streams, descending in a series of waterfalls, to the floor of the valley proper. The Norsemen left their mark here, as in Swaledale, with their name for summer grazing pasture—*saetr*—which became simplified into 'sett' or even 'seat', so that around Hawes, which really marks the start of the dale proper, we find Appersett and Countersett and Burtersett.

Hawes itself is a delightful market town, unless you are trying to motor through it on a Tuesday, when market day has been held since King William III gave it a charter nearly three hundred years ago. Then, the narrow road to the east becomes heavily congested with farmers' cars, usually towing boxes of sheep,

LEFT *Surrounded by potential buyers, an auctioneer commences the bidding for a fresh lot of lambs at a sheep sale in Malton.*

BELOW *A farmer takes note of likely-looking animals at auction— if he doesn't manage to pick up a few bargains, it certainly won't be for want of research!*

plying to and from the auction mart just off the road to Leyburn. To the north of the town is the 100-foot waterfall of Hardraw Force, which is set in a natural amphitheatre and forms a spectacular backdrop for the brass-band concerts that are staged there in the summer—a nice day out for the family, as the sounding brass booms back from the rock face.

The world-famous Wensleydale cheese—milky-white, crumbly and delicious— is now factory-produced in Hawes, but it is still possible to find an isolated farm where the wife might sell you a pound or two of the real farmhouse Wensleydale, usually made to a recipe that has been in the family for generations. There's nothing like apple pie eaten with a bit of Wensleydale.

From Hawes, the Ure winds along the valley bottom (though still around seven hundred to eight hundred feet above sea level) to Bainbridge, the historian's dream village. Here, the Bain, having splashed its way down from Lake Semerwater, joins the Ure to earn itself the title of the shortest river in England. Its course runs just three miles, yet, unlike the dozens of 'becks' that have by this time swelled the waters of the Ure, the Bain alone gets the title of a fully fledged river. Bainbridge is a sheer delight, with the Rose and Crown overlooking a picturesque village green, and the whole scene dominated by a huge grassy mound that once housed a Roman fort.

The inn itself, which can trace its ancestry to the reign of Henry VI, is a place of immense character. The horn once used to summon foresters from their labours is kept there and is still blown during the evenings between Michaelmas and

ABOVE *Proclaimed Queen of Scotland a week after her birth in 1542, Mary Stuart was forced to abdicate 25 years later by disaffected Scottish nobles. As a rival claimant to Elizabeth I's English throne, Mary was imprisoned upon crossing the border, and spent several months incarcerated in Bolton Castle.*

ABOVE RIGHT *When imposing Bolton Castle was erected in the late 14th century, it cost the then princely sum of £12,000. The stone used in its construction was quarried locally.*

Shrovetide. In the days when Tom Woodmass was the landlord I've seen orphaned foxcubs, which he's taken in and reared as family pets, running around a pen at the back of the pub with his own dogs. I've drunk at the bar in the company of a donkey, and of a duck with a liking for brown ale. And, of course, I've enjoyed a glass or two with customers of a more orthodox character, too.

A few more miles to the east and we move into the history of England in the Middle Ages. On the northern side of the valley stands Bolton Castle, built by the powerful Scropes (pronounced 'Scroops') in the 14th century. In those rough-and-ready days it must have been a very desirable 'mod. res.', designed as it was to give the maximum amount of comfort as well as military protection. This was one of several English 'homes' of Mary, Queen of Scots, in flight from her rebellious Scottish lords; it held out staunchly for King Charles in the Civil War.

The Scropes must rank as one of the county's greatest families. They appear in Shakespeare, they were Kings of Man, they produced two earls, a Lord Chancellor, a Lord Chief Justice or two, and innumerable barons and baronets. They fought in the Crusades and were at Crécy and Agincourt. They intermarried with the Nevilles, produced an Archbishop of York who was beheaded by Henry IV, and were granted the right to a private family chapel by a papal bull.

Aysgarth is perhaps the most popular tourist centre, because here the Ure dashes over limestone platforms, providing three series of spectacular falls, all backed by curtains of trees; and if catering for the modern tourist's requirements has taken something away from the village's charm, mercifully all this has been kept well clear of the natural beauty of the falls themselves.

Leyburn, which can claim to be Wensleydale's capital—certainly since the tragedy of Wensley itself—figures in the Domesday Book. It has town fairs in May and October, is the home of the Wensleydale Agricultural Society Show and the Wensleydale Tournament of Song. From here the valley begins to flatten out into the Vale of York and the traveller has the choice of straight ahead, towards the

Great North Road and an early meeting with the River Swale, or a gentle diversion southeast to Middleham and back into medieval history.

Middleham is the centre of stables that have a proud name on the turf going back as far as 1845, when Charles Kingsley, author of *The Water Babies*, described it as 'quite a racing town...jockeys and grooms crowd the streets and I hear they are a most respectable set and many of them regular communicants'.

It was Robert FitzRandolph who built the first castle at Middleham and his Norman keep still stands. Then came that most powerful of medieval families, the Nevilles, to add great walls and new turrets. It was the chief home of the Kingmaker, Richard of Warwick, the dominant figure of the Wars of the Roses until he changed sides and was killed supporting the Lancastrian cause at Barnet.

It was under the protection of Warwick, at the time when he was the greatest of the Yorkist magnates, that that grossly maligned monarch, Richard III, spent a happy childhood at Middleham Castle. Here, as the young Duke of Gloucester, he learned the knightly virtues and martial arts; here he enjoyed hunting in the Dales with the earl and his retinue, who would eat six whole oxen in a single day. Here, too, Richard first met the young Anne Neville, who, for another brief period of happiness in his life, became his queen.

The great days of Middleham Castle ended with Richard's death in 1485; the buildings were subsequently dismantled, but the ruin is still impressive. A walk of only a minute or so, after parking in the marketplace, brings you up against the massive curtain walls; but if you are prepared to take a slightly longer walk to the south of the castle, the view from there is much more rewarding, looking down a gentle slope at the buildings as a whole. Here it is much easier to picture its life in the 15th century, the young Richard growing up, and then returning to Middleham as King of England. Here, in the southwest tower, his son was born and died as a small boy, but not before he had been proclaimed Prince of Wales at York—possibly the only trip he ever made out of Wensleydale.

So Middleham had its great days of pageantry and its grim days of royal sorrow. It's a little corner of Wensleydale that merits several pages in England's story. So too, I suppose, does Jervaulx Abbey, although, compared with some of the other Yorkshire abbeys, the ruins are not so interesting. Here settled the industrious Cistercians rather than the more academically inclined Benedictines. Apart from being credited with the original recipe for Wensleydale cheese, they were great horse breeders. The abbey's dissolution came in 1537. The last abbot was Adam de Sedbergh, who had taken part in the most gently named of all northern uprisings, the Pilgrimage of Grace.

On now to Ripon, steeped in its own traditions, some of which go back to Alfred the Great, who granted a charter of incorporation in 886. The traffic can be a bit tricky in that splendid old market square but it's worth the struggle. Until 1604, Ripon was ruled by a 'Wakeman', who was responsible for dealing with all crimes committed in the night, i.e., between the hours of curfew and sunrise. The last Wakeman, who became the first mayor, was Hugh Ripley, and the office is remembered by the blowing of the Wakeman's horn each evening at the corners

BELOW *Old traditions die hard in the Dales: here, the Wakeman blows his semicircular buffalo horn during Ripon's nightly 'setting of the watch' ceremony.*

of the marketplace. It is a great tourist attraction and Americans in particular love to record the ceremony. I have a personal interest in that square too—some of the best pork pie in Yorkshire can be bought there, if you can find somewhere to park!

Between Ripon and Pateley Bridge, with estates in both Wensleydale and Nidderdale, stands one of the loveliest abbey ruins in the country and certainly one of my favourite beauty spots: Fountains Abbey, the greatest Cistercian abbey in England. I sometimes wonder if the Christmas story of Good King Wenceslas was not drawn, in part, from the tale of those thirteen monks from St Mary's in York, who were, in fact, Benedictines when they first decided to found an abbey in that wild and inhospitable stretch of country (as it was in the first half of the 12th century). The story goes that during their first two years at Fountains, living in terrible poverty, beset by winter weather and predatory beasts, they were asked for food by a blind beggar. The monks and lay brothers were near to starvation themselves, with only two loaves of bread to share among the lot of them, but from the first they had established a principle that no man might ask for help and be refused. The abbot, accordingly, ordered one loaf to be given to the beggar

THE PILGRIMAGE OF GRACE

ABBEYS LIKE JERVAULX and Fountains might still ring to the sounds of monks' chants, had a 16th-century Yorkshire rebellion called the Pilgrimage of Grace fared differently.

In mid-1536, royal commissioners toured the country effecting the Dissolution of the Monasteries, Henry VIII's systematic closure and sale of England's religious houses, designed to raise revenue. In the North, where the imposition of new taxes and Protestant doctrines already rankled, irritation festered into revolt.

Led by Yorkshire lawyer, Robert Aske, the Pilgrimage soon numbered up to 30,000, even enjoying support among local nobility. Aske confronted Henry's local representative, Thomas Howard, the 3rd Duke of Norfolk, and demanded the ending of monastic closures, an assurance that a northern parliament would be held to consider local grievances, and a

pardon for all rebels. Lacking sufficient troops, Norfolk undertook to carry these demands to Henry, and granted the pardon. The rebels duly dispersed.

Norfolk's magnanimity was borne of necessity. The merest hint of renewed trouble in 1537 provided Henry with an excuse to avenge the rebellion. In the following months, over 200 rebels died in executions staged across the North as warnings to prospective dissenters. Aske himself was hanged in York in July 1537.

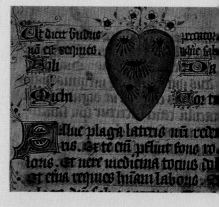

ABOVE *Banners carried by Aske's pilgrims are known to have displayed the five wounds suffered by Christ on the cross, represented here as five piercings to a heart.*

LEFT *Henry VIII gained nearly £1,500,000 by selling off or leasing lands appropriated during the Dissolution of the Monasteries.*

FAR LEFT *Religious treasures, such as this silver-gilt chalice from Dolgellau in Wales, swelled the royal coffers of Henry VIII after his systematic rape of the Church.*

and the other shared by his flock. And scarcely had this been done than the starving monks saw a wagon, laden with food, coming down the hill from a landowner in Knaresborough.

From that moment the monks in that 'wild and rocky place, thick set with thorns and a fitting lair only for wild beasts', began to prosper. What faith those men must have had, clearing the land, chasing off predators, and building day after day. After thirteen years their work was almost complete, when it was destroyed by fire and they had to start all over again. The nave, aisle and transepts that you see today date from the resumption of their labours in 1147, and it is still possible to see much of the beauty of the original masonry.

Meanwhile, the River Ure has moved quietly on through Ripon, with its modern marina and army barracks, across the Vale of York to join the Swale.

NIDDERDALE: POTHOLERS' COUNTRY

Nidderdale differs from the other four dales in that it is, as far as the motorist is concerned, a cul-de-sac. All the others have a western outlet, whether it is a major road like the A65 through Airedale or the B6270, which climbs spectacularly out of Swaledale. For those who explore Nidderdale by car, it peters out at Scar House and Angram reservoirs, and even these reaches of the High Pennines are attainable only by use of a waterworks road. But they are well worth a visit for the magnificent scenery on all sides, for a series of picnic areas and for the fascinating labyrinth of caves leading from Goyden Pot, though, as ever, warning to the inexperienced is necessary about keeping well away from any pothole system when the water level is high, or when sudden rain may bring about a dramatic rise in level.

The Nidd rises on the northeastern slopes of Great Whernside, although this 2,309-foot peak is really one of the Wharfedale hills, towering as it does above Kettlewell. This is very much potholers' country and it has seen many a nail-biting rescue of the unwary and the foolhardy. One of these, in 1958, went on for two or three days and brought, in the wake of the cave-rescue organisations, a great gathering of newspapermen who were far less at home in this territory even than the unfortunate band of explorers trapped below. One *Daily Express* reporter, panting and wild-eyed, arrived back at his base headquarters (comfortably established in the Bluebell Hotel in Kettlewell) to report that he had been pursued down the fellside by a wolf! It was, of course, a wolf in sheep's clothing and I cannot see its 'pursuit' being of a particularly energetic nature, but there is something rather endearing about a born-and-bred Londoner, in the middle of the 20th century, being utterly convinced that wild beasts still roamed the Yorkshire Dales.

From Great Whernside, the infant Nidd, like the Aire, quickly plunges underground and can be seen rushing through its subterranean courses by those who go to explore the cave system of Goyden Pot; then, towards Lofthouse and Ramsgill, it resumes a more orthodox march to the sea. This is the land of the walker and the caver, the angler and the birdwatcher.

There are superb circular walks around the fells, and a ten-mile tramp over into Wharfedale from Stean provides panoramic views of two dales and a visit to the old lead-mine workings of Yarnbury, on the moors above Grassington.

Gouthwaite Reservoir is a private nature reserve of endless fascination for those privileged to be granted access to it. The reservoir itself was built around the turn of the century and as its wildlife has been rigorously guarded for more than eighty years some very rare specimens indeed have been observed here—golden eagle, pied-billed grebe, red and black kites, Temminck's stint and red-necked phalarope, for instance. Ramsgill, at the head of Gouthwaite Reservoir, is, without much argument, the prettiest of the villages in the dale, though Wath, at the foot, would certainly put forward claims as a haven of peace and tranquillity.

Another mile and we reach the metropolis of Upper Nidderdale—the attractive market town of Pateley Bridge, surrounded by high moors that are reached by steeply sloping roads and footpaths. In fact, the area was called Little Switzerland when the railways opened it up to the townsfolk of the industrial West Riding in the mid-19th century, and its popularity as a 'day-out' venue grew and continued over the next fifty years to such an extent that, when the reservoirs were built at the head of the valley, a single-line light railway was constructed, giving access to the more remote areas above Wath. It was the first municipally owned passenger railway in Britain, when it was opened in 1907, taking 'trippers' as far as Lofthouse, until the valley was made more accessible by the arrival of motorbus transport. The plant and equipment were sold in 1937.

LEFT *The furrowed limestone of Knipe Scar, north of Grassington, shows up chalk-white against the Wharfedale landscape. Knipe Scar is a popular hang-gliding launch pad.*

BELOW *A golden eagle surveys its lofty domain. These magnificent— and rare—creatures are known to drop by at Gouthwaite Reservoir, some 10 miles east of Grassington.*

For some reason that is not quite clear, the locomotives and coaches for the six-and-a-half-mile line from Pateley Bridge to Lofthouse were brought from London—from the Metropolitan Railway. If railway engines have souls, as steam enthusiasts insist they have, then those cockney locos must have felt pretty lonely in rural Nidderdale. One of them was called 'Holdsworth', very much a North Country name, which suggests it was either christened, or rechristened, on its arrival in Nidderdale via the great railway centre of York, and there is a famous photograph of it outside the engine sheds there in 1907.

The annual show of the Nidderdale Agricultural Society is held at Pateley Bridge in late September and if it is now shorn of some of its former glory (such as a visit from the Yorkshire County Cricket Club, travelling by horsedrawn wagonette), it is still a popular and important date in the diary of the farming community and, indeed, of the whole dale.

By the time it reaches the attractive village of Ripley, the river has begun to leave behind the high fells and uplands. It skirts Harrogate on the northern side. Harrogate grew up around its mineral springs and now, with a population of more than sixty thousand, is by far the major centre in this particular dale.

I am very fond of Harrogate. There are few more pleasant towns in the whole country to visit during those weeks when the icy grip of winter is being prised loose at last, and first the snowdrops, then the crocuses and finally the daffodils lay down their carpets over the wide green spaces of the town centre. On a personal note, I have taken part in a number of epic matches on the pleasant

AGRICULTURAL SHOWS IN THE DALES

COMPETITIVE LIVESTOCK SHOWS have long been a linchpin of the Dales farming community. Since the late 18th century, local farmers have welcomed the chance to catch up with advances in farming machinery, methods and science, and generally chew the cud. Most importantly, they come to parade their livestock in the hope of winning prizes. More than pride is at stake: entering stock in a competition is a form of advertising, with prize-winners subsequently commanding higher prices at market. Today, shows are more popular than ever. The region's premier agricultural event, Harrogate's Great Yorkshire Show, draws up to 110,000 people each July, of whom almost a quarter are farmers.

Top billing at agricultural shows goes to cattle and horses, and to sheep—among them local breeds, the Swaledale, Wensleydale and Dalesbred. Animals are judged within classes arranged according to breed, sex and age. Entries are led past a panel of judges, who award cups, trophies and rosettes—usually red for first prize, blue for second and yellow for third. Judging is typically followed by a grand parade of prize-winners. Smaller creatures, like pigs, pigeons, rabbits, dogs and ferrets also feature regularly on show schedules, as do sheepdog trials, ferret races and falconry.

Shows celebrate not just livestock, but all facets of country life. Dry-stone walling, fell-racing, gun-dog training, fly-fishing, horse-shoeing—any or all could feature in display or competition form, and for the gumbooted Damon Hills of this world, there are even tractor-handling contests from time to time. More sedate events variously include shepherd's crook-making, baking, jam-making and knitting competitions; and prizes for the most impressive onion and finest runner beans are also up for grabs.

If you can't orchestrate your trip to Yorkshire to coincide with the Great

ABOVE *Judges get to grips with onions of truly monstrous proportions.*

ABOVE *Dressed up to the nines, a shire horse draws admiring looks at the Rye Dale Show. In medieval times, the shire's ancestors were valued for their ability to bear the weight of knights in full armour.*

BELOW *A Highland cow peers out from beneath its foppish fringe as it swaggers into the ring at the Great Yorkshire Show.*

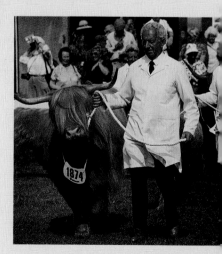

Yorkshire Show, there are plenty of other shows to check out, including late September's Nidderdale Show at Pateley Bridge. The Otley Show, first held in 1796, takes place in May; the Upper Wharfedale Agricultural Society's Kilnsey Show, and the Wensleydale Agricultural Society show at Leyburn, both take place in late August; and Wetherby held its 145th annual show in June 1997.

St George's Road cricket ground and I have drunk champagne more than once there when Yorkshire have rounded off another season as champions. I can't help thinking of Harrogate in the feminine gender, perhaps because it has grace, elegance and charm so different from the more rugged qualities of most other Yorkshire towns, perhaps because it is renowned as a shopping centre. A gentle walk around the middle of Harrogate in March is calculated to warm the heart of anyone.

Once clear of Harrogate, the Nidd plunges straight into a narrow limestone gorge, where tiny cottages with red-tiled roofs cling precariously to the steep slopes and where a defensive fortification has existed for more than a thousand years. This is Knaresborough, which had a recorded existence in King Alfred's time, was an important centre when the Domesday survey was carried out, and was a royal burgh of Edward III. Beside the 12th-century castle ruins is the cave of Mother Shipton, a 16th-century soothsayer, who foretold:

Iron in the water shall float
As easy as a wooden boat.
Learning shall so ebb and flow
The poor shall most wisdom know.
Carriages without horses shall go
And accidents fill the world with woe.
Under water men shall walk
In the air men shall be seen
In white, in black and in green.

Not bad, for a view of the 20th century from around 1500, was it?

The Nidd has now but a short journey to join the Swale and Ure, at this stage flowing together as the Ouse, and, as if reluctant to relinquish its identity, it starts to twist and loop and turn back on itself before finally giving up the struggle at Nun Monkton, six miles from York. But first it has passed the boyhood home of a most famous Yorkshireman, Guy Fawkes. He is supposed to have been a bell-ringer at Cowthorpe, just south of the river, and it's pretty certain that, as his triple bob majors rang out over the water meadows of the Nidd, he had no idea that, for the next three hundred years, his name would live on, as bonfires blazed over the whole country on the night of November 5.

He was, of course, pretty daft to imagine that, along with his fellow plotters, he could ever get away with such a far-fetched and ill-conceived conspiracy, but I like to think he showed a bit of Yorkshire character when it was discovered. One of his judges recorded: 'This handsome young redheaded Yorkshire captain lies tonight in the deepest dungeon of the Tower. Tomorrow for him is nothing but torture, ruin and death, yet he sleeps the sleep of a child whilst we, his judges, toss uneasily beneath the canopies of Hampton Court.'

ABOVE *A defiant Guy Fawkes kneels before King James I, after being caught in an attempt to blow up Parliament, in 1605. Initially tightlipped, he was persuaded to yield the names of his co-conspirators by a few turns of the torturer's rack.*

THE SOUTHERN DALES

ABOVE *The Dales' dramatic limestone outcrops make them enduringly popular among enthusiasts of rock-climbing.*

W HARFEDALE, OF ALL THE YORKSHIRE DALES, has a characteristic loveliness of its own, compounded of steep valley slopes crisscrossed by miles of dry-stone walls; of peat-brown water rushing over polished limestone platforms; of old grey villages huddled round their greens, where summer sports take place in much the same way as they have since the first Queen Elizabeth; of woodlands carpeted by springtime violets and primroses; of good pubs with good ale and marvellous characters in their taprooms.

Wharfedale is not historic in the sense that Wensleydale is with its clearly recorded history. Wharfedale goes back into the misty realms of Celtic folklore and Viking saga. It is not a valley of ghostly legend like Swaledale, but its ghosts are there just the same. It claims none of Airedale's industrial archaeology and yet it has its old mills by its old streams. Above all, Wharfedale delights the eye and sets the pulse racing. The ponderous face of Kilnsey Crag makes you doubt your eyes, whether viewed from two miles away or close-up as you stand under that overhang, especially if you happen to catch a couple of climbers suspended beneath it by the highly technical hardware of modern mountaineering.

FOLLOWING THE WHARFE

The Wharfe starts its life very close to the birthplace of the Ribble, which chooses to plunge southwest and head for Lancashire. The Wharfe, however, chooses an easterly route out of the wilderness of Langstrothdale Chase. Over its first six or seven miles it splashes merrily beside one of the roads linking Wharfedale and Wensleydale as it climbs dramatically over Fleet Moss. Down in the valley the farms and hamlets seem snug and secure, even if you do tremble a little at the

thought of their isolation in the winter snow. But in summer there is no thought of snow as families choose from a score of ideal picnic spots at the riverside.

At length the river reaches Hubberholme, which, although merely a collection of farms grouped around a pub and St Michael's Church, may reasonably be described as the first community of any size. Here, a Viking chief named Hubba ruled the roost a thousand years ago and he might well have been the man who instituted the village 'Parliament', which sits once a year, on New Year's Day, in the bar of the George. There is only one item of business—the letting of Poor Pasture, a piece of grazing land owned by the church—and it doesn't take very long, not with the more pressing business of drinking the first New Year pint at hand. Next comes Buckden, where a road goes left over Kidstones Pass and into Wensleydale.

And then there's Starbotton; here, the Wharfe is trickling for the first time into recorded history, for the existence of Starbotton was recorded in the Domesday Book. Then, as it reaches Kettlewell, the valley of the Wharfe begins to broaden, which has the effect of enhancing the beauty of the dale.

The B6160 crosses the Wharfe at Kettlewell, although a narrower road will obligingly take you down the northern bank of the river if you prefer, under the shadow of Great Whernside, giving you an earlier view of Kilnsey Crag. The main road, however, leads direct to the shadow of the great crag.

First, though, it joins the little road winding out of Littondale and the Wharfe is joined by its main tributary, the Skirfare. Between the two valleys stands the massive rampart of Old Cote Moor, all outcrops and scree and grazing for thousands of sheep. There are walks over this moor for the ambitious and energetic, involving a precipitous ascent and an equally dramatic drop on the other side, but these were paths of necessity for, first, the shepherd monks and later the lead miners.

Littondale, taking its name from one of the valley's five villages (Arncliffe, Halton Gill, Foxup and Hawkswick are the others), is largely unspoilt because its visitors are mainly walkers, anglers or birdwatchers, all of whom respect the

ABOVE *In one of the highlights of the Kilnsey Show, contestants in the Crag Race run to the summit of Kilnsey Crag, a limestone buttress that was carved out when Ice Age glaciers ground their way through Wharfedale.*

countryside. Arncliffe's church has a roll of honour for those who fought, not, as one might expect, in either of the two world wars, but at Flodden Field in 1513, when the flower of Scottish chivalry was decimated and James IV killed. Charles Kingsley loved Arncliffe, and if *The Water Babies* was conceived and part written high above on the Malham plateau, much was also written here.

Back in the main valley, the Wharfe has now reached the twin villages of Kilnsey and Conistone. The huge crag forms a remarkable backdrop to the annual show and sports day of the Upper Wharfedale Agricultural Society, held immediately after the summer bank holiday. Here you can see the few remaining exponents of dry-stone walling at work; they start at the beginning of the day and their work is judged at the end of it. For those who demand more energetic forms of entertainment, there is the race to the top of the crag (via the steep grassy surrounds—not up the face itself) and back to the showground. Kilnsey Show is one of Wharfedale's most colourful annual events. Across the river, Conistone church is perhaps the oldest in the dale and both villages have a road that leads directly to Grassington, the capital of Upper Wharfedale.

TRADITIONAL SKILLS FOR COUNTRY LIFE

YORKSHIRE MAY HAVE CRADLED the Industrial Revolution, but it never turned its back on its traditional country crafts, many of which are still practised today. Some, like dry-stone walling, date back 5,000 years. Since their heyday after the enclosure laws of the 18th century, many dry-stone walls have been dismantled to allow for larger pastures, yet the lichen-stained wall still endures as a quintessential Dales image.

Instead of mortar, the wall-builder relies on gravity and an educated eye. Building from a shallow foundation ditch, he methodically lays stone upon stone, intuitively knowing which shape to choose to plug a gap. Wider tiestones are added to bind the wall, which is capped with flat, upright topstones. Such arduous work pays dividends: dry-stone walls are equipped to withstand both the brutal Yorkshire climate and the butting of even the most determined sheep!

Similarly, the ancient craft of thatching makes use of locally available materials to provide roofing, making up in charm and skill of construction for what it may lack in sophistication. The thatcher's basic laying skills have not changed over the years, and nor have tools like leggets, spar hooks and hand shears. However, newer techniques of securing the straw, often in a diamond pattern, allow thatchers to express their individuality. Working in teams and often battling the elements, thatchers use different materials for specific effects:

LEFT *Dry-stone wallers at work in the Dales. Their freestanding stones will expand and contract in varying temperatures without causing damage to the wall.*

For a spot with a population of around twelve hundred, Grassington is remarkable. On the lower slopes of the moors (where there was once extensive and profitable lead mining), it is possible to trace the outlines of a large Celtic settlement. Edmund Kean and Harriot Mellon performed classical tragedies in a theatre that is now a couple of cottages. John Wesley preached in what is now a barn. Down the main street stood the smithy of Tom Lee, who was hanged for murder in York, his body brought back to hang on a gibbet near Grass Woods (just a step northwest of the village). There are those who will not walk past that spot at night, even today. Iron Age, Bronze Age, Celtic settlements—all have left their mark in or near Grassington, which sprawls across the northern slopes of the valley and so has a splendid aspect, with its back to the cold winds of winter and its face looking happily into the summer sunshine. The river itself is serenely beautiful in the valley bottom as it winds towards the picture-postcard village of Burnsall.

Burnsall must stand very high on any list of England's prettiest villages. Its setting is one of perfection, on a loop of the river that is crossed by a bridge so attractive that I would be happy just to sit and look at it all day long. The village

LEFT *His forge glowing orange behind him, a farrier sets about shoeing a horse. Racehorses are shod at least weekly; for others it is a less frequent requirement.*

BELOW *Perched on a ladder high above the ground, a thatcher carries out repair work. Depending on the materials used, thatched roofs can last as long as 100 years.*

long straw for smoothness, durable Norfolk reed for a close-cropped brushlike texture, or combed wheat-reed for a rowed design. Happily, changing fashions have revived the thatcher's craft, and the need to replace weatherworn coverings ensures employment well into the 21st century.

The blacksmith was another village mainstay, the 'ting!' of his hammer blows as familiar a sound as a sheep's bleating. Working on an anvil fixed to a wooden block, he could turn his hand to making anything from weather vanes to fire grates. The farrier had similar skills, as well as a thorough knowledge of horses, and, before veterinary surgery became a profession, doubled as horse-doctor. The age of motor cars and spare parts drastically cut the work of the blacksmith and the farrier, but they still survive, their forges enflamed not by bellows but by electric fans, and their horseshoes now often factory-made and preshaped.

ABOVE *Mossy rocks shoehorn the River Wharfe through the chasm known as the Strid. This white-water ravine has claimed the lives of many down the centuries.*

green borders the river itself and here the summer sports have been staged for at least four hundred years. Looking down on the village is Burnsall Fell, the course for England's oldest fell race, and to the east the craggy summit of Simon's Seat presides benignly over this section of Wharfedale.

As the valley narrows, the woods hurry down to escort it through a series of grottoes and glades, past the picturesquely named village of Appletreewick. Here, towards the end of the 16th century, lived a youngster named William Craven. At the age of thirteen, he was sent off to London to be apprenticed to a mercer—a dealer in expensive fabrics. He learned his trade well, was made an alderman of the City of London, became Sheriff, then Lord Mayor in 1610, and finally was knighted. Now, have I heard that story somewhere before, dressed up a bit? That's it—Dick Whittington. However, there's no mention of a cat in the story of young William Craven. Let's see what the local-boy-who-made-good did for his part of Wharfedale: he founded and endowed Burnsall Grammar School, restored and embellished the church, and built that bridge I was telling you about. And his son became the first Earl of Craven. Not bad for a lad from Appletreewick!

The valley is now narrowing every step of the way and the suspicion grows by the minute that just round the next corner something dramatic is going to happen. Before that, however, we reach Barden Tower and here, for a moment, our story overlaps that of Airedale, for the tower was built by Henry Clifford, Lord of Skipton Castle, just over the hill. Henry led the men of Craven to battle at Flodden, and those lads whose names hang in the church further up the valley, at Arncliffe, would have been alongside him.

From Barden, a road winds over a stretch of moorland called Black Park and down into Skipton, and the views from the top of the hill are so breathtaking that it's worthwhile making a little detour from the valley of the Wharfe.

The Wharfe now narrows to a marked degree with beech and birch and alder crowding down through the rocks to the water's edge. But as the volume of water is compressed into an ever-narrowing defile, the lovely Wharfe becomes a death-trap at the Strid. This is probably the most famous, or notorious, stretch of water in the North of England, largely because of its toll of victims over the years. As the river plunges among the rocks, it reaches a width that seems to invite the adventurous spirit to jump across it. But beware. The leap itself is something of an optical illusion—it's just a little further than it looks—and the landing is uncertain on tilted, and sometimes moss-covered, rocks. The Strid's list of victims is formidable because, once in the water, it is difficult to get out. Violent undertows drag you down deep beneath the rocks and there have been few survivors. In such a sylvan setting, the Strid seems to me to be rather like an exotic jungle plant that attracts unwary insects with its beauty and then traps and devours them.

Once through this narrow glen, the river then broadens and has a bland innocence as it flows through the water meadows of Bolton Priory, where generations of mill workers from the industrial West Riding have taken their picnics. The local parish church is actually the nave of the old priory. Surrounded by the ruins of the remainder of the priory, the buildings show a variety of architectural styles—Norman, Early English, Decorated and Perpendicular, and, as you drive down the road from Burnsall, the route takes you under an ornate stone arch that was built by the monks to bring water from a moorland stream to operate their flour mill.

From the past, we move very quickly into the present as far as I am concerned, because the sixth, fifth and fourth holes of Ilkley golf course soon appear on the left bank. I've spent a lot of time there trying to ignore the existence of the Wharfe. The first three holes are even more hazardous, because while it is a very simple matter to drag one's opening tee shot into the water, the second and third (both par-3 holes) are built on islands in the river itself.

Ilkley was Olicana to the Romans, who had a small garrison here to protect one of their roads, but to the Victorians it was an inland watering place noted for its mineral springs and the bracing quality of the air on its world-famous moor. 'On Ilkla Moor Baht 'At' is Yorkshire's personal anthem, sung whenever expatriates gather together in far-flung outposts. It is, in truth, a long and rather boring song and not a particularly good advertisement for those moorland breezes, as it tells of the sad consequences of wooing a young lady named Mary Jane while bereft of headgear. It goes on for about eight verses and describes, as I remember it, the whole span of life and death. Grim stuff!

Still, Ilkley is always worth a visit. Apart from its hospitable golf club, the walks over the moors (on both sides of the valley) are exhilarating; there is an abundance of good hotels, and communications are excellent. For the ambitious walker it is first class because it marks the start of the Dales Way, which, using old-established tracks, leads the whole length of Wharfedale, over into the valley of the Ribble, through Dentdale and the Howgills, to end at Bowness on Lake Windermere—a fine hike.

Many smaller towns felt deep resentment at being gobbled up by the newly created metropolitan districts in the seventies, and I don't blame any of them. It was supposed to streamline local government and effect all kinds of economies, but I'm blessed if I can think what they were. The cost of new letterheaded civic notepaper alone must have been enormous. But all this must have paled into insignificance beside the sense of civic outrage at the loss of age-old identities and I doubt if any felt this more strongly than Otley, the next town on the Wharfe.

Since the early part of the 13th century, Otley has had a charter to hold a market, and market day in Otley (with the pubs open all day on Friday) is rather like having Christmas once a week. The Butter Cross in the town centre marked the spot where dairy products were sold from the Middle Ages right up to the outbreak of the Second World War. Chippendale was born here and Turner painted landscapes of this part of Wharfedale for his friends. The agricultural show is the oldest of its kind in England and a great social event, not just for the farming community. And after all this, the town now finds itself part of the Metropolitan District of Leeds. Otley is livid about it, and I'm not surprised.

BELOW *Completed in 1888 to mark the golden jubilee of Queen Victoria, Otley's Jubilee Clock is very much a product of the Victorian age: constructed with four faces but no chimes, it may be seen yet never heard.*

Skirting the eastern end of the ridge called Otley Chevin and its continuation, Harewood Bank, the Wharfe now reaches Wetherby before at last developing a utilitarian character at Tadcaster. Here the Romans had a river crossing (Calcaria), and here, nearly two thousand years later, the town is easily identifiable by the smell of hops: Tadcaster is very much a brewery town.

By now the Wharfe is near the end of its travels. I doubt if there is a river course in the country to match it for beauty in so many guises before, at Cawood, it joins the waters of the Swale, Ure and Nidd to become part of the Ouse.

AIREDALE AND ITS WORKING RIVER

For a river that gave so much practical help to the Victorian industrialists, the Aire has a singularly romantic start to its travels—on the high limestone plateau above Malham Cove. This is great country for the geologist and naturalist alike, for the archaeologist, the botanist—and for the angler and fellwalker.

As England emerged from the Dark Ages the Malham area was an Anglian settlement, but after the Norman Conquest in 1066 the land was divided between the Norman barons, who got the good bits, and the monks, who got the swamp and scrub and, by sheer industry, turned their wildernesses into gardens. Malham went onto the books of Fountains Abbey, miles away over what is difficult country even today, and communication with this outpost of monastic empire must have been something of a problem way back in the 12th century.

LEFT *Charles Kingsley is said to have claimed that the black markings across the vertical limestone crescent of Malham Cove were fingerprints left by grubby chimney sweeps.*

BELOW *The glassy waters of Malham Tarn, the highest lake in the Pennines, once served as a trout farm for the monks of Fountains Abbey.*

BELOW *Heath Robinson's illustrations conveyed perfectly the other-worldly magic of* The Water Babies, *Charles Kingsley's tale of the subaquatic adventures of a chimney sweep named Tom.*

The Aire begins as a clear little stream flowing out of the great natural lake of Malham Tarn, which inspired Kingsley to write *The Water Babies*; indeed, much of the book was actually written at Tarn House on the northwestern shore of the lake. This, in the 19th century, was the home of Walter Morrison, one of the outstanding personalities of Victorian Yorkshire. More than that, he was a national and international figure, since his business interests extended to owning a railway in Argentina. But he enjoyed nothing more than to go home to Tarn House, where he entertained friends like Kingsley, Darwin and Ruskin.

Morrison loved the high fells and after travelling 250 miles by train (to Settle on the magnificent Leeds–Carlisle line), he would often dismiss the coachman, who was waiting for him with a landau, and walk the six miles or so to Tarn House, a climb that is almost precipitous at times. Morrison did a great deal for the area and it seems absolutely right that his home should now be an important centre for the Field Studies Council, which welcomes students from a very wide circle (both geographical and academic) to its residential courses.

No sooner has the Aire emerged from Malham Tarn than, perversely, it disappears into the limestone courses behind the face of the Cove, the massive limestone scar that encloses the village of Malham in an amphitheatre. At the foot of the Cove the Aire is reborn as it bubbles up out of the ground at a point that has been named Aire Head and that, to many, is the real source of the river. South of the village, it is joined by Gordale Beck, but the two

YORKSHIRE DIVIDED: THE ENGLISH CIVIL WAR

LEFT *A Victorian painting depicts Cromwell surveying the carnage of the Battle of Marston Moor. Of the estimated 3,000 Cavaliers that perished there, Cromwell wrote 'God made them as stubble to our swords'.*

Oliver Cromwell beat the Royalists at the Battle of Marston Moor, west of York, in July 1644—decisively seizing the initiative by attacking while the Royalists were taking their evening meal—it took the efforts of a Yorkshire-born general, Sir Thomas Fairfax, to help swing the war in Parliament's favour. Fairfax was charged with training and commanding Cromwell's crack 'New Model Army'. In June 1645 this irresistible army routed the Cavaliers at the Battle of Naseby, Northamptonshire, from which point Charles's execution, in 1649, was almost inevitable.

Cromwell was soon at the helm of a Commonwealth of England; but after his death in 1658 the country's dalliance with republicanism collapsed, and in 1660 the monarchy was restored.

BELOW *Posing stiffly for a portrait artist, Charles I displays the haughty demeanour that would later alienate Parliament and lead to his execution in Whitehall in 1649.*

T HE ENDLESS column inches pondering the role of the monarchy that choke our dailies would have bemused King Charles I. To his mind, monarchs ruled by divine right, with Parliament a tool to be convened only to do their bidding. Others disagreed, and so arose the English Civil War, a conflict whose reverberations were felt as much in Yorkshire as in the rest of England.

Charles brooked no parliamentary meddling in his affairs and would dissolve Parliament if it came to it.

BELOW *A line of muskets spit fire in a modern-day re-enactment of a Civil War confrontation.*

Between 1629 and 1640 he did without Parliament altogether. But in 1640, with Scottish hordes banging on the northern gates of the country, he was forced to swallow his pride, summon his MPs and request money from them. Like a genie released from its bottle, Parliament set about trying to curb royal powers. In January 1642, mutual antagonism boiled over when Charles marched into the Commons to arrest John Pym and four other MPs whom he regarded as troublemakers. Though Pym and company were absent, Charles's action united Lords and Commons against him, and war soon commenced.

The war split the country. Charles's support came mainly from the North and West of England and from Wales, though in Yorkshire Parliament had the support of the manufacturing towns of Leeds, Halifax and Bradford, and of the port of Hull, which refused entry to Charles in 1642. Southeastern England, including London, was for Parliament.

To impose his will, Charles raised an army of mounted Cavaliers; his foes, the Parliamentarians, led by Oliver Cromwell, became known as Roundheads after their cropped haircuts.

Initial encounters proved inconclusive, and though the mounted 'Ironsides' of

together still constitute nothing grander than a stream a few feet wide that saunters amiably past the villages of Kirkby Malham, Airton, Calton and Bell Busk.

Calton Hall was the home of 'Honest John' Lambert who, though born of a wealthy family, was a captain of horse in the Parliamentary forces during the Civil War. He rode with Cromwell and Fairfax in that decisive Battle of Marston Moor and was left in command of the North when Fairfax went south at the head of the New Model Army. He was renowned for his rectitude, yet Lambert lived in an age when you just couldn't win. He was anti-Stuart, but he opposed plans to advance Cromwell to a status more exalted than that of Lord Protector and died an exile for his principles. In the church of Kirkby Malham the bells bear inscriptions commemorating the Lambert family.

From Gargrave, where householders have built attractive little bridges across the stream to the main road, the Aire skirts Skipton to the southwest. The Springs Canal, a spur of the Leeds and Liverpool Canal, cuts right into the heart of this lovely old market town, sweeping spectacularly round the back of the splendid castle. Skipton is the model medieval town, with the High Street running straight to the door of the Norman parish church and the gate of de Romille's great castle. Here, the imperious instruction 'Desormais' ('Henceforth') in letters of stone provides a chilly welcome for visitors. For five hundred years, from the reign of Edward II, this was the home of the Cliffords who, like the Tempests just a step down the road, were one of the great warrior families of the Middle Ages. In both cases they fought at Crécy and at Agincourt, and on most of the other battlefields of France.

Here, in the heart of Yorkshire, the Cliffords were Lancastrian supporters in the Wars of the Roses, which might seem strange to some but not when it is remembered that the civil strife of the 15th century was not so much about individual allegiance to one's home territory as service to one's overlord. Some historians 'credit' the terrible 'Black-faced' Clifford with the murder of young Edmund, Earl of Rutland and the brother of Richard III, after the Battle of Wakefield. Just a year later it was Clifford's turn, in the Palm Sunday slaughter of the Lancastrians at Towton. His son was spirited away to more remote family estates in Cumberland, there, in contrast, to be brought up as the gentle Shepherd Lord, returning to Skipton when the Tudors were securely on the throne of England.

So the Aire flows on, out of a bloody era and, beyond Skipton, into the Industrial Revolution. Its waters powered the mills of the wool textile industry and even its smaller tributaries played their part. Keighley, first of the major industrial towns, takes its motto 'By Worth' from the stream that tumbles out of the Brontëland moors to join the Aire just southeast of the town. While cartographers dignify it by the title of River Worth, to those who live beside it, it rates nothing grander than 't'beck'.

The Brontë village of Haworth became part of the Borough of Keighley, which in turn was swallowed up in the 1970s by the Metropolitan District of Bradford, but to literary aficionados I suppose Haworth will always remain a community in its own right. Indeed, the pilgrims flock there from every part of the world.

The Parsonage is now a museum and the present landlord of the Black Bull will gently discourage you from drinking yourself to death as Branwell did. A few steps beyond the Parsonage and you are in another world—a world of high, inhospitable moors that stretch for miles before spilling down into Lancashire's answer to Yorkshire's wool—the cotton towns of Rochdale, Oldham and Bolton. Here, in the plaintive cry of the curlew, it is possible to hear the anguish of Heathcliff searching for his lost love.

Haworth is the headquarters of the Keighley and Worth Valley Railway, beloved of steam enthusiasts and invaluable to film-makers. Here *The Railway Children* was made and those who know the line well will have identified many a shot in television plays that call for a steam-railway sequence. It was, in fact, one of the first lines to be saved from the axe of Dr Beeching, and an immense amount of hard work went into restoring and preserving the permanent way, the bridges and the tunnels, acquiring locomotives and rolling stock, and putting it all on a sensible financial basis. One of the Worth Valley line's six stations serves a hamlet called Damems which, in the 1930s, had its own claim to fame as the smallest

THE BRONTË SISTERS

RAPT IN THE pitching emotions chronicled by Emily Brontë's *Wuthering Heights*, it is hard to believe that its creator was a young woman of humble origins, who wrote from a parsonage in the remote Yorkshire village of Haworth. Incredibly, Emily's sister, Charlotte, penned an equal masterpiece, *Jane Eyre*, in the same year, 1847, and Anne, the youngest sister, wrote *The Tenant of Wildfell Hall* a year later. That three young women who knew so little of the world were able to portray such intense passions has long confounded critics. Certainly, each carried the seed of genius within her. Yet their isolated upbringing was also instrumental in nurturing their talents. Removed from the real world, the girls were avid readers, and invented imaginary worlds inspired by the toy soldiers of their brother Patrick, known in the family as Branwell.

The Brontës became Yorkshire folk by adoption: their father, Reverend Patrick Brontë, was of Irish stock, his wife

Cornish. Yet Yorkshire had a profound impact on their work—never more vividly than in Emily's depiction of the bleak moors in *Wuthering Heights*.

The sisters' first book, a volume of verse, was published in 1846, under the names Currer, Ellis and Acton Bell—male pseudonyms assumed for privacy and to ensure that their work would be judged on equal terms with that of male writers. It sold only two copies, but within two years they were the toast of London's literary salons.

The Brontë saga is a very tragic one: Branwell's death from alcohol and opium addiction in 1848 was quickly followed by the loss of Emily and Anne to TB. Charlotte died in 1855 from complications during pregnancy, following her marriage to Arthur Bell

RIGHT *The Brontë sisters—from left, Anne, Emily and Charlotte—in a portrait painted by their brother Branwell, c.1834. A fourth, painted-out figure, probably Branwell himself, can be made out in the centre.*

Nicholls. Yet visitors to the Haworth Parsonage, now the Brontë Parsonage Museum, will notice something else— the caricatures, scribblings and everyday artefacts speak of a family who supported one another in the face of adversity, and of the spirit and vitality that imbue their much-loved novels.

standard-gauge station in the country. Then, I am told, the company built the stationmaster a house to save him a three-mile walk. It doubled the size of the station and the title was lost!

Reinforced by the Worth, the Aire marches on through a forest of mill chimneys, skirting Bradford. (From this great industrial complex ringing Bradford was born perhaps the greatest nursery of county and Test cricketers in the world—the Bradford League. Herbert Sutcliffe, Sir Leonard Hutton, Brian Close, Ray Illingworth were just a few of its products.) First, though, it casts a nostalgic eye upon Saltaire, built by Titus Salt.

As Bradford wrenched from Norwich its pre-eminence in wool marketing, so the manufacturers began to diversify on the outskirts of Britain's fastest-growing town. Huddersfield, Halifax, Keighley all had their own areas of specialisation in the type of cloth they spun, and the area around Dewsbury and Batley, south of Bradford, is still known as 'the heavy woollen district' for the rough but durable qualities of its products. Titus Salt built up a great business with a huge supply of alpaca wool (which for some reason no one seemed to want) lying on the dockside at Liverpool.

Titus Salt built his mill on the banks of the Aire, just three or four miles north of Bradford. As his business prospered, he passed on benefits to his workers in the form of houses, all laid out in uniform streets; and he built churches, schools, institutes, baths and a library. A whole town sprang up and, combining his family name with that of the river, he created Saltaire.

The sad decline of such staple industries of the West Riding as wool and engineering has meant less industrial pollution of the Aire and, although new chemicals now sour its waters, the indefatigable anglers still sally out at weekends in search of chub and roach. How different it must have been in 1152 when a handful of monks trudged down the Aire Valley in search of a place to settle. When they founded Kirkstall Abbey they could fish happily in the clear waters of the Aire and graze their sheep in the water meadows.

They were industrious chaps, those Cistercian monks. Their day started as early as one in the morning and went through until around eight at night! They pioneered the use of iron ore, started a tannery and a pottery, and introduced spinning and weaving using the wool of their own sheep. And when you think that some of these sheep were grazed as far away as Holderness, in the East Riding, they'd have had a bit of walking to do as well. Just to keep them out of mischief, these busy lads were simultaneously building their monastery, which was not quite complete when their first abbot, Alexander, died, thirty years after they had settled there.

In the 12th century, the market in the village of Leeds, a couple of miles downriver, sold the monks' wool at a better price than it fetched at other markets. Seven centuries later, the city of Leeds took the cloth made in the satellite towns around Bradford and made it into clothing. But it all started with, and grew around, those monks who first set up shop down the hill from one of my favourite cricket grounds—Headingley.

BELOW *The enlightened industrialist Sir Titus Salt maintained an unflagging concern for the welfare of his staff. When he died in 1876, 100,000 people are said to have turned out for his funeral procession.*

A SEASONAL TRANSFORMATION

ABOVE *Farndale's famous floral showpiece— countless spring daffodils, or 'Lenten lilies', turn entire hillsides into rolling yellow waves.*

LEFT *Sheep can scarcely graze when the Rosedale winter snow lies thick. But thanks to fodder supplies stored in stone barns, most should survive through to the spring thaw.*

YORKSHIRE'S COUNTRYSIDE is immensely varied—that is part of its fascination. The variation derives not just from the terrain—panoramic dales, austere Pennine peaks, coastal cliffs and limestone scars, riverside glades, blustery moorland heights—but also from the cycle of the seasons. The uplands, in particular, undergo an almost unsettling transformation: it is difficult to believe that a bleak February snowfield is one and the same place as the glorious sweep of purple-heathered moorland in August.

In the remoter parts of Yorkshire, winter can be very long and hard. Heavy snows may isolate distant farms. When spring finally breaks, colour surges back into the countryside's cheeks. Bluebells abound in the valleys. In Farndale, the banks of the River Dove turn yellow with wild daffodils. Later, in June, it is Swaledale's turn to dress in yellow—with buttercups, this time. In the meadows lurk the purples of cranesbill and melancholy thistles, or patches of red clover. The palette grows richer as the summer deepens and the heather blossoms of August and September turn plateaus into mauve seas. On grassier fells, the blue-green base of moor grass is flecked with wild thyme, harebells and yellow rockroses.

LEFT *A russet sunset glow bathes the Pennine landscape near Hebden Bridge.*

RIGHT *A summer carpet of purple heather adorns the Hole of Horcum in the North York Moors National Park, which boasts England's largest expanse of heather moorland.*

Down in the Dales, while the lambs fatten and cavort the long summer days away, wagtails have been tending their nests in the dry-stone walls. But a restlessness sets in as the blackberries ripen and the red hawthorn and rowan berries emerge. The Swaledale curlews prepare to head off to winter in coastal resorts. Autumn descends. Deciduous woodlands transmute their green foliage to shades of gold and red, a last fashion parade before being stripped of their finery by the onset of another winter.

Now the Aire is right out of its river valley. It joins forces with the Calder south-east of Leeds, and enters coal-mining country—and Rugby League country, too. Many of those hard-as-nails League players come out of the mines around Castleford and Featherstone. Over the northern edge of the Yorkshire coalfield slides the Aire and out, once again, into low-lying farmland—a very different river from the sparkling stream that trickled out of Malham Tarn, sixty miles back. It winds between the great cooling towers of the power stations that take the coal hewn from the earth and turn it into energy, until, poisoned and spent, it gratefully starts a new life as part of the Ouse.

EASTERN YORKSHIRE

In spring, the little North Riding valley of Farndale is a glowing mass of gold as the wild daffodils come into bloom; five months later the moors just to the north are an eye-dazzling mass of purple as the heather sings its hymn of praise to high summer. And the road that winds up and down precipitous banks on its way from the picture-postcard delights of Hutton-le-Hole, north to the Cleveland villages of Castleton and Danby, is a route through a Technicolor fairyland. The colours on a bright sunny day, whether it is spring or summer, are spectacular.

This is all part of the immense variety of the countryside that is one of Yorkshire's greatest attractions. The moors that stretch between Pickering and Whitby, for instance, with the weather-beaten old village of Goathland as their capital, are totally different in character from those that separate Yorkshire from Lancashire, far to the west, and this is not merely because the surrealistic outline of the Fylingdales early-warning station looms out of the morning mists to the right, halfway along the journey. These, somehow, are more hospitable moors than those of the Pennines. But though one can certainly visualise the A169 being blocked by driving snowstorms, the moors that straddle the county border far to the west are more easily associated with pitiless, driving rain, and their peat hags with squelchy treachery.

At the southwest corner of the North York Moors are the gentler Hambleton Hills with the chalk outline of a horse carved above Kilburn easily visible from places as far afield as Harrogate and Wetherby. At the foot of the hills we find picturesque villages—the Coxwold of Laurence Sterne, and Kilburn, which has that 314-foot-long white horse carved in the year of the Indian Mutiny by school-master John Hodgson and his pupils. There is Ampleforth, with its great Roman Catholic public school, the ruined abbeys of Byland, Rievaulx and Rosedale, and Hutton-le-Hole where two small streams meet and ramble among the grey stone cottages and green lawns.

Helmsley is a lovely old market town with red-roofed houses entwined with flowering creepers and the ruins of a 12th-century castle, as well as some splendid pubs with a distinctive market-day atmosphere. Eastwards runs the Vale of Pickering, which, topographically as well as geologically, separates the North York Moors from the Yorkshire Wolds, and here again is a valley that provides architectural magnificence with its market towns and villages and, as a bonus,

a great horse-racing, training and breeding tradition—the superb racecourse on York's Knavesmire, the stables of eminent trainers around Malton, and the Sledmere Stud of the Sykes family. Here, too, is Hovingham Hall, family home of the Duchess of Kent before her marriage, and of her father, Sir William Worsley, who, as President of Yorkshire County Cricket Club from 1961 to 1973, was a man for whom I had a profound respect and affection. Pickering, from which the Vale takes its name, is just one more of those characteristic market towns that abound in the area, again with a 12th-century castle ruin to provide an indication of its place in history as a significant centre of population.

On the south side of the valley, through which run the two main roads to the seaside towns of Scarborough, Bridlington and Filey, are the Wolds, which are really a continuation of the ridge running north–south through mid-Lincolnshire. They do not rise much above 600 feet at any point but, because they are flanked by flat and usually fertile plains, the view from any vantage point is always impressive. And as the roads wind through these mini-hills there is always the prospect of a superbly crafted stately home, or a village that looks as though it has been custom-built for the pages of a tourist brochure, round the next corner. This is the home of people different in character and in language from those of the industrial West Riding and, indeed, from the Dales of the far northwest as well. They take time to make up their minds; they weigh their words more carefully, I think, than the townsmen of Leeds and Bradford and Sheffield; and they take life at a more leisurely pace. But they're Yorkshire no less for that.

We have now reached the most southeasterly point of the county, the land that constitutes the northern shores of the great estuary of the Humber. This is Holderness, clearly given its name by the Norsemen, but I doubt if they would recognise much of the coastline eleven hundred years on. At the northern end is the inland lake of Hornsea Mere, over five hundred acres in area and popular with sailors and anglers alike, but the low coastline has been subjected to a battering from the North Sea over so many centuries that it has changed shape and character quite dramatically. And yet, with that marvellous compensation that nature provides, as the coast is eaten away, much of it is swept round into the estuary, to extend and rebuild the great talon of Spurn Head, which claws its way far into the mouth of the Humber. This is a land of the birdwatcher and the naturalist, lengthening by about a yard a year, yet in places no more than a few yards wide.

Looking back westwards, it is infinitely sad to see the outline of the once-great port of Hull, its trawler fleet now decimated and its trade in decline. I looked the other day at a reference book, published only in 1971, and read:

> Fishing fleets, cargo ships, oil tankers and now streamlined modern car ferries nose past Spurn Head, twenty-one miles southeast, and head for the forest of derricks and cranes along miles of Hull's dockland. The docks grow almost annually to cope with a surging tide of cargo: wool from Australia and New Zealand for the West Riding mills, timber from Scandinavia, dairy products from Denmark, grain and seed for the flour mills and oil-extraction plants that punctuate the Hull horizons.

It is strange and tragic to reflect that this was written when Hull was Britain's third-largest port. Alas, few would recognise it today from the description. And yet Hull always has been a city of the sea and, even now, amid the industrial decay of the end of the 20th century, it remains so in its pride and dignity and personality.

THE ULTIMATE DALESMAN

In April 1939 a new magazine appeared on the counters of booksellers and newsagents—largely those in the North of England, but some through more adventurous agents in other parts of the country. Today, the magazine goes into homes in more than fifty countries. It found its way through to the Falklands during the war with Argentina; and through the Iron Curtain into Moscow; it flies to remote islands like Ascension, in mid South Atlantic, and Tuvalu in the South Pacific; it reaches picturesque addresses like 'Cutter's Corn, Norfolk Island' (between New Zealand and the Queensland coast). And it arrives each month at the homes of thousands of countryside enthusiasts throughout Britain and of nostalgic expatriates living in Australia, Canada, New Zealand and the United States.

The Dalesman magazine is one of the outstanding success stories in journalism of the most wholesome kind.

It started life as *The Yorkshire Dalesman*, created and produced from one room of a house in the pretty village of Clapham, deep in the heart of northwest Yorkshire's limestone country—the inspiration of a man called Harry J. Scott, and indeed it could only have been the creation of a man like him. He was a Quaker, the kindest and most generous of souls, with a gentle humour and a tongue and pen incapable of malice. He wrote with love about lovable things, and the greatest of these to Harry Scott (after his family) was the limestone country of the Yorkshire Dales. He worked on newspapers in Leeds but yearned for the country life and at every opportunity fled with his wife, son and daughter to a cottage in the

ABOVE *Harry Scott, founder of* The Dalesman, *and his wife Dorothy (seated in the centre) pose for a photograph with the magazine's staff.*

TOP RIGHT *Home to Harry Scott, and the original headquarters of his beloved* Dalesman, *the cottage named Fellside (centre) sits beside a beck in the village of Clapham.*

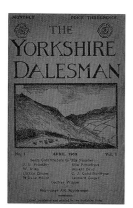

ABOVE *A monthly magazine celebrating life in the Dales,* The Yorkshire Dalesman *would in time shorten its name, to become simply* The Dalesman.

Washburn Valley. Since these opportunities occurred only at weekends and in holiday time, they were not enough. In the mid-thirties—not exactly a time of prosperity in the industrial West Riding—he took a dramatic and daring step. He gave up the security of his salaried job on the *Yorkshire Post,* rented an old, stone-built house in Clapham and moved there with his young family. His economic planning had a simple innocence: if he could make £3 a week by free-lance writing, they could live well in surroundings that seemed to them idyllic.

There he could dream, amid the stream of articles he wrote under his own name and a variety of pseudonyms, on every kind of countryside topic, of ultimately pouring all his energy into a magazine of his own, a publication that would reflect the leisurely tempo of life in the Dales, the quality and standards of that life, and at the same time capture the dynamic changes of nature. Quietly he laid his plans and, with his own savings and a little help from friends, *The Yorkshire Dalesman* was launched in the spring of a momentous year—1939.

J. B. Priestley welcomed the first edition. 'I am glad to learn,' he wrote in that original issue, 'that our beloved Dales are to have their own magazine.' Priestley went on to recall having been commissioned to tramp through Wharfedale and Wensleydale to write a series of articles shortly after the First World War: 'I have never found again—no, not even in the romantic islands of the West Indies or the South Seas, not in the deserts of Egypt or Arizona—the sunlight that set all the dewdrops glittering about my path that morning.' A beautiful recollection of 1919; I wonder if Priestley realised, as he wrote, how close we were to another, even more cataclysmic war that was to involve most of the world.

Certainly Harry Scott didn't, or perhaps wouldn't, allow himself to think so. By August 1939, he was enthusiastically writing to potential advertisers: 'Already circulation has reached 7,000,' and inviting them to take advertising space in the magazine at 3s. per column inch. Exactly one month later, the world was at war.

This had the immediate effect of pegging the circulation of *The Yorkshire Dalesman* to the figure that had given Scott so much delight after only four issues. Just about every penny he possessed had gone into the magazine's launch. Now came the problem of keeping afloat amid the most appalling difficulties.

Scott was not the sort who could contemplate his own well-being while thousands were dying every day in a war in which he could not take part himself. Regular subscribers were asked to return their copies, once read, to that one room in Scott's home, by now named Fellside, where they were recycled, so to speak, and sent to members of the forces. Many of them found their way to ships, airstrips and battlefields, where the first enemy might well be a German or a Japanese or an Italian, but the second was most certainly boredom. Scott's little magazine provided the perfect answer to it. In those pages of gently humorous anecdote about Dalesfolk, articles on shepherds and dry-stone wallers, servicemen and women found an antidote to the horrors of war. In the drawings and photographs and reproductions of watercolours of Dales scenes and characters, they could escape.

Scott's simple act of kindness in seeking to offer a little comfort to those who were involved quite accidentally assured the success of *The Yorkshire Dalesman*. By the end of the war it had a new public that might never otherwise have been tapped, and the Dales themselves had a new fan club.

By 1946 the magazine was on a sound financial basis and expanding in every direction. *The Yorkshire Dalesman* became *The Dalesman*. Later came a flood of specialist books and booklets covering every aspect of country life. The Dalesman Publishing Company was born. It is still alive and well and flourishing in Clapham.

Shortly after the war, as the front room of Fellside began to overflow with manuscripts, reference books and typewriters, headquarters were moved to the other side of Clapham Beck. The editorial offices were in what used to be the vicar's coachhouse, and commercial and sales offices were in adjoining buildings. The publication of books began to grow and the list of titles at times exceeded three hundred, covering subjects ranging from countryside walks around York to the confessions of a Swaledale poacher, from Pennine birds to Roman forts, brass rubbings to farmhouse recipes, battlefields to water mills, witches to sheepdogs.

But still the flagship of the fleet, *The Dalesman*, sails out across the continents and oceans. Mr and Mrs Ashworth, in Port Stanley, Falkland Islands, are subscribers for whom *The Dalesman* staff experienced a special concern in the summer of 1982. When the fighting ended in those far-off islands, Mrs Eileen Plumridge slipped a note into the envelope containing the September edition of *The Dalesman*, anxiously enquiring how many copies they had missed during that brief, sad war. Back came the answer: 'None, thank you—all our copies got through. And by the way, we had a white rose sticker attached to the windscreen of our Land-Rover throughout the Argentine occupation.'

There is a sublime wholesomeness about the contents of *The Dalesman*, which somehow protects it from the mess of war. It is good for the soul to read a publication that has no reference to conflict, mugging, hooliganism, dishonesty, cheating, lying or deceit. It may not reflect life in general in the world today, but it does reflect those qualities of rural England that it is still possible to find if you search industriously enough—the qualities that Harry J. Scott loved and prized sufficiently to want to encapsulate in one magazine, half a century ago. He lived to see his dream come true before he died in January 1978.

CHAPTER THREE

MUSIC OF THE INDUSTRIAL NORTH

ABOVE *Shadows of Yorkshire's industrial past lend a touch of poignancy to this sunset over the Leeds and Liverpool Canal.*

TWO OF THE MOST SIGNIFICANT STRANDS of Yorkshire's cultural heritage developed, indirectly but clearly, from the Industrial Revolution—choral singing and brass band music—and if we illustrate this by taking one example of each of these art forms this is not meant to disparage Yorkshire's many other choirs and bands. The Huddersfield Choral Society and the Black Dyke Mills Band are the tips of two enormous icebergs, for both traditions have spread far and wide, most notably in the mill and mining towns of the West Riding.

John Wesley, the evangelist, played a major part in establishing choral singing by bringing in a form of Christian worship that appealed to the working class of northern England—passionate preaching and fervent singing. Apart from his Christian message, Wesley gave his new chapels hymns that he or his brother Charles had written, with stirring words and rousing tunes. Sunday services in Wesley's chapels became more than an act of worship. There was joy to be experienced in singing well-loved hymns, and they were sung with fervour. And as the home crafts of spinning and weaving were swamped by the advancing tide of industrial mechanisation in the early 19th century, so workers were thrown together in increasing numbers. They sang together on Sunday and worked side by side during the week. Why not combine the two and sing together during the week?

And so the first choirs were born. As oratorios and other forms of sacred music filtered into England from Germany, repertoires became more ambitious, even though few of those early choristers can have had any formal training in reading music. If they had a voice, they learned to use it by standing next to a singer who knew the music, and they learned every note, every cadence, every inflection, every rhythm, every tempo, simply by listening.

This, then, is what music meant to the mill-working, chapel-going populace of the industrial north in the 19th century. It brightened a drab existence; and it has given us magnificence to enrich our more sophisticated society.

THE HUDDERSFIELD CHORAL SOCIETY

The beginning of the Huddersfield Choral Society was as unlikely as anyone can imagine. When Wesley first visited the area in the middle of the 18th century he said of the local populace that 'a wilder people I never saw in England'. But he left behind his Nonconformism and from those Wesleyan chapels and Anglican churches came sixteen men, on the evening of June 7, 1836, to meet in the Plough Inn, in Westgate. They soberly drew up a 'Preamble' establishing a choral society and ordaining that the first meeting was to be held in the Infant School, Spring Street, on Friday, the 15th day of July 1836, at eight o'clock in the evening, the succeeding meetings to be held on the Friday on or before the full moon in every month. Full moonlight was necessary to find one's way home along unlit roads!

LEFT *Yorkshire's Heptonstall Chapel is the oldest Methodist chapel in the world in continuous use. The foundation stone of the hexagonal building was laid by John Wesley in 1764.*

BELOW *John Wesley spreads the word of God. After Wesley's death, Methodism continued to grow throughout the English-speaking world and now has a following of some 26 million.*

From the first there was a discipline that we see reflected in the present-day rules. Late arrivals for practice were fined threepence—increasing to sixpence if they were more than fifteen minutes late or absent altogether (unless through sickness), and here you see the common sense of it: if you are going to have a choir, the absence of even one voice can affect the balance of its singing. Today, the members register their attendance at rehearsals (rather in the manner of clocking on at the mill) and those who do not make the required number of appearances meet a fate far worse than a sixpenny fine—they risk missing a concert.

In 1837, there were fifty-four men but only eight 'female performers', a balance that is greatly changed today. The first conductor was Henry Horn, who was organist at St Paul's parish church, so he was one of the founders who was not from the Nonconformist fraternity, and his principal lieutenants were twin brothers, James and Edward Battye, librarian and secretary respectively. James Battye was an accomplished musician and some of the glees—unaccompanied part songs—and anthems he composed are still sung. Perhaps his finest epitaph lies in a minute of the society for November 20, 1848: 'Resolved that a selection from the works of Handel, Haydn, Mozart, Battye, etc, be performed...' That's what I call moving in distinguished circles.

By 1837 the society was performing in Huddersfield's Philosophical Hall, which was hired for four 'quarterly meetings'. Hiring fees might have presented a problem, but not to a group of Yorkshiremen accustomed to watching their brass carefully. The choir simply gave one extra concert, in December or January, to pay the rent.

By the middle of Queen Victoria's reign the society was firmly established and its concerts had become major musical and social events in the growing textile town. Choir practice took precedence over everything short of family bereavement—and this tradition has been maintained amid the sophisticated counterattractions of today.

Susan Sykes, the daughter of a Brighouse gardener, was found to have a remarkable singing voice as a child. She first sang in public at the age of fourteen, and four years later she married a local butcher to become Mrs Sunderland; to this day, in Yorkshire music circles, the name has a real ring to it. It is perpetuated by the Mrs Sunderland musical competitions, held annually, which have started many singers on their careers. So great were her natural gifts that by the time she was twenty-three she was giving recitals in London. Queen Victoria was a staunch admirer, and after one of her many private concerts at Buckingham Palace, the Queen handed Mrs Sunderland her own autographed score of the *Messiah*, with the tribute: 'I am Queen of England, but you are Queen of Song.' For ever afterwards, Mrs Sunderland has been known as 'The Yorkshire Queen of Song'. Yet for all the fame her superb soprano voice brought her, Mrs S. sang for twenty years as the Huddersfield Choral Society's principal soprano.

Despite those palmier days, the society had serious problems in the 1870s. Its concert hall had been converted to a theatre and there was no other suitable

ABOVE *The soprano Mrs Susan Sunderland, whose vocal talents were discovered by choirmaster and blacksmith Luke Settle; she is said to have rehearsed by keeping time to Settle's rhythmic hammering upon an anvil.*

building in which to perform before the public. Naturally enough, support drained away. Fees for guest soloists were getting higher, income from concerts lower. The society found that in a number of ways the pace of change was too swift for it. Yet there was enough perspicacity in the membership to ask, when Huddersfield was about to be incorporated as a borough, to be allowed to collaborate in the design of the first town hall. When it was opened, in October 1881, it included a concert hall and an organ.

So what better way to open the building than with a three-day music festival? The choral society, more than two hundred and fifty of them, assembled in their serried ranks and for three days and nights the music poured out of Huddersfield's brand-new town hall: Mendelssohn, Berlioz, Rossini—nothing frivolous, you understand. World-famous principals were called to Huddersfield for those three days of song. Sir Charles Hallé brought over his orchestra of growing reputation and at the end of the festival said, 'I have conducted many choruses but have never found a better, or, indeed, one so good. For refinement, perfect truth of intonation and expression, and especially for power, it cannot be surpassed or equalled for the same number.'

The 'Huddersfield' was back on course after a few troubled years and, what was more, it had found a true home. Even while the choir continues to travel the world and to startle new ears with the sound Hallé admired so much, Huddersfield Town Hall has remained its spiritual home. This period, which the society itself refers to as its renaissance, saw the membership rise to 450.

Then came the new century and a new era for the society when, in 1901, Dr Henry Coward became the conductor. Coward, who was later knighted, was

ABOVE *Thumbnail sketches capture some of the personalities who took part in 1881's Huddersfield Musical Festival, among them the conductor Sir Charles Hallé (top right).*

ABOVE LEFT *Framed against the magnificent fixtures and fittings of Huddersfield Town Hall, the massed ranks of Huddersfield Choral Society in full voice are an impressive sight.*

ABOVE *The Choral's part in the centenary celebration of Vienna's Choral Union of the Society of the Friends of Music earned it both rapturous applause and a silver medal cast to mark the occasion.*

TOP *The Sir Malcolm Sargent years were captured for posterity in recordings such as this mid-fifties interpretation of Handel's* Messiah.

not only technically brilliant as a musician; he was a man of vision, imagination and sensitivity. 'Under him,' wrote W. L. Wilmshurst, in an early history of the society, 'rehearsals become not merely formal practices but occasions of valuable education, both vocally and intellectually, which no one wished to miss.'

Coward took a choir with a reputation for immense volume ('Sledgehammer singing', according to London critics) and really shaped the singing of the society as it is today. He created a sound that in its full, disciplined volume can make the hairs stand out on the nape of the neck, and then be hauled down from those soaring heights to a pianissimo 'above which,' as Coward said, 'the ticking of a clock can be heard.' Remember—many of those 400 voices belonged to men and women who spent their days in spinning and weaving sheds. Any kind of conversation at all between workmates had to be conducted at full fortissimo to be audible above the rattle of the looms. There was no great need to develop voice production among Coward's cohorts. He had the base material and he worked on it.

Coward remained with the Huddersfield Choral Society for thirty-one years and the value of the association is incalculable. He was succeeded by Malcolm Sargent, who was to become the much-loved 'Flash Harry' to a future generation of final-night Promenaders. So came another golden age for the Choral. Sargent worked on Coward's 'flexible instrument', refining its already splendid qualities until that pianissimo moved critics to a new extravagance of description: 'In *The Dream of Gerontius* the choir could give a diminuendo so delicate that it was difficult to decide where the tone ended and the silence began.' Sargent took the society to Vienna, Berlin, Brussels and the United States. Austria found their *Messiah* to be 'sensational'. Magnificent recordings flowed from the presses—*Messiah, Elijah* and *Gerontius*. If any had doubted the international reputation of the society, these recordings alone would have dispelled the doubts, but Sargent marched his choir around the world as if to establish that the acclaim was not due to the skill of recording engineers.

Sir Malcolm Sargent was followed by Wyn Morris (1969–72) and John Pritchard (1973–80). Then came the dynamic and imaginative Welshman, Owain Arwel Hughes, with a briefcase full of new ideas, one of which was the Workshop Weekend, when members travelled to a seaside hotel to refresh themselves, to concentrate hard on their music-making, and also to enjoy something of the good fellowship of an artistic association.

What is it that creates the unique Huddersfield sound, the sound that soars and shimmers and hovers and then flies to join the angels, from whom, it seems, it must have come in the first place? It is not mere quality that marks it as different. The 'Hallelujah Chorus' of that incomparable 1950s recording of the

Messiah is as distinctive, musically, as the Taj Mahal is architecturally. Sir Malcolm Sargent is reputed to have explained it thus: 'Northern people are accustomed to speaking their minds. They are not afraid to open their mouths to report what is in their hearts and the singing of the Choral is an expression of their thoughts and feelings.'

But how do you equate that with the view of a lady member of the Huddersfield who outraged a few million Celts by offering the view: 'The Welsh sing with their hearts; we sing with our heads'? From Arnold Harrop, the longest-serving member of the society, came this explanation: 'It's something to do with the moors, the wide open spaces which surround us. You can go up there and let rip as loud as you like to develop the voice.'

Arnold Harrop is part of the Nonconformist tradition of entry into the Choral, 'graduating' from the Mount Pleasant Wesleyan Methodist chapel at Lockwood. But there are not so many Arnold Harrops around these days. Often where there were once three Methodist chapels there is now one—and in some places none at all. Those stately buildings have become school annexes, builders' offices, even car showrooms; the voice of the choirs is stilled and one great area of recruitment to the Huddersfield Choral Society is gone for ever.

However, there is a steady flow of applicants and membership is still highly prized. There is a growing interest among young professional people and, as the standards and reputation of the society hold firm, many members now travel long distances (without having to wait for the light of the full moon!) to Friday-night rehearsals, drawn by those standards and stirred by the challenge of the audition.

THE BLACK DYKE MILLS BAND

At the top of the bare wooden staircase that leads to the bandroom of the Black Dyke Mills Band hangs a print that I dare say epitomises the archetypal Yorkshireman—at least to a lot of the southern gentry. He sits, eighteen stone of him, in shirt and trousers, a plate bearing the remains of his evening meal in front of him, with the mandatory dish of pickled onions and a pint bottle of stout.

A thin curtain covers the entrance to the next room from which comes subdued conversation of a technical nature. 'I think that's a B flat at bar twenty-seven, Ian...Right. Let's try it again.' There is the light tap of a thin baton on a music stand. You know that music is about to be made. But no way in the world are you prepared for what now comes surging through that curtain, swelling through the stout gritstone walls, rolling and roaring around the rafters. It is a juggernaut of sound, picking you up and tossing you like matchwood in an Atlantic gale. You are carried away on a sea of molten brass. It dies away to a tender pianissimo, held on the boundary of credibility...gently, delicately, tremulously held. And then, with an upward sweep of an unseen, baton-clutching hand, away we roar again. In the concert hall the sound of the Black Dyke Mills Band is majestic, imperious; here, at rehearsal in the bandroom, which just finds room for the twenty-six players and their conductor, it stuns the senses. And yet for all the sheer volume of sound, it is controlled, ordered, disciplined—and magnificent.

The band won the first Crystal Palace contest ever held, back in 1860, and it has been used to winning ever since. Its record in the National Championships shows wins in 1902, 1928, 1947, 1948, 1949 (after three successive wins Dyke had to miss the 1950 contest), 1951, 1959, 1961, 1967, 1972, 1975, 1976, 1977 (another year's exile for another hat trick), 1979 and 1981. Eleven second placings, nine thirds and three fourths are regarded as unworthy of mention. The band won the European Championship in 1978, 1979 and 1982, and were World Champions in 1970. And for good measure, Black Dyke were the BBC's Band of the Year in 1967, 1970, 1975, 1976 and 1979. So it's not difficult to see why, to me, they are the foremost representatives of a form of self-entertainment that grew from the poverty of Victorian England.

Perhaps I should make that 'Victorian Britain', because the first-known all-brass band was formed in Blaina, South Wales, in 1832, where the poverty of the working class was just as grinding as that of the West Riding. The delicate touch required for stringed instruments was not a natural attribute among the workers of these industrial regions and, apart from that, they must have found the playing

YORKSHIRE AND THE INDUSTRIAL REVOLUTION

PROFOUND INDUSTRIAL ADVANCES swept through Britain in the 18th and 19th centuries. In less than 100 years, our country's mainly agricultural economy was transformed into one based primarily upon urban manufacturing; a process that came to be known as the Industrial Revolution. This epochal period in the history of mankind derived much of its momentum from the Midlands and the North, where the raw materials requisite to change were to be found in bountiful supply—if England became the 'workshop of the world', then these regions comprised its furnace.

For centuries, what little manufacture went on had taken place largely in the home, and by hand. Families had long produced cloth in their cottages, to supplement their income. The Industrial Revolution changed all this. As machines grew bigger, and the division of labour more marked, manufacture shifted from the home and into the factory, and the face of Britain was altered for ever.

Several factors combined to spark the revolution. The 18th century witnessed

an outburst of inventiveness spawning labour-saving innovations, like the spinning jenny and Compton's mule, whose colourful names often belied their importance. This glut of new machinery coincided with the harnessing of coal and steam as new energy sources. Shadowing these industrial advances were equally profound developments in the field of transport, with canals and steam trains greatly easing the passage of freight from source to market.

ABOVE *Bradford chokes in a soupy industrial smog. 'If anyone wishes to feel how a sinner is tormented in Purgatory,' wrote German poet Georg Weerth, 'let him travel to Bradford.'*

The Industrial Revolution transformed the sociological complexion of Yorkshire, whose rich coal reserves made it attractive to industrial magnates. Whole cities developed around single industries: Sheffield around steel; Leeds around wool; and Bradford around worsted cloth.

of brass a braver, more stirring experience, than scraping a violin. Consequently, the brass band became to the horny-handed sons of toil what the string quartet was to the occupants of stately homes.

The origins of the town band can be traced back to the 'Waits', small groups of musicians who wandered the streets. A brass band in the early 19th century would have been incapable of making anything like the sound a modern band makes, because the brass instruments of those days had no valves so the range of notes was limited. Repertoires were extended by adding reed instruments like the clarinet, flute and piccolo, giving greater range, but there were few working men who played woodwind. Army units were able to train musicians to play them, however, and today a combination of brass and wood-wind (with percussion) is still called a 'military band' as distinct from the brass band, which has no woodwind. It was the perfection of the valve, to develop the range of brass instruments, that played a major part in establishing the brass band tradition of the working man's music-making.

Queensbury, which straggles over a ridge between Bradford and Halifax, was a tiny village called 'Queenshead' when Peter Wharton formed a brass and reed band there in the year that Wellington and Bonaparte were having their little ding-dong on the fields of Waterloo. Eighteen years later the village got its second band, still a 'military' combination, with a French horn player called John Foster in its ranks. Foster owned the local woollen mill and he bought a set of brass instruments to form a band for his workers in 1855, and the Black Dyke Mills Band was born.

Fred Ellis is secretary and treasurer of the Black Dyke and a former player. His pride in his association is manifest but, just like the current players, the first thing you notice about him is that he radiates a sense of personal pleasure—joy, even—in his work. The Black Dyke take their pleasure, and their music, to fifty concerts a year. They have toured Europe and the United States. They have broadcast well over five hundred times and made forty records. They have played for the Queen, the Duke of Edinburgh and Prince Charles. They have been conducted by Edward Heath and backed a 'single' by Paul McCartney. They have played in Henry Wood Promenade Concerts and staged a BBC 2 television 'spectacular'.

Yet their enjoyment of their own music-making never seems to flag. Perhaps it comes from a sense of release from the tensions of the two great contests a year—the British Open, traditionally held in Manchester, and the National Championships in London.

'Everyone wants to knock Black Dyke off their perch,' says Fred Ellis. 'We don't listen to the other bands. If we are drawn to play early, we do it and then disappear until the adjudication. If we are late in the draw, we get back into the bus and go for a drive into the country until it's our turn. No, not to a pub. There's no drinking before we play. Afterwards? Ah, well, we might relax a bit then. But we generally know when we've won without waiting for the results.'

ABOVE *The euphonium, a brass wind instrument with valves, resembles the tuba in shape but has a somewhat higher pitch and a mellower sound.*

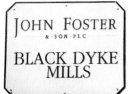

ABOVE *The band's name doffs its cap to the company that spawned it, though the 'Mills' was dropped in 1997.*

TOP *Black Dyke, dressed in full regalia, pose for a photograph outside Park House, Queensbury. The house was one of many built by the Foster family of Black Dyke Mills.*

How can that be if they don't listen to the other contestants? Well, here we find the natural confidence of men who know quite simply that, in top form, they are the best. If they have played well, they know it. And they know that at their best they are unbeatable.

Fred gave me a cassette of one of their recent recordings (Russian music— Shostakovich, Rachmaninov, Mussorgsky, Rimsky-Korsákov, Prokofiev, Glinka, Tchaikovsky, Borodin) and a car sticker proclaiming me a 'Pondasher' of the Black Dyke Mills Band. 'Pondasher' was the pseudonym of a *Sunday Times* writer who produced an article on the band and they delightedly seized on it as a generic term for their aficionados.

The band is a Yorkshire institution, as much as cricket and fish and chips and Ilkla Moor and batter pudding. Wherever music is played in the world, they've heard of the band from that windswept hilltop of Queensbury, but let's leave the last word to Frank Dean, probably Black Dyke's greatest Pondasher: 'A slip or a "fluffed" note is a national crisis and there are no allowances for reasons and certainly no place for excuses. They aim higher than is possible to achieve and usually arrive at a point which is as near perfection as human frailty will permit. When a collection of plumbers, joiners, teachers and clothworkers can assemble and produce the sounds which Dyke do, then there has to be a God.'

ELIZABETH HARWOOD: A LIFE OF MUSIC

Just as the choirs were born out of a need to create one's own entertainment, they in turn produced men and women with outstanding voices to be the soloists at their concerts. Many of these went on to win international reputations on the concert platform and the stage. But there were also those who were quite simply born to sing, whose natural gifts were developed through private tuition and training in the great musical academies of the North of England. One such singer is the soprano Elizabeth Harwood.

Strictly speaking, as she was born in Northamptonshire, Elizabeth Harwood is not a Yorkshire lass at all—but it would not be advisable to give her an argument about it. Her father, a 100 per cent thoroughbred Yorkshireman, moved back to his native county when his daughter was just five months old. Sydney Harwood was a Scarborough-born local government officer and in 1938 he became clerk to the Skipton Rural District Council. So the young Elizabeth spent the whole of her childhood in the Gateway to the Dales.

Elizabeth was brought up in a home filled with music. Father was a chorister. Mother (Constance Read in her professional life) was a beautiful soprano. Miss Read, against her father's wishes, enrolled at the Royal Academy of Music, took her Licentiate of the Royal Academy of Music in singing and teaching, and performed as a soloist in the early days of broadcasting. After the Harwood family had moved to Skipton— their home was actually in the village of Embsay, just outside the town—Mr and Mrs Harwood (tenor and soprano) teamed up with their friends Dr and Mrs Merlin (baritone and contralto) for Sunday musical evenings in the delightful Edwardian tradition. And so for the young Elizabeth began a life of music.

'I remember those Sunday evenings of singing, all through the war. They were wonderful. And, of course, with Mother teaching, there were always pupils in the house. Mother tells a lovely story about one of them—a very pretty girl who took a long, long time to learn. Mother was trying to teach her pupil an aria from *The Magic Flute* while she could hear me, upstairs, at the age of four, singing it perfectly. So it was all being taken in. I was learning music, absorbing it, becoming steeped in it, at that age.'

Elizabeth went to Skipton Girls' High School and as she moved up the school she learned the piano, the violin and the double bass. It was while she was a pupil there that Elizabeth first met Sir Malcolm Sargent.

'I joined a country-dancing class in Skipton and met a boy who was away at school but whose father was Captain Fordyce, agent for the Skipton Castle estate, and his mother was, for a while, secretary to Sir Malcolm Sargent. John was home from school and asked me if I would like to go to a concert Sir Malcolm was giving in Leeds. I leapt at the chance because I had never been to anything like that, and at the concert John sent a little note round—written on Skipton Castle notepaper, which had the desired effect—asking if we could meet him. The conductor replied that he'd

ABOVE *Soprano singer Elizabeth Harwood during a performance of* The Count Ory *at Sadler's Wells in 1963.*

like us to have dinner with him afterwards at the Queen's Hotel in Leeds and I couldn't believe it. I had to pinch myself. I was no more than sixteen but I remember telling Sir Malcolm that I was going to be a singer and he patted me, metaphorically and indulgently, on the head and said, "Of course you are, my dear." I insisted, "Yes, I am. I know I am going to sing with you, one day," and he again indulged me, very pleasantly, thinking I'm sure, The poor little thing doesn't know what it's all about. Five years later I went to London after winning the Kathleen Ferrier Memorial Scholarship and in fact Sir Malcolm gave me some of my first big chances, to sing at the Royal Albert Hall and in the Proms.'

Elizabeth was still only sixteen when she sang her first *Messiah*. It was an engagement her mother was due to fulfil in one of the villages near Skipton— 'I think it was Beamsley but Mother says it was Bradley'—but Madame Read went down with a cold and sent her daughter instead. The fee was to be one guinea but Elizabeth was given 25 shillings 'because she showed a lot of promise'. Elizabeth Harwood has since sung in nearly every major opera house in the world.

Her mother, at seventy-seven, looks twenty years younger than her age. She has eight pupils who go to her regularly for lessons, and every Wednesday morning twenty members of the local Women's Institute choir arrive for rehearsals. She runs a harvest festival concert, compering the hour-long show herself. She has an incredible zest for life. Perhaps that's the secret, the unbroken link, spanning the years since she and her husband sang in the chapels and village halls of Beamsley and Hebden and Giggleswick and Appletreewick. For Elizabeth, too, now settled in Essex, those days are fresh in the memory—Mother pedalling away at a little harmonium and joining Father in a duet, 'Love Divine, All Loves Excelling', and the harvest festival days with suppers of 'wonderful Yorkshire cooking and baking'.

'I treasure my memories. So many of them are of Yorkshire...the happiest of childhoods with the music that my parents gave me. I miss the Yorkshire people; I miss their warmth. I used to walk a lot at home in Yorkshire and I love the seclusion of being alone. When I go back North, to Ilkley, I've got to go on the moors.

'You can have all the Swiss mountains in the world, but to go up onto the Cow and Calf...the beauty, the fresh air...it's sheer therapy. Nothing can take its place.'

Anyone who has climbed up to Ilkley Moor will know exactly what she means.

THE GOOD OLD DAYS

In 1953, the newly established northern outpost of BBC Television submitted to London a one-off programme on the history of the music hall. The superb City Varieties Theatre in Leeds was the ideal setting for the documentary, which traced traditional music-hall entertainment from the Victorian era up to 1953. One box in the theatre was set aside for shots of the audience and, as the different eras were portrayed onstage, the eight occupants had to leap out of the box after each act for a quick change of costume. It was an historic moment for the theatre, for television, and for those people in the box. The traditional chairman of the show was Don Gemmell, from the Players' Theatre in London, where the idea for the documentary had first occurred to its producer, Barney Colehan.

OPPOSITE *The Cow and Calf Rocks form stark landmarks above the town of Ilkley. According to local hearsay, a Bull Rock once stood beside them, but was broken up in the last century and used to build a hotel in Ilkley.*

The programme was enthusiastically received at television headquarters in London and back came an enquiry to Barney Colehan: 'Can you do some more?' 'Well,' said Barney, 'we can't do the history of the music hall again, but we'll take the best of the idea and develop it.' And the best of the idea was the participation of an audience not only willing, but wildly enthusiastic to don Edwardian dress, to grow (or glue) side-whiskers of the most luxuriant quality and generally to enter into the spirit of a music-hall performance as it originally developed. The first *Good Old Days* was recorded at Leeds City Varieties in July 1953 and, like Topsy, it growed and growed.

Thirty years later, when the BBC decided to take the show off, there was a waiting list of 25,000 people clamouring for a chance to put on hooped skirts, starched shirtfronts, tails or dazzling military dress uniforms, to boo and hiss, to join in choruses, to acclaim or deplore the articulate artistic alliteration of Leonard Sachs, its chairman for all but the first four programmes. It would have taken nearly ten years for the last people on that waiting list to reach the head of the queue for a seat in the stalls or circle of the City Varieties at *The Good Old Days*.

The beginnings were modest. In 1953 there was no 'run-out' at the front of the stage where the chorus line could kick their collective legs, or the balladeers serenade the audience, and no separate box for the chairman, who simply had a seat onstage. The playbill for the first show on Monday, July 20, 1953, reads like

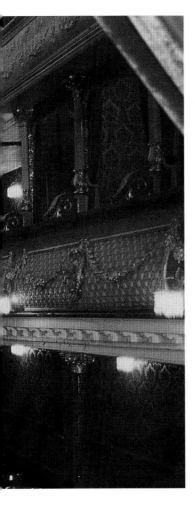

this: Billy Wareham (acrobat), Florrie Ford (played by Marjorie Manners, one of the great principal boys of pantomime), Eric Williams (magician), Joe King (comedian), Jack Pleasants (played by Geoffrey Hibbert, doing 'Twenty-one Today'), Pop, White and Stagger (comedians), Vesta Tilley (played by Joan Sterndale-Bennett) and the Cancan Girls.

As the show grew in popularity with both theatregoing and television public, so the big-name artistes of the theatre began to show more interest. Within a few years Morecambe and Wise, Bruce Forsyth, Des O'Connor were all happy to appear on *The Good Old Days*. The audience became ever more enthusiastic and a queue for seats began to form. Then colour television arrived to add a completely new dimension to the scene and there was a positive explosion in the demand for seats. They became more precious than Cup Final tickets and theatrical costumiers who might well have been ready to close their businesses in the sixties and seventies suddenly found a new demand for frills and feathers and furbelows. The theatre itself, a glory of scarlet and gold Edwardiana, became another star of the show.

The Good Old Days had by now reached the stage when the audience was better dressed than the artistes; the decor of the theatre was more elaborate than the sets. So producer Colehan had to prise a bit more money out of the BBC to dress up his show and to buy really big names to open and close it. It began

ABOVE *A trip to see* The Good Old Days *at the City Varieties Music Hall in Leeds always provided a good excuse for delving into one's dressing-up box.*

ABOVE LEFT *Lush and exotic, the interior of the City Varieties Music Hall in Leeds was constructed according to the oblong layout typical of early music halls.*

RIGHT *Barney Colehan, producer of* The Good Old Days*, gets a close shave from a Wild West knife-throwing act.*

as a vehicle for the real music-hall performers like Rob Wilton, G. H. Elliott, Randolph Sutton; after twenty years it had entered the age of the television star—still with a nostalgic appeal of its own but now, in the more sophisticated era of the small screen, having to compete on its merits as a television programme. Yet over the years the style of *The Good Old Days* basically never changed. It got better in terms of content, dress and sets (and audience participation). It survived competition from the big-budget spectaculars like *The Shirley Bassey Show* and *The Morecambe and Wise Show*; it saw one situation comedy series after another wax and wane. But *The Good Old Days* for thirty years retained its appeal to the public by simply putting on a music-hall performance.

The programme has gone out live and as a recording; it has gone out on every night of the week, at one time or another, from Monday to Sunday; it has been screened as early as 7.00pm and as late as 11.30pm, and yet it has always found a television audience. The programme has been sold to Norway, Denmark, Sweden, Holland, Belgium. It gained a big audience in Australia.

The big stars had come to love it, not only because it was the last bastion of music-hall entertainment, but because it was difficult—virtually impossible—to 'die' in front of such an overwhelmingly friendly audience. Dear old Arthur Askey perhaps summed it up best of all. 'If you can't succeed on *The Good Old Days*,' he said, 'you can pack it up because the audience have been waiting years to come, and when they get there, they nearly eat you.'

AN INNOVATIVE PRODUCER

According to Barney Colehan, the success of the world's longest-running television show was based on a mixture of ingredients—the nostalgia, the joy of hearing and joining in the singing of favourite old songs, the delight of dressing up in colourful and flamboyant costume, the communicated pleasure of the artistes and the perfection of the theatre itself. Leeds City Varieties developed from what was really a large bar where people went for a social drink and the entertainment was a secondary attraction. It developed with the addition of stages and a custom-built theatre.

And Barney Colehan the television innovator was virtually immortalised by having the original bar named after him. His name was in use in just about every household in the country in the forties and fifties. Remember 'Give him the money, Barney'? The words were those of Wilfred Pickles, whose rich Halifax voice was heard on one radio programme after another at a time when television had not reached the North (or very many other parts of the country outside the London area, for that matter), but 'Barney' was none other than B. Colehan, producer of the homely, slightly vulgar, but greatly loved programme, *Have a Go*.

Producers are the unsung heroes of television and radio. They are the men and women who conceive the ideas for programmes, decide on the personnel they want, work out the budgets, set up the mechanics of the programme, supervise its

VICTORIAN MUSIC HALLS

F OR THE BEST part of a century, from mid-Victorian times to the aftermath of the First World War, music halls delighted northern audiences with acts ranging from stand-up comedy and saucy songs to clog dancing and tightrope walking. The halls began life as singing rooms attached to busy pubs, and were strictly for men only. At first they were attacked from the church pulpit; but their acts became steadily more respectable as sweethearts and wives insisted on going along too.

The Leeds City Varieties—the only music hall still going strong today—started as a singing room, and was rebuilt in plush and gilded grandeur in 1865. Other Yorkshire towns, among them Bradford and Huddersfield, also had their popular music halls. There were at least ten in Sheffield—among them, the London Apprentice, which carried a notice stating 'Women Without Escorts Not Admitted'. Singers in the halls had songs they made very much their own, like George Leybourne with 'Champagne

Charlie' and Nellie Power with 'The Boy I Love is up in the Gallery' later taken up by Marie Lloyd, the much-loved music hall artist who became a household name.

The first silent moving film was shown in London in 1896, after which the days of music hall were numbered. The advent of talking pictures and radio

ABOVE *A programme dating from 1904 advertises 'High Class Music and Varieties' at The New Sheffield Empire Palace, one of several music halls in Sheffield at the time.*

dealt the final blow, and by the late 1920s music hall had all but disappeared, its theatres converted into cinemas.

transmission or recording, and stand or fall by the end product. To the public, I suppose, they are just names at the end of the credits, causing those viewers and listeners who notice the name to wonder, 'What does *he* do?' Well, the answer is quite simple: without him you wouldn't have been watching or listening to the programme that has just ended.

Such an anonymous creator was Barney Colehan. He was born in Calverley, five or six miles from Leeds, and started his working life as an apprentice to a chemist. He joined the army as a private and the end of the Second World War found him a major, commanding a company of engineers in Germany. To this day he retains what is known as a military bearing, that is to say, he has kept his middle-aged figure in good trim, his back is as straight as a ramrod and he sports a magnificently curling moustache that is very much his trademark. In Hamburg, while still in the army, he felt he had a few ideas that might work on radio so he approached the British Forces Broadcasting station there. He was asked to present a programme called *A Melody, A Memory*, which a few old soldiers will remember. They were invited to write to the radio station requesting a piece of music that

ENTERTAINMENT IN THE NORTH

EVERY CONCEIVABLE TYPE of music-making features in Yorkshire, from sailors' shanties to modern jazz.

Music-lovers travel from afar to enjoy the York Early Music Festival, which includes music ranging from the songs of the medieval French troubadours to pieces for string quartet by Haydn. The festival sometimes includes the cycle of medieval mystery plays, performed on pageant-wagons. Equally prestigious is Leeds' triennial piano competition, which attracts brilliant young players from around the world. Leeds is also the headquarters of Opera North, one of England's leading opera companies, and plays host to a variety of other events, especially in summer, when audiences can take their pick of opera in the park, pop concerts, and salsa under the stars.

Hull is another important music venue and holds an international jazz festival and a festival of sea shanties set against a backdrop of sailing ships. The spa town of Harrogate holds an international arts festival embracing street theatre, stand-up comedy and chamber music concerts. Picturesque Whitby has a week-long folk festival, as does the minster town of Beverley. Smallest of Yorkshire's many musical venues is Marsden village, on the fringe of the Pennines, where a weekend of jazz is held each autumn, confirming that music-making is alive and well in even the smallest corner of Yorkshire.

BELOW *Costumed musicians re-create the past at the York Early Music Festival, which includes concerts, lectures and exhibitions.*

ABOVE *Three salty sea dogs strike up at the Hull International Sea Shanty Festival. Shanties developed as a rhythmic accompaniment to the more laborious shipboard tasks like hoisting the sails.*

evoked special memories for them. The programme was popular and a BBC career can be said to have begun right there for the apprentice chemist-cum-Royal Engineers major.

A BBC executive came over on the lookout for new recruits and Barney was invited to present himself at the studios in Woodhouse Lane, Leeds, with a view to joining the Corporation 'should a vacancy arise'. One did, and Barney Colehan joined the staff of the BBC and, among other programmes, produced *Have a Go* for six years. As the television service started to develop he was invited to remuster, and, as a television producer, Barney remembered a series on which he had worked in radio called *Top Town*. This brought together artistes representing the talent of one town or city to compete against others from another. Civic pride was very much involved and the series proved popular, so when Barney transferred to television, he resurrected the *Top Town* idea.

Soon, representatives of French television came across the Channel to look at the programme with the idea of developing it as a co-production with games and physical contests rather than artistic performances. The BBC, apparently, were not then quite ready for an international contest, but they tried out the idea on the sands at Morecambe with competition

ABOVE *Never one to take himself too seriously, Eddie Waring opts for a light-hearted alternative to a referee's usual black garb in* It's a Knockout.

from the neighbouring Lancashire resort of Blackpool. However, everyone seemed to have forgotten the rate at which the tide comes sweeping across Morecambe Bay. The first *It's a Knockout* was almost literally swept away by the sea. But with two humorists like Ted Ray and Charlie Chester in charge of the presentation, the assembled throng managed to laugh away the problems and a successful show was in the can. *It's a Knockout* went round the country, pitting one town against another, with David Vine as the presenter and Eddie Waring as referee, and finally it went into Europe as *Jeux sans frontières*.

So Barney Colehan emerged as one of the creative talents of television, operating for more than thirty-five years from his base in his home town of Leeds. The man whose ideas have provided spectacular but harmless, wholesome fun for millions of listeners and viewers, shrugs it away modestly. 'I've been lucky to have had the best years of television because I got into it when we were all innovators, inventors, experimenters. Nowadays, everyone is a specialist of some sort, but in my early days, like everyone else, I had to be prepared to turn my hand to anything...an excerpt from a theatre, a Rugby League match, I even did the first televised High Mass from Leeds Cathedral. It's a good life. At least it's never dull.'

A PASSION
FOR SPORT

ABOVE *Leather and wood collide—the defining moment in the game of cricket.*

THE EARLY YEARS of Yorkshire County Cricket Club were, in many ways, as stormy as those of the 1970s and 1980s. In the mid-19th century, the Yorkshire character and temperament was as blunt, obstinate and uncompromising as it is today. Spades were called bloody shovels; fools were never suffered gladly; and, to complete the metaphorical sequence, a lot of dirty washing was aired in public.

The county club was formally constituted in January 1863, in Sheffield, with a minimum subscription of half a guinea a year. It would, therefore, have been something of a gentleman's club or at least a club for those who, if not perhaps gentlemen in the MCC's interpretation of the word, had a bit o' brass. Half a guinea in 1863 would buy a lot of material possessions, and membership of a county cricket club would not rank very high in a working man's list of priorities. The first committee consisted entirely of Sheffield men and there was immediate bridling in such areas as Bradford and York where, it was felt, there was an equal, if not greater, right to speak in cricketing terms for Yorkshire. The first county side, which played against Surrey at the Oval on June 5 and 6, 1863, included three players from Sheffield and three from Huddersfield, but two from Bedale, in rural Wensleydale, and one from Ripon, the tiny cathedral city in the North Riding— unlikely bedfellows. And it was ill feeling between the different factions that led to George Anderson declining the committee's invitation to captain the side in 1865, and to four other players also refusing to take part. Two years of depression followed until the rebels were persuaded to return to the fold.

A CENTURY OF YORKSHIRE CRICKET

The two years of eclipse (1865–6) saw the emergence of a great pair of bowlers, George Freeman and Tom Emmett: in seven matches of the 1867 season Freeman took 51 wickets at an average of 7.4 runs apiece, and Emmett 30 at 5.2. Freeman was the greatest fast bowler of his day, according to the greatest

batsman—W. G. Grace. While these two bowlers were proving the irresistible force, Ephraim Lockwood and his uncle, John Thewlis, were setting themselves up as immovable batting objects, and Yorkshire cricket was established as the force which, with a few lean years, it remained until 1970. Emmett perhaps goes down in history as one of the first characters of a game in which much of the folklore has been based on the dry one-liner—like Emmett's comment after a day in the field against Gloucestershire with 'W. G.' in full cry: 'It's Grace before meat, Grace after meat and Grace all bloody day.'

By the 1870s the great dynasty of slow left-arm bowlers, which was to be Yorkshire's pride for the next hundred years, had been established. Edmund Peate averaged 7 wickets a match over three years in the 1880s and had, according to Lord Hawke, 'the most perfect action of any man'. He was succeeded by Bobby Peel, who topped the 100-wickets mark in nine successive seasons—seasons in which far fewer matches were played than today. The 1890s saw the arrival of George Herbert Hirst, with 125 wickets in 1893, and, with two other bowlers doing even better, Yorkshire won their first county championship—the first of thirty they were to win up to 1968. It was an early illustration that bowling and fielding win championships, a lesson that Yorkshire were never to forget. They developed a system of specialist fieldsmen and it was a system that brought great rewards in the years to come.

If 1893 had been the bowlers' year, 1895 was the batsmen's, highlighted by a score of 887 against Warwickshire at Edgbaston. Peel made 210 and Lord Hawke 166. The following year saw the introduction of winter pay for the professional

ABOVE *The formidable W. G. Grace notched up over 54,000 runs and nearly 3,000 wickets in a career spanning more than 40 years.*

TOP *Successive Yorkshire captains Tom Emmett (with bat on shoulder) and Ephraim Lockwood (third from right) were included in this assemblage of eminent English cricketers, dating from 1880.*

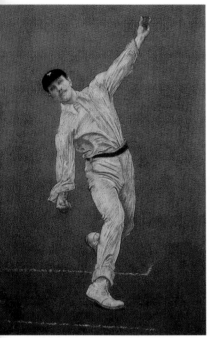

ABOVE *Wilfred Rhodes became the oldest player ever to appear in a Test match when in 1930 he turned out for England in Kingston, Jamaica, at the grand old age of 52 years and 165 days.*

players, who consequently became established as men with financial security as well as tremendous kudos in the county.

A Yorkshire player was by now something of a demigod, though relatively few of the cricketing public 'knew' players as they do today. There was no television to bring the great players under the scrutiny of every household in the country, no cult-of-personality writing in the newspapers to detail the most personal habits or outside interests of the players. They stood or fell by their achievements on the field while retaining a general anonymity off it. There was, in consequence, a marvellous mystique about the great ones and the idolatry that their talents induced was wholesome. Yet even in this era—perhaps especially in this era—the public image had to be maintained with dignity. When Bobby Peel's fondness for a tipple was somewhat ostentatiously manifested, Lord Hawke sacked him, for all his greatness. It was well for Yorkshire that a replacement was waiting off-stage in the one and only Wilfred Rhodes.

Now when people talk about the great all-rounders of the recent past, I raise my cap, as I happily do to all great players of any generation. But I think I raise it just a little higher to Wilfred Rhodes. I was privileged to know him as a marvellous old man until his death in 1973. Rhodes's career spanned cricket's greatest golden age. He bowled at Grace and he bowled at Bradman. He shared a record first-wicket partnership for England and another for the last wicket. He scored 1,000 runs in a season seventeen times and took100 wickets in a season twenty-two times, twice topping the 200 mark. He did the hat trick against Derbyshire in 1920 when he was forty-three, and he gets no fewer than fifty-two entries in the Yorkshire CCC handbook under the heading 'Exceptional Bits of Bowling'. Rhodes played in fifty-eight Tests for England over a thirty-one-year period, scoring 2,325 runs at an average of 30.19 and taking127 wickets at 26.96. For Yorkshire he scored 31,156 runs at 30.10 and took 3,608 wickets at 16.

Wilfred was not a colourful character in the way that Gary Sobers or Ian Botham can be called colourful. He was, in many ways, the epitome of the dour Yorkshireman. He was not a man to lose graciously. On the contrary, he *hated* to lose. The ground was his battlefield and while the Hawkes might be the generals, Rhodes was the sergeant major, the leader of the fighting men, the man who made things happen. Neville Cardus, reporting in the *Manchester Guardian*, on Yorkshire v. Lancashire, Bramall Lane, 1919, provided this picture of Rhodes as a slow left-arm bowler:

> Rhodes was easily the best of the Yorkshire bowlers. In his forty-second year, Rhodes has recaptured a characteristic which made his bowling unique twenty years ago. There were slow bowlers before Rhodes who had his enormous finger spin, but they could only get it to operate on the average wicket by tossing the ball well into the air, which had the defect of giving quick-footed batsmen time to jump in and drive. Rhodes seemingly set

a scientific principle at defiance by spinning at a tantalisingly slow pace, yet with the low flight of the medium-paced man. The result is a twisting ball that defies the offensive tactics best calculated to cope with it and one has, perforce, to wait for the ball and allow the spin to come off, which, of course, is the very thing one wants to prevent.

This combination of a characteristic of the slow bowler with one belonging definitely to the medium-paced bowler got Rhodes his wickets yesterday. He is a delightful bowler to watch even when he is working destruction against Lancashire.

I have gone on at some length about Wilfred Rhodes because, although he was in teams that had many other great players, somehow he seems to me to sum up more completely than anyone else the essential character of Yorkshire cricket in its greatest days. There were more accomplished batsmen (though never a greater bowler), more athletic fieldsmen and more picturesque personalities. There were grim and gritty men in abundance and there were droll and whimsical

THE ORIGINS OF CRICKET

CRICKET'S ORIGINS are every bit as mysterious as its rules may appear to the layman. Its name probably derives from the Anglo-Saxon *cricce*, meaning 'shepherd's crook' or 'staff'. A rival theory has it as a derivation of *krickstoel*, Dutch for a church kneeling stool—a possible reference to the low, wide, early wickets. As for its evolution, perhaps the most plausible theory traces it back to a rural sport in which players used a *cricce*, or some more rudimentary club, to defend a target—the wicket gate of a sheep pen, possibly, or a tree stump—from projectiles like stones and pine cones.

The first reliable reference to cricket dates back to 1598, and many mentions—mostly uncomplimentary—follow. Contemporary accounts of popular pastimes rank it with bear baiting and wrestling, and tell of enthusiasts being fined for playing on the Sabbath. Only during Cromwell's Commonwealth (1649–60) did cricket assume its noble status: with no court to dally in, aristocrats returned to their estates,

where many would have found tenants playing this compelling new game.

Cricket's first known rules were drafted in 1774, possibly in response to the increased betting taking place around matches. But the game had to wait another year for its final evolutionary step, when a third stump was added after a Hambleden v. Kent match in

ABOVE *An early cricketer prepares to bowl. Pioneering batsmen wielded curved bats, enabling them to scoop up the underarm, ground-level bowling then prevalent.*

which Edward 'Lumpy' Stevens repeatedly bowled the ball through John Small's wicket, without ever once managing to dislodge his bails.

PLAYER'S CIGARETTES.

G.G.MACAULAY, YORKSHIRE

CHURCHMAN'S CIGARETTES

H. VERITY

ABOVE *Hedley Verity's star never faded: in his last match for Yorkshire before his untimely death he claimed seven Sussex wickets for just nine runs.*

TOP *This contemporary cigarette card of George Macaulay captures the gritty determination of the famous bowler.*

players, lovable and heart-warming players. But Wilfred Rhodes seems to have embodied just about everything that set Yorkshire cricket apart from that of other counties. There were the Sutcliffes and Huttons, the Veritys and Boweses, all great men and great players. But if the county decides some day to put up a statue at Headingley inscribed simply 'Yorkshire cricket', then I think it would have to look like Wilfred Rhodes.

But let us not neglect some of the others who helped to win those thirty championships, starting with Lord Hawke, the most notable 'non-Yorkshireman' to play for the county. He was born in Lincolnshire in 1860 while his father was rector of Willingham. But that father was a proud Yorkshireman and the family estates included the battlefield of Towton, where Edward IV destroyed the Lancastrian forces on Palm Sunday, 1461. You can't get much more Yorkshire than that! The rector inherited the title and young Hawke lived at Wighill Park, near Tadcaster, for fifty years from 1874, and he led Yorkshire from 1883 to 1910 (he was also president of the county for forty years from 1898 to 1938). His background—Eton and Cambridge University—could scarcely have been in greater contrast to that of the forces he commanded and yet he probably did more than anyone else, before or since, to give standing and dignity to the professional cricketer. And he did it in what was the age of the gifted (and not-so-gifted) amateur.

WAR STOPS PLAY

George Macaulay was a bowler whose sustained aggression towards, and blatant hatred of, batsmen would have earned him high marks from me every time. Jim Kilburn, the cricket correspondent of the *Yorkshire Post*, wrote of him:

> Batsmen, temporarily, and groundsmen, permanently, were Macaulay's sworn enemies and he never dissembled. He wanted to be taking wickets all the time from half past eleven to half past six and he resented the interruptions of luncheon and tea. He once caught Lancashire on a crumbled wicket at Old Trafford and when he had bowled them out twice in a day regretted they could not be given a third innings. On an occasion of sunshine after rain at Hull, when there was a delay until the storm waters soaked through, Macaulay was observed pacing the pavilion enclosure in an agony of impatience. 'Seven left-handers,' he was muttering. 'Seven left-handers in the side and I can't get at them.'

Macaulay played from 1920 to 1935 and by then we had seen the development of Bill Bowes, my coach and my friend after the Second World War, and Hedley Verity, the next of our marvellous slow left-armers who, sadly, did not survive the war. He died of wounds sustained in the landings in Sicily when he was a captain in the Green Howards. These two, in their contrasting styles of bowling, were the Yorkshire spearhead through the 1930s, when the county won seven championships in nine seasons, and counted their third place in 1936 and their fifth in 1934 as wasted years. In 1931 Verity took all 10 wickets against Warwickshire for 36 runs and finished with a haul of 169. In 1932 he took

LEFT *When England first lost to Australia on home soil in 1882, the press bemoaned the death of English cricket; since then, its 'ashes'— actually the charred remains of a cremated stump in an urn—have been contested regularly by the two countries, in a confrontation depicted in this* Punch *cartoon as a tug of war between the lion and the kangaroo.*

a total of 146 wickets, including that never-to-be-forgotten 10 for 10 against Nottinghamshire. From then on, until the war put an end to county championship cricket, he took successively 168, 100, 199, 185, 137 and 189 wickets. To my great regret I never saw him play, but Jim Kilburn has summed him up for me.

> He looked his part. At first glance he was obviously a student of something, and he loved his art. He thought about it, talked about it, experimented with it and was never happier than when a bowling problem was set before him...
>
> Every now and then he bowled a faster ball which was far above medium pace and which very rarely failed in accuracy of line and length. During his run-up to bowl this batsmen's surprise, the wicketkeeper (Arthur Wood) would stretch out his hand and back would scuttle the slips and gully. Dozens of spectators, players and critics watched for years to discover the signal between Verity and Wood but the secret was never known until after Verity had been killed. Wood then confessed that there had been no secret at all. 'I just sensed it,' said Wood.

Bill Bowes I did see play, but obviously not at his greatest. Like Hedley Verity, he had fought in the war and, while he was fortunate enough to survive, years in prisoner-of-war camps wrecked his health and he was never really a fast bowler when he returned to play Yorkshire cricket again in 1946 and 1947. But I have spent hour after hour yarning with Bill. He has always been an essentially modest man, particularly about his own achievements, but he has a superb memory and a great gift for describing cricketing occasions, like the time he bowled Bradman for a duck at Melbourne in 1932.

'The crowd applauded him all the way to the wicket. It was deafening. And just as I started to run in, the applause started up again. He walked away from the wicket and I stopped. Just for something to do while the noise died down I waved the deep fine leg to come up closer. There was nothing clever about it, no deep-laid plot. But when the applause started once more, again, for something to do, I waved the mid-on to move in a bit closer. And at last the clapping stopped. I started to run in. Suddenly I sensed that Bradman expected me to bowl a bouncer. As I got near the wicket I saw him start to get into position to hook and I bowled a ball of full length. He saw it and tried to get back into position. He was so good that he nearly got there and just got the faintest nick on it before it hit the stumps. Well, the silence…it was something you could really feel. It was awesome. You could hear the rattling of the trams down in the middle of Melbourne. And as Bradman started to walk slowly back to the pavilion just one spectator started to applaud him. Just one. It was a woman and we could see her out of all the vast crowd.'

It's a marvellous story—as any account of Bradman bowled for nought has to be—but the thing is really to hear Bill tell it himself. You can feel that silence as he and Jardine's touring team experienced it in Melbourne.

HOW CRICKET BATS AND BALLS ARE MADE

I N OUR INCREASINGLY AUTOMATED world, there's something reassuringly low-tech about top-class cricket bat manufacture. Machinery may take the slog out of preparation, but the craftsman's eye does the rest.

Lightweight English willow is used to make bats. Lengths are split into 'clefts', stacked and left for nine to twelve months to season, then machine-pressed to harden them and locate hidden flaws. A machine saw is used to hew the flat face and convex rear ('meat') of a bat; but subsequent shaping is by hand, as craftsmen plane, shave and sand to create a well-weighted blade. The handle's shock-absorbing qualities are achieved by

LEFT *Hand tools are preferred to power machinery in the crafting of a bat's 'pod', or blade. The bat-maker's painstaking work earned him the nickname of 'pod-shaver'.*

RIGHT *A craftsman deftly stitches a new ball; his handiwork will need to withstand strokes that propel it at over 100 miles an hour.*

BELOW *Sited at the far end of the spectrum from green, the cherry red of a ball means it shows up perfectly against cricket pitches.*

gluing together strips of rubber and Asian cane. Once worked into shape, the handle is bound with cord and sheathed in rubber. Handle and blade are expertly mortised, and fine-tuning balances the bat. Bleaching and waxing conclude the process.

Traditional skills are also at work in ball production. Tanned and dyed leather is cut into diamonds, which are stitched into hemispheres. Meanwhile, the stuffing, or 'quilt', is prepared. The quilt is now commonly a machine-moulded composite of cork, synthetic rubbers and fibre. Two leather hemispheres are clamped round a quilt and seamed

together, in a raised herring-bone pattern, with waxed thread. Machine sewing is common, but for top-class balls, hand sewing is best. Now the finished product is ready to do the bowler's bidding.

The 1930s was, too, the period that saw the rich maturity of Herbert Sutcliffe. Herbert Sutcliffe was probably the greatest player on bad wickets that Yorkshire and England have ever known. He was, of course, a magnificent batsman on good pitches, but eminent critics have long felt that he came into his own when batting was at its most difficult. He became a great friend in his later years—especially when I retired from cricket and he retired from the Yorkshire committee. There had been, you might say, a personality clash on one or two occasions when we were both in office! But afterwards, particularly when he lived in a nursing home near my home, he used to join us regularly for Sunday lunch and we spent hours talking about his cricketing days and mine.

In an entirely different way from Lord Hawke, Herbert Sutcliffe made an immense contribution to raising the status of the professional cricketer. Lord Hawke did it by exercising a kind of patriarchal benevolence; Herbert did it by example. His kit was always quite immaculate; he was the very model of what a well-turned-out cricketer should look like.

Cardus wrote of Herbert Sutcliffe that he could play at and miss six balls in an over, then lean nonchalantly on his bat at the end of it as though he had middled every one. This infuriated Herbert when he read it. 'Never,' he exploded, 'never did I play at and miss six balls in an over in my entire career.'

His opening partnership with Percy Holmes was immortalised by the record 555 at Leyton in 1932, but let's not forget that together they had three other first-wicket stands of more than 300, fourteen others of more than 200 and fifty of 100 or more. Percy Holmes had not the style of Sutcliffe, either on the field or off it. He was very much more of a homespun character than his dapper and dignified partner. But each had a deep appreciation of the other.

The 1930s also saw the start of Len Hutton's career as the greatest batsman I played with. Len Hutton was dogged by poor health in his teens and, although a family background in cricket plus his unmistakable talent had brought him to the notice of Yorkshire when he was little more than a boy, he was nursed rather gently into the first team. Indeed, he had won his regular place only two years before he startled the world with 364 against the Australians at the Oval in 1938: in a game that started at 11.30 on a Saturday morning, he batted until half past two on Tuesday afternoon in the timeless last Test of the series. It was an unprecedented piece of concentration and, quite apart from making him every Yorkshire schoolboy's hero, it established him as Public Enemy No. 1 with succeeding generations of Australian bowlers.

During the war, Hutton, an army physical-training instructor, suffered a broken left forearm, which never healed entirely satisfactorily. With this disadvantage (and five years out of his sporting life) he carried on a career that brought him eighty-five centuries for Yorkshire and a total of 24,807 runs (average 53.34). He scored nineteen centuries in his seventy-nine Tests, in which he made a total of 6,971 runs (average 56.67), and in 1952 he became England's first professional captain. As a captain, he believed less in inspiration and flair than in ruthlessly minimising the possibility of error. England won eleven Tests under him, drew eight and lost

ABOVE *The late, great Sir Len Hutton was one of cricket's true legends; his innings of 364 for England against the Australians at the Oval in 1938 set a world Test record that only Gary Sobers and Brian Lara have ever exceeded.*

ABOVE *In an England career spanning 13 years and 67 Tests, Fred Trueman's aggressive, pacy bowling yielded over 300 Test wickets.*

TOP *Out! A stump is ripped from the wicket, and bails are sent flying, during a county match between Surrey and Yorkshire.*

only four. My relations with Len as a Test captain were not the most cordial, but my respect for him as a player has always been, and will remain boundless.

After winning the county championship immediately following the war, Yorkshire shared it with Middlesex in 1949 and then had to wait ten long years for their next success, partly because Surrey dominated the competition almost throughout the fifties, and partly because Yorkshire, despite a tremendous playing strength, did not always pull together. I had come on the scene in 1949, and over the next twenty seasons I was to take 1,745 wickets for the county at 17.13 each and score 6,852 runs. During that period I played sixty-seven times for England, taking 307 Test wickets at 21.57, held sixty-four catches and scored 981 runs. It doesn't need me to tell anyone that those were the happiest days of my life.

YORKSHIRE'S CRICKET GROUNDS

It is not widely known that the Yorkshire County Cricket Club does not have a ground of its own. A fee is paid for the use of each ground whenever Yorkshire play a game on it. Even Headingley, for so long the scene of Test cricket, belongs to the Leeds Rugby League Club, which operates on the other side of the great back-to-back stand on the southern side of the cricket ground. But, since the 1890s, Headingley has been the very heart of Yorkshire cricket even though it was not until the county club had been in existence for 100 years that its offices were moved from the centre of Leeds to the new building on the cricket ground.

The story of cricket at Headingley is an integral part of the history of the game. Going back a mere fifty-odd years, we have the immortal Bradman hitting over 300 in a day on July 11, 1930. It was an historic innings in many ways by the Boy from Bowral—105 before lunch, 115 in the middle session and 89 between tea and the close—309 runs in a day. It has never been equalled and with the present-day over rates it is never likely to be, either! Bradman returned to Headingley in 1934 to score another triple century, and on his next visit, in 1938, I suppose you can say he failed with only 103. On his last appearance there, in 1948, he made 173 not out—against the clock.

Of course, I was always going to have the fondest personal memories of Headingley from the moment I made my own Test debut there on June 5, 1952, against Vijay Hazare's Indian tourists. England had a professional captain for the first time in Len Hutton and I was on leave from the RAF at Hemswell, east of Gainsborough. It was on the third day that my memorable moment arrived and the Headingley scoreboard read: India 0–4. Four wickets had fallen in the first fourteen balls of India's second innings, and when Hazare, coming in at No. 6, played and missed, I was deprived of a hat trick in my first Test by nothing more than a cat's whisker. That apart, I used to get weekend leave from the RAF to play as a professional for the Leeds Cricket Club for £10 a match, which was a bit more than I got for a week's duty as a national serviceman.

Dickie Moulton, the groundsman in the forties and fifties, was a magnificent preparer of wickets. Not for him the lavish application of marl or use of scientific aids. He believed in watering and rolling in delicate quantities of natural fertiliser—cowdung. You could smell Headingley wickets, quite literally—and you didn't bother to lick your fingers when bowling.

HEADINGLEY, HEART OF YORKSHIRE CRICKET

CRICKET IS LIKE a religion to many Yorkshiremen, and they've long worshipped at the Headingley Ground in Leeds. But in fact Yorkshire County Cricket Club (YCCC) was formed not in Leeds, but down the road in Sheffield, in 1863. It was only in 1893, when the YCCC leased a plot of land from Leeds Cricket, Football & Athletic Co. Ltd, that Headingley became county headquarters for Yorkshire.

Leeds has witnessed some memorable cricket down the years, none more so than England's sensational fightback to beat Australia in 1981. Despite an innings of 149 by Ian Botham, Australia's target of 130 runs seemed a formality. Enter English fast bowler Bob Willis. Producing the performance of his life, Willis brushed Australia aside with Test career-best figures of 8 wickets for only 43 runs. In an outrageous reversal of fortune, England triumphed.

Sadly Headingley's first-class cricketing days seem numbered. It's long been a source of frustration for the club that its ground is rented from the adjacent Leeds Rugby Club, and, with the advent of summertime rugby starting to compromise the fixture list, it is felt that the time has come to move on. A site in Wakefield has been earmarked, and designs are circulating for a state-of-the-art stadium. One name mooted is the White Rose Bowl. Assuming the club raises funds of around £45 million, YCCC could be calling in the removal vans before the millennium is out.

ABOVE *Odds against a home win midway through 1981's Leeds Ashes Test were long enough to tempt Australians Dennis Lillee and Rodney Marsh into a flutter! Their win proved scant consolation for losing the match.*

LEFT *A sunny session of play at Headingley.*

ABOVE *To don a cap bearing the white rose of Yorkshire has been an ambition of untold thousands of Yorkshire lads.*

ABOVE *The old enemy: the rose of Lancashire has much the same effect upon your average Yorkshire cricket fan as a red rag has upon a bull.*

Headingley is not the loveliest of grounds and it is not the best equipped, but it has a North Country character of its own, a very clearly defined personality. The line of tall, elegant trees that stand sentinel along the northeastern perimeter are as well known a landmark as the gasholder at the Oval and a good deal more attractive. (Debates on their origins and species take place in our BBC commentary box during every Test there.) The red-brick pavilion still stands, now divided into many uses, as a reminder of the more gracious days of cricket. And to the west there are the wide-open spaces of the 'popular' side terraces, from where many a pungent comment on the day's activities is bellowed across the green acres. On Test match days, as with Roses matches of yesteryear, the atmosphere in the ground is vibrant. Somehow, everyone feels a part of the game, and, indeed, everyone is.

There will always be a soft spot in my heart for Bramall Lane, Sheffield. It was there that I took my first steps along the road to first-class cricket, when I came under the wing of Cyril Turner, who had been a Yorkshire all-rounder before the war and was now responsible for developing the young talent of South Yorkshire. As Headingley is owned by a Rugby League club, Bramall Lane belonged to the Sheffield United Football Club, which has known great days in the Football League.

Bramall Lane had one of the most colourful and knowledgeable crowds in the world. They addressed all Yorkshire players by their first names, bellowing across a hundred yards of sward as though engaging in intimate personal conversation. I am convinced this was done not so much out of any presumptuous familiarity as from an intimacy with the game in all its nuances, which extended to its practitioners. The opposition were not accorded the same courtesies and the crowd was quick to seize on any name that might lend point to their collective or individual wit. Thus, Bernie Constable of Surrey, playing resolutely up and down the line with one eye on the clock as it approached 6.30, was informed: 'Constable—you'll be back on't beat tomorrow.' The pun was as popular as the *double entendre*. Winston Place, as representative of the mortal enemy (and nowhere was the Roses rivalry more fervently expressed than at Bramall Lane), was exhorted to 'get back to t'fish shop'.

Bradford's ground at Park Avenue is homely and lovable rather than majestic and historic. Here there is a 'popular' side where the wiseacres have offered their advice and comment from time immemorial. Here it was that Norman Horner, after a two-match career with his native county in 1950, played in the colours of Warwickshire on his first return to Park Avenue and fielded on the boundary. A shot climbed high from the bat towards Norman as the umpire's cry of 'No ball' echoed round the field, unheeded as it happened by two venerable observers close to its point of arrival. Norman let it bounce in front of him and threw back to the wicketkeeper as the two watched in mystified silence. Finally, one turned to the other and asked, aghast, 'Did tha see that?' 'Ah did.' 'What's tha mak on it?' Long deliberate pause for reflection, then, 'Well, it were our Norman. Ah suppose blood's thicker na watter.'

At Park Avenue it was, in the days before the First World War, that Alonso Drake bowled to Jack Hobbs and was struck for 6 into the face of the football-stand clock with such force that the hands stuck at three o'clock. Ruefully the bowler lamented to his teammates, 'Ah wish 'e'd knock it to 'arf past six.'

I had my moments at Park Avenue, like the time I had to stay at one end until close of play on a Saturday evening. Carefully I put a straight bat to ball after ball until one exasperated spectator yelled at me, 'Are you cummin' back 'ere on Monday, Trueman? 'Cos if you are, Ah'm not!'

St George's Road, Harrogate, is the smallest of the Yorkshire grounds and one of the most pleasant. It is ideally suited to the Festival atmosphere and I have always thought how marvellous it is to see the Festival developing there in recent years, while almost all the traditional end-of-season seaside gatherings have gone. The people at Harrogate are different, too, 'involved' in their cricket in quite a different way from those at Leeds, Bradford and Sheffield. We had to beat Glamorgan there in 1962 to win the championship and the supporters drove up and turned on their car headlights so that they could work through the night before the game, helping the groundsman to get the pitch ready after a lot of rain. They were rewarded with a 7-wicket win for Yorkshire.

My abiding memories of the Circle Ground, Hull, are associated with water. It always seems cold and windswept at the best of times (and if the wind was out of the southeast it invariably wafted with it a pointed reminder of the fish docks in my day), but I seem to remember the ground for rain, rain and more rain. In 1958, Ronnie Burnet and Reg Simpson surveyed a ground under four feet of water. Yorkshire and Nottinghamshire might have arranged a swimming gala, but there was not the slightest chance of playing a game of cricket there, even two days later. The two captains went off to ring Lord's about an immediate cancellation and were told

BELOW *Bramall Lane may no longer have a place in the cricket calendar, but the rivalry of the Roses matches continues: here, the two counties do battle in the semifinal of the 1996 Nat West Trophy, at Old Trafford.*

ABOVE *So close is Scarborough's cricket ground to the rolling waves of the North Sea, that it seems Yorkshire's more robust batsmen must be in danger of losing cricket balls in the surf.*

there was no precedent for abandoning a match on the first day. So while the rest of us went home, the captains booked into a hotel for the night so that they could return solemnly next morning and formally call off the fixture.

And so to Scarborough, where the Festival was Mecca for so many supporters—and for one or two players, too, who looked to complete their 'double' of 1,000 runs and 100 wickets in a season in those closing days of the summer. It was a great social cricket occasion, the games played with something less than the grim intensity of county championship matches and the evenings enlivened by a round of parties. Like most Festivals, Scarborough's lost some of its glory when players' sentimental attachment to it began to wane in the face of financial rewards to be gained elsewhere, but, I am proud to say, Yorkshire flatly refused to let it die as others had done. With the help of sponsorship, and under the presidency of our Test Match Special colleague Brian Johnston, a revival began in the 1980s and long may it continue.

Apart from the Festival, the North Marine Road ground has also traditionally staged a county match in the height of the holiday season when thousands of holidaymakers have flocked to the resort during the traditional 'feast' weeks in the industrial areas of the county.

Scarborough has seen all the great personalities of the game, all the great touring sides, at its end-of-season fireworks. It has seen mighty hitting like the straight 6 of Cec Pepper, which cleared the boarding houses—sorry, private hotels—at the seaward end of the ground and landed in Trafalgar Square. It has seen annual gatherings of friends who came together just once a year for t'Festival and departed swearing undying brotherhood, to meet again in a year's time. And it has seen the greatest emphasis of all on the axiom that, in the last analysis, cricket is meant to be fun. It is as if Yorkshiremen, at the end of a season in which they have been locked for four months in the decidedly grim business of competitive cricket—from their county side down to the humblest of leagues—have come together to let their hair down at last. Only for a day or two, you understand.

RUGBY LEAGUE

Rugby League is a game that was conceived and born in the North, and, as befits a contest so utterly northern in character, it came into existence because of a row with them fancy fellers down South. While we cannot claim it exclusively as a Yorkshire game, it was certainly founded here and its headquarters have always been here. It was in the George Hotel, Huddersfield, that Rugby League effectively started life on Thursday, August 29, 1895, and the circumstances that created it have not changed all that much over the years.

The game of Rugby Union then, as now, was played right across the whole spectrum of society—but some parts of it were more equal than others. In the North it was (as it is now) generally believed that southern clubs were made up of more affluent members, men who didn't have to work too hard for a living and were substantially better paid. In the North (where they still tend to believe that everyone living south of Birmingham is a banker, a stockbroker, an accountant or a lawyer), rugby was played by working-class men from working-class homes, side by side with teams of grammar school old boys and university graduates. Those working men—from textile or engineering factories, or from the mines— worked a hard, five-and-a-half-day week of long shifts for an average wage of 26s a week. They simply could not afford to lose their pay for a shift on Saturday morning when they were required to travel to an away fixture; so many employers, enthusiastic about the game, were willing to give a bit of a helping hand to star players. Thus, certain suspicions grew in the minds of southern clubs and administrators that the purity of rugby as an amateur sport was being tainted by 'broken time' payments to some players in the North.

BELOW *In an early encounter, Oxford and Cambridge do battle on the rugby field. The modern game originated in 1823, when a Rugby schoolboy named William Webb Ellis picked up the ball and ran with it during a football match.*

Allegations were flung and denied; the row simmered for several years, just below boiling point. Much, I think, of North–South rivalry in sport, where there is more than a touch of bitterness, can be traced to this period and the breach that followed. It was the northern clubs that finally took the initiative and broke away from the Northern Rugby Football Union, in 1895, as the Northern Union. It operated games on a competitive basis with Senior Leagues in both Yorkshire and Lancashire. In its second season of existence, the Northern Union introduced a knockout competition for the Challenge Cup and the first final, on May 1, 1897, was watched by 13,490 spectators who paid £624 to see Batley beat St Helens at the splendid new stadium built at Headingley by the Leeds club.

The Challenge Cup that year, and those that followed, saw many stirring encounters between the best clubs of Yorkshire and Lancashire, which otherwise did not meet each other with any regularity, and gradually the clamour grew for a Super League of the top sides from each county. This, not unnaturally, caused dismay among the less successful clubs, which relied on fixtures with more glamorous sides for their best gates, but the proposal to form a Northern Rugby League, composed of the twelve best clubs, was accepted by a meeting, again in Huddersfield, in 1901. In the 1902–3 season there were now two divisions of the Northern Rugby League, each consisting of eighteen clubs with a two-up, two-down promotion and relegation system, but it was disastrous for the smaller clubs in Division Two. Some went to the wall and after three years the League reverted to one division of thirty-one clubs, with each club compiling its own fixture list, much as Rugby Union clubs had always done, without a formal competition for any championship. The Leigh club topped the table and were rewarded with a contemptuous sneer for allegedly rigging their fixtures to include all the weaker sides!

From the first, the Northern Union placed strong emphasis on the more attractive elements in the game. If they were going to be professional then they needed income, and to get that they had to draw in crowds as Association Football did. Spectators seemed to want the game to flow; they wanted strong, fast running and expert passing of the ball. Mauling in the mud was all right for the chaps who played in front of two men and a dog for the sheer love of mauling in the mud, but the Northern Rugby League was going to be dedicated to more attractive stuff than that. In 1906 the step was taken that separated the game utterly from Rugby Union—the number of players in a side was reduced from fifteen to thirteen. Which two positions to eliminate? Logically at that time, the League decided to dispense with the wing forwards, arguing that the role of those two gentlemen was (a) to block the scrum

BELOW *Contested on the first weekend of May each year, Rugby League's Challenge Cup Final remains the sport's showcase game, and turns London's Wembley Stadium into a part of northern England for a day.*

half; (b) to bury the stand-off; (c) generally to prevent the ball reaching the fleeter members of the side by any means at their disposal. In short, their job was to spoil. So out they went and for the next sixty or seventy years League was indeed a much more fluent, spectacular and entertaining game to watch.

A QUAINT NORTHERN RITUAL

Why, then, has the game of Rugby League never caught on in a real sense outside Yorkshire, Lancashire and Cumbria? It was tried in South Wales in 1907 with clubs at Merthyr Tydfil and Ebbw Vale; the following year Aberdare, Barry, Mid-Rhondda and Treherbert joined, but the venture did not survive even until the outbreak of war in 1914. True, these were essentially working-class communities with great sporting traditions, but Rugby Union has a hold on the Welsh heart that nothing will ever break. Rugby Union in Wales owes nothing to the old-boy network but everything to national pride.

Between the wars Rugby League was tried, without gaining any hold on public affection, in London and in Newcastle-upon-Tyne. Then another attempt was

ABOVE *Rugby balls have come a long way since the days when the game was played using an inflated pig's bladder encased in leather.*

RUGBY LEAGUE VERSUS RUGBY UNION

RUGBY LEAGUE AND RUGBY UNION are like twin brothers that have fallen out. Since 1895, the two have existed as separate games or 'codes', and it is League, with its two fewer players to a team, and simpler rules, that has grown into the more fluid and entertaining of the two.

Events in Rugby League's centenary year, 1995, shook the game to its foundations, when its leaders voted to accept a contract with Rupert Murdoch's BSkyB TV corporation worth £87 million over five years. The deal promised financial security and a higher profile to a sport long blighted by poor gates, decrepit grounds and its limiting 'cloth caps and whippets' image. Its most radical element was the shift to a summer season. Overnight, a game of mud, mayhem and muscle became one just of mayhem and muscle.

Despite its new-found wealth, these are uncertain times for Rugby League. Now deemed a valued commodity, it needs to prove it can pay its way. Its ability to do so will depend upon how far this traditionally northern sport can broaden its appeal.

League's relationship with the newly professional Union is another unknown. Murmurings of a remerger between them are probably misguided—with the codes now playing at different times in the year, there seems no danger of their treading on one another's toes. Still, these traditional enemies are showing conciliatory signs. Players move between codes; cross-code

ABOVE *Va'aiga Tuigamala of Wigan bursts through a Bath player's tackle during the teams' 1996 cross-code challenge.*

ground shares occur; and in 1996, Bath and Wigan contested a two-match series in which both triumphed in their own code, presenting the happy possibility that both disciplines are in robust health.

made to establish League in the Welsh valleys shortly after the Second World War, but again it soon foundered (perhaps to the relief of northern fans who had a hell of a time trying to say 'We're playing Ystradgynlais next week'). More recently it has been tried once again, at Cardiff, but this is partly in the nature of an economic move—using a soccer ground that would otherwise be empty every other week while rates and other overheads have still to be paid.

Even then it was just a quaint northern ritual observed by those quaint northern peasants. It got no coverage in the London-printed editions of national newspapers, except once a year when the Challenge Cup final took the wild Northerners to town to let blood at Wembley. But no one could ever say there was hooliganism or crowd misbehaviour. Rugby League fans have always been and still are fanatically proud of standards of conduct which are fit to set before a Queen or a Princess or a Prime Minister who accepts an invitation to be a guest at the final. London hoteliers and even the hard-to-please cabbies will tell you they look

BELOW *Match night in a dark, stormy Halifax in 1980; Rugby League's recent deal with Sky has since offered the game a much-needed shot of glamour.*

forward to that modern Rising of the North. The League fans are not afraid to spend their brass without feeling it necessary to kick in the front door.

There is a warmth, a homeliness about the game that is infectiously endearing. Which brings us to Eddie Waring. More than any other individual, he drew attention to the game through his commentaries on BBC Television and created a public that had never existed before. His tortured accent and fractured English made him a cult figure. An Eddie Waring Impersonation Club even sprang up. His style did not make him universally popular in the areas where the game is played. Indeed, a St Helens-based group lobbied Broadcasting House in London, in an effort to have Eddie removed from commentaries. But his supporters within the BBC were staunch and his fan club around the country far outnumbered his critics in the North, even if they felt they had legitimate grounds for complaint.

The argument against Eddie was that his extraordinary style stamped the game with a sense of the ridiculous, and there is no doubt that this school of thought had a point. Although they never knew it, these critics had rueful allies among succeeding generations of TV directors within the BBC who groaned in despair at Eddie's refusal (or inability) to achieve programme requirements by following instructions. He was always liable to digress into pigeon fancying or the contents of a letter from South Wales as a winger was screaming down the touchline en route to a spectacular try. Indeed, when the BBC, in response to a clamour from devotees of the game, tried to mount a Try of the Month sequence (to match goal-scoring spectaculars in their soccer coverage), they found that a remarkable number of tries had been televised with no identification of the players involved! It drove the purists mad, but it seemed to endear Eddie more and more to a huge band of followers in the southern areas of the country and perhaps it was this, more than anything else, that augmented the anti-Waring faction in the North: he was painting a picture of the North as southern people wanted to see it, a picture of quaint, uncouth, unlettered barbarians performing one of their quaint, barbaric northern rites. Eddie retired in his own time, with legions of fans in unlikely places. We shall never know how many laughed with him and how many at him. But there can be no doubt that his commentary was unique.

Media coverage of the game has thrown up many characters, almost all of whom had a devoted allegiance to the club they followed and wrote about week after week. There was dear old Bert Foster who travelled far and wide with York just after the war as Rugby League correspondent of the *Yorkshire Evening Press*. The club was in a sorry state at the time and heavy defeats followed one after the other. It was this, I think, that prompted the paper to put the result (in Bert's Monday review of Saturday's game) at the end of the article, arguing perhaps that the scoreline would deter even the most hardened reader from pursuing the report further. Thus Bert's pieces used loyally to begin, 'York were distinctly unlucky to lose at Wigan on Saturday...' Then would follow around a thousand words of eulogy before the stark last line was reached: 'Wigan 54, York 2.'

The economics of Rugby League are something to marvel at. Regularly, something like one-third of the clubs play before home crowds of fewer than a thousand, yet

they soldier on, Huyton bravely flying the flag in the most fervent of soccer citadels—Liverpool—and Doncaster, against impossible odds, chalking up defeat after defeat in the sporting wasteland of the Yorkshire–Nottinghamshire border. It is difficult to see how clubs like these, and Rochdale Hornets, Bramley, Keighley, can remain in existence. But they do. As one board of directors succeeds another (retreating, impoverished, to lick its collective financial wounds), hope springs anew that this time the success that has eluded the club throughout its entire Rugby League history is just over the horizon. At the other end of the scale it is, of course, a different story and there is nothing quite like seeing an entire town shut up shop and set off for Wembley at the beginning of May.

Hull FC, to give it its formal title, provided the success story of the early 1980s, when, just seven years after it faced extinction, it was involved in two successive Challenge Cup finals. Hull's turnover in 1981–2 was £650,000 and, the following season, three-quarters of a million. Hull paid more to the Rugby League in levies on its gate receipts than clubs like Huyton and Doncaster take, in aggregate, in a whole season. As the soccer club, half a mile down the road, teetered on the brink of total insolvency, Hull FC at the Boulevard was building a new stand, bringing over not one, not two, but three players from New Zealand.

Hull had had great sides before, in prewar days, and in the fifties and sixties, but around 1976 they had reached just about rock bottom. Playing strength was, to put it mildly, modest; gates had dwindled and the finances were in a terrible state. In fact, one new director put it like this: 'If we had known then what we know now, we would never have taken office.' But they didn't know, and they did go in, and the city, reeling under the burden of its unemployment figures and the murder of its centuries-old fishing fleet, came to sporting life. In the northeast of Hull, the rival club, Kingston Rovers, was already enjoying a degree of success and together they went to Wembley, with families divided and father shouting against son.

The team manager, Arthur Bunting, was a scrum half with Hull Kingston Rovers, so his crossing of the Humber to lead the arch rivals to glory is looked upon with more than usual disfavour in the northeast of the city. He believes that the game is very much on the way up.

Hull have sixty players on their books—miners, plumbers, car salesmen, a welder, an insurance man, carpet cleaners—and 'six or seven hundred more who want to get in'.

It's good to get into this atmosphere and enthusiasm and drive and optimism. It's infectious and you come out of it with a spring in the step. But then you think about what a different atmosphere it must be down at Tatters Field, Doncaster, and the thought is sobering. There is a sort of heroism in the existence of Doncaster Rugby League Club. It came into the game with nothing but hope and it still has nothing but hope around thirty years later. Generations of players have come and gone, conditioned to accept defeat as virtually inevitable, yet still driving themselves to play their guts out. The Hulls of the world still play it just as hard against Doncaster as against St Helens or Wigan or Leeds because among players throughout the game there is mutual respect. It's a man's game.

OPPOSITE *It is the game's fluid blending of athleticism and brute strength that makes Rugby League such a compelling sport.*

A BRIEF HISTORY

E ARLY IN 1983 came an announcement that raised a few eyebrows in the world of tourism—the city of Bradford had achieved a greater percentage increase in visitors than anywhere else in the country. Bradford? Tourists? Somehow the two just don't go together. It's easy to see why York attracts visitors, and it wouldn't be a surprise to learn that many more had decided to visit a spa town like Harrogate, the traditional coastal holiday centres of Scarborough and Bridlington, or the quaint resorts of Whitby, Redcar, Saltburn, Withernsea and Hornsea. But Bradford, deep in the heart of the industrial West Riding? It didn't make sense if you considered simply the traditional aspects of tourist attractions.

THE STORY OF BRADFORD

The more you dig into the story of Bradford, the more you realise that it deserves this new status. It is 20th-century in its general appearance but essentially 19th-century in character because modern Bradford was built on wool. The façade of a marvellous 19th-century development has created a whole city history in itself. Also for around two thousand years the area has been peopled by tribesmen and townsmen belligerently opposed to outsiders. It was pretty certainly a tribal centre of the Brigantes before the disciplined organisation of the Legions finally quelled the last enthusiastic aggression of the natives. It was most assuredly a rallying point for the organised resistance to the Normans to such a degree that Duke William swore a great oath that he would not leave a soul alive in the northeastern area of the England he had conquered. And, by and large, he kept his vow. One Norman chronicler recorded that, in what was to become Yorkshire, no fewer than 100,000 people perished and the survivors—there can have been few of them out of an 11th-century population—lived on rats, mice and 'other vermin'.

Ilbert de Lacy, one of the knights who had fought with William, was granted 150 manors in West Yorkshire for his

BELOW *Commissioned by William the Conqueror late in the 11th century, the Domesday Book provided a census and survey of English landowners and their properties.*

services, but that cannot have been such generous payment as it sounds after the army had taken toll of the area for its resistance to conquest. The Domesday Book said tersely of Bradford: 'Ilbert has it and it is waste.' Yet it clearly took more than a touch of genocide to suppress the Yorkshire spirit, for the population began once again to increase; land came under the crude plough and various forms of trade and handicraft began to develop. By 1277, with the de Lacys still in feudal control and now Earls of Lincoln, a 13th-century census revealed that 'Henry de Lacy hath many liberties in the town of Bradeford: to wit a gallows, assize of bread and beer, a marketplace and a free court from ancient times.'

The free court imposed fines for such offences as 'unruly temper', card playing at night and assault (a 10s fine for an assault in which blood was shed, 3s 4d for an assault with no spilt blood—pretty hefty fines considering the value of money in those days). The assize of bread and beer was a sort of weights and measures inspectorate, adjudicating on whether quantities and ingredients were correct.

Bradford was staunchly Lancastrian in the Wars of the Roses, as the town, at that time, was part of the lands of the Duchy of Lancaster. In the Civil War of the

THE WARS OF THE ROSES

LATE IN THE 15th century, two rival lines of England's royal family, the Yorkists and the Lancastrians, clashed in a prolonged struggle for the Crown. The wars drew their romantic name from the badges—red roses for the Lancastrians, white for the Yorkists—that their followers are thought to have worn to display allegiance.

It was the weak rule of Henry VI, a Lancastrian prone to mental illness, that triggered the wars. Yorkist Richard, Duke of York, attempted to unseat his king, and though he died in battle at Wakefield in 1460, his son, Edward, succeeded a year later. Now Edward IV, he underlined his sovereignty by dealing the Lancastrians a sound thrashing at Towton. He reigned until 1470, when disgruntled noblemen jumped ship to the Lancastrian side and reinstated Henry; but victory at Barnet saw the Crown returned to Edward within the year.

Upon Edward's death in 1483, events took an even bloodier turn, when his

two sons were murdered in the Tower of London—possibly by their uncle, who became Richard III. Alienated Yorkists rallied around Lancastrian Henry Tudor who, triumphant at Bosworth, became Henry VII.

After 30 turbulent years, England was battle-weary, and Henry VII's marriage to Edward IV's daughter, Elizabeth, came as welcome news. Henry's dynastic badge, the Tudor rose, diplomatically combined the red and white of Lancaster and York.

LEFT *Fought on the snow-whipped Palm Sunday of 1461, the Battle of Towton was said to have dyed the waters of the River Wharfe red with blood.*

BELOW *Edward IV holds court. Neither of his sons, the ill-starred Princes in the Tower, would live to enjoy the fineries of kingship.*

ABOVE *According to one witness, the rains that lashed the grand opening of Bradford City Hall caused its clock to 'go deranged and toll lugubriously'.*

ABOVE RIGHT *Silhouetted against a bruised and foreboding sky, Bradford's Lister's Mill appears the very embodiment of Blake's 'dark satanic' vision of industrial England.*

1640s Bradford was Parliamentarian and suffered greatly for its convictions. It was, in fact, the scene of one of the first engagements and was twice under siege. It was a gallant Captain John Hodgson with a well-armed body of Halifax men who drove off the troops sent by King Charles to occupy the town almost as soon as his breach with Parliament had been opened. The Royalists retreated to Leeds and as Sir Thomas ('Black Tom') Fairfax rode in from Selby to take command of the Parliamentarians, Hodgson and his men were reinforced by hundreds of Puritan clothworkers armed with clubs and scythes tied to long poles.

A second siege followed quickly, as the Royalists, led by the Earl of Newcastle, gave Bradford a tremendous hammering with their vastly superior artillery, until Fairfax was reduced to just one barrel of gunpowder (with, it is said, no tinder to ignite it!). While Black Tom was hacking his way to safety, his lady wife was taken prisoner in Bradford High Street. How had the great Parliamentarian general come to leave her behind? Did he, while detesting the Papist leanings of the Royalists, still respect their reputation for chivalry and knightly attitudes towards the fair sex? If so, how right he was, because the Earl of Newcastle sent her off to join her husband in his own carriage. If things like that could happen, it makes you wonder what the hell they were all fighting about.

A PHILOSOPHISING SPIRIT

Bradford can very rightly be proud of its pioneering work in the field of free education. Bradford Grammar School has long been one of the outstanding educational establishments in the county with a great sporting, as well as academic, tradition. There is evidence of the existence of a free grammar school in the town in the mid-16th century, the records of a Duchy Court held in the reign of Edward VI showing it to have an endowment of three acres of land worth 2s 5d in rent. In the next hundred years or so the school obviously received other and greater endowments because a formidable list was recorded by a panel of charity commissioners in 1655. It was not until eight years later, however, that letters patent were issued to 'the Free Grammar School of King Charles the Second at Bradford, for teaching, instructing and better bringing up children and youth in grammar and other good learning and literature to consist of one master or teacher and one usher or under teacher'. There were to be thirteen governors, of whom the vicar of Bradford was one, to be drawn from 'the most discreet, honest and religious persons in the neighbourhood'.

So was formal education established in Bradford, but obviously the grammar school could benefit only a fraction of the population of a town that was growing steadily, if slowly, after the Civil War had ravaged it so seriously. Ten years after the execution of Charles I, the number of baptisms and marriages in Bradford was half that of 1639, immediately before the war began. If the town could claim to have been on the winning side, it had certainly paid for it in the number of deaths among its male population.

For the next century and a half, learning was restricted to a privileged few and even when Joseph Priestley set up a Philosophical Society in the late 18th century, it was disbanded after a few years. In 1823, they tried again, this time led by one Samuel Hailstone Esq, with a rather broader-based Literary and Philosophical Society in which forty-two people subscribed £50 each to build a hall and set up a 'library, apparatus, etc'. Once again it was going to be something of an elitist society, but it was sabotaged by the vicar who preached a sermon in which he enlarged upon the irreligious tendencies of a philosophising spirit! Several of the subscribers, reports mid-Victorian writer John James, 'took fright and withdrew their subscriptions. Thus was a society, so auspiciously formed, broken up.'

But there were still some pretty persistent chaps around in Bradford, even in those days, and in the winter of 1838–9 a course of lectures on several aspects of natural philosophy was delivered by a local man, William Sharp, a Fellow of the Royal Society. At the end of the course, Mr Sharp invited his students to form—wait for it—yes, a Philosophical Society in the town and it came into being on April 12, 1839. One of the society's rules called for 'the formation of a local museum, or a collection of the natural productions of the district within fifteen miles of Bradford'.

The idea was that if this lead were followed by all the towns in the country the value to science generally would be enormous. Bradford had set a challenging lead and Mr Sharp, his exciting new educational development well and truly launched, followed up by bombarding the British Association for the Advancement of Science and the Royal Society with propaganda for his local museum. It was taken up by several of the top scientific minds in the country; the idea had got under way.

BELOW *An 18th-century portrait of theologian and scientist Joseph Priestley (1733–1804). As a child he is said to have displayed an enquiring mind; one of his juvenile experiments, in which he corked spiders into bottles to test how long they could survive, was a precursor to his discovery of oxygen in 1774.*

At the same time, the Bradford Philosophical Society was pressing on with enthusiasm. Nearly two hundred members were enrolled in the first year and here the founders showed a bit of good Yorkshire cunning. They invited fourteen of the country's top scientific thinkers to become honorary members. Flattered, most of them accepted. It cost the society nothing at all, but the honorary members felt it was only right to send a book to the library, or an exhibit for the museum.

Side by side with this rather up-market form of education was growing the Mechanics' Institute, which was aimed at that section of the populace to whom contributing £50 towards the construction of a hall would be unthinkable. The aims of the institute were: 1) The provision of a library for the use of all members and subscribers. 2) The supply of popular instruction, through public lectures. 3) The formation of classes under well-qualified masters in which every facility should be afforded for pursuing the various branches of useful knowledge. It was set up in 1832 and in the first year had 352 members, 800 volumes in its library and issued them to 4,642 borrowers; by 1838, there were 541 members and 2,249 books, which were issued on 19,000 occasions. By the time Princess Victoria had become Queen there was a growing literacy among the population, but the numbers were still painfully small in relation to the now rapidly growing factory towns. How could working-class children get any form of basic education?

EDUCATION FOR THE MASSES

The Sunday schools, which had come in the wake of John Wesley, preceded the day schools by many years. A National School had been opened in 1831 and was 'kept' in a Sunday school belonging not, in this instance, to a Wesleyan chapel, but to Christ Church. Fifteen years earlier, the Quakers had opened a British and Infants School off Leeds Road. It cost the enormous sum for those days of £2,300, all of which was raised by subscriptions from the Society of Friends, but was open to children of all denominations. As with the National School, there was a charge of 2d a week for each pupil and an extra penny for those who learned to write! Here we see the vicious circle that so retarded the improvement of general education through the early and mid-Victorian years. Child labour was extensively used because it was cheap. Parents needed the miserable pittance of the kids to supplement their own small wages (if, indeed, they had jobs); to send the youngsters to school, even part-time, was to lose that pittance, or part of it. To have to pay 2d or 3d as well was enough to deter all but the most farseeing and caring parent.

However, while the first crude elements of formal education for the masses attracted only a tiny percentage of working-class children, Sunday schools bulged at the seams with huge intakes on the Day of Rest. Here the children could at least have some sort of window on the world outside the gloomy factories, the narrow streets, the tiny cottages that were the whole of their world for six days a week.

At this time there were around seventy worsted spinning mills in the greater Bradford area, housing roughly two thousand frames, each of which spun between 700 and 850 hanks of yarn a day—each hank measured 560 yards. In 1830, a total of 43,736,386 pounds of wool was devoured by machinery that was becoming more efficient every day. Child labour was an essential part of this industrial activity so that, as more day schools began to open, the cheapest section of the labour force was in danger of being lured away. The mill owners had a problem. Some, like Titus Salt, had a paternal, benevolent approach to their workers; others were cast in the Dickensian mould—greedy, grasping, ready to exploit. 'Half-timers' provided something of an answer—children who spent half their time in school, half working in the woollen mills. It was not an ideal solution, but at least by the beginning of the 1870s almost every child had a chance of some rudimentary education.

The village of Clayton, which was a half-industrial, half-agricultural community on a hillside to the west of urban Bradford, has long since been engulfed by the spread of housing but still retains something of the nature of a village community. Indeed, its inhabitants talk naturally of 'the village' and it retains a strong sense of identity. Ben Ashton, first headmaster of the school that opened there following the 1870 Education Act, taught the great-grandparents of people still living in 'the village' and his meticulously kept school journals make fascinating reading.

THE QUAKERS

ABOVE THE DIMINUTIVE River Bain in the Wensleydale hamlet of Countersett, stands a small, stone-built meeting house. Dating from 1710, it was built by Michael Robinson, son of Richard Robinson, one of the first Yorkshire Quakers. Countersett is typical of the remoteness of such places of worship, because early Quakers were persecuted by the Established Church, who saw them as a threat to the religious status quo, along with all other Nonconformists.

Founded in about 1650 by preacher and missionary George Fox (1624–91), the Society of Friends soon became known as Quakers after Fox's admonition that mankind should 'tremble at the Word of the Lord'. They rejected ordained ministers, church ritual and music, and were pacifists, as they are today. Fox travelled widely in Yorkshire, and in 1677 stayed at Countersett, where Richard Robinson had been holding Quaker meetings since 1652.

Quakerism took firm root in the North, especially in the more prosperous farming districts. It also appealed to no-nonsense industrial entrepreneurs, such as the Rowntrees of York. The Quakers' most prominent member was cocoa manufacturer and social reformer Joseph Rowntree (1836–1925). His employees worked reasonable hours and earned adequate wages, and

a pension scheme was set up for them in 1906, two years before state pensions began. He also appointed a works dentist to combat the effect of cheap chocolate on workers' teeth and provided amenities like gardening and photography clubs.

ABOVE *Yorkshire Quaker wool merchants do business in one of 77 panels comprising the Quaker Tapestry, on permanent display at the Friends Meeting House, Kendal, Cumbria.*

LEFT *A photograph taken in 1910 depicts female employees packing chocolates in the Rowntree factory in York; workers were strictly segregated according to sex.*

ABOVE *A roomful of little Oliver Twists make the most of a simple workhouse meal.*

ABOVE RIGHT *Built in 1854, Ripon Workhouse boasted a vegetable garden, an orchard, piggeries, and even an in-house mortuary.*

MARCH 25, 1872: Clayton British School was opened this morning at nine o'clock. During the day 126 scholars were admitted.

MARCH 28: This week I have selected two boys out of the first class to teach the Infants. We broke up today for Easter (a five-day break).

APRIL 3: Admitted five new scholars.

APRIL 8: Admitted twenty-two new scholars.

JULY 11: I cautioned a half-timer about absenting herself without leave.

OCTOBER 12: The upper part of the school have, during the past week, taken their dictation on paper instead of slates. Some of them have, so far, written it very neatly.

By the end of the first year of the school's existence the education inspector reported: 'The work is, as far as it goes, of a satisfactory character. Separate accommodation, however, is required for the infants.' This was duly reported to the managers, with a request for the provision of more accommodation, and signed by the entire staff—Benjamin Ashton, first-class certificated teacher; Bessie Day, assistant; Herbert Barker, pupil teacher. By May, an infants' room had been set up and the school advertised for a certificated infants' mistress, who arrived on June 9.

Then we get a glimpse of a darker side of life in this world of part-time education as, on November 20, Mr Ashton reports: 'A deplorable event has happened last week. A boy named Henry Illingworth (a half-timer at Messrs Benn's mill) was kicked by an overlooker and died a few days after.' (An inquest was held, the overlooker was committed for trial on a manslaughter charge and he got twelve months' hard labour.)

Tragedy struck again in the winter of 1882:

NOVEMBER 11: Much sickness. Two children died.

DECEMBER 2: Another four died. Scarlatina.

On December 9, 1893 it was reported that 'workhouse children were admitted on Monday last' and two years later we learn something that makes you wonder how the workhouse children could bear to leave the portals of Mr Bumble. 'Fifty children,' reads the school record, 'are being taught in a classroom measuring 21ft by 10ft and 49 in a room 16^1/2ft by 14^1/2ft. In the smaller room the air is so bad as to be positively injurious to health of both teachers and scholars.'

Mercifully, in September 1898, the school took possession of the new board school and, I'm sure, with as much relief as pride, 'marched in procession round the cricket field and entered the new school'. Their troubles were not ended, however. In July 1900, 'Moved from classroom into Assembly because of rain coming through ceiling.'

As we reach the Great War, the school's story begins to take on the character of Noël Coward's *Cavalcade*. The headmaster in these days was Mr Arthur Senior.

MAY 12, 1915: Received notice to report for duty with 5th Battalion,
   West Yorkshire Regiment. Mr Catherall takes over as acting headmaster.

AUGUST 31, 1916: Lt Senior visited school and took afternoon prayers.

MAY 18, 1917: First batch of potatoes planted.

JANUARY 14, 1918: Captain Senior visited school this morning.

MAY 29, 1918: King and Queen visited Bradford. Attendance affected.

OCTOBER 10, 1918: No woodwork classes today. Teacher had to report
   for military duty.

JANUARY 16, 1919: Captain Senior recommences duty after three years eight
   months' leave of absence on military duties.

But now let's skip through eighteen years to July 14, 1937, when the head logged this little bit of social history:

'I have had occasion to report to the Office the case of Joe Hollingsworth. This boy is fourteen years of age but not qualified to leave school until the end of term. His attendance has been most irregular and after a day's absence on an excuse of illness I have met him on my way home from school taking out meat for a butcher. On Monday of this week he was taking out meat during school hours. I reported the matter to the Education Office and this morning an official from the Office warned the boy's mother and also the butcher concerned. On my way to school this afternoon I was stopped by the father who was most threatening and abusive.'

It seems things hadn't changed very much over the years.

ABOVE *News of Captain Cook's violent death in Hawaii spurred King George III to grant a coat of arms to his family; its Latin motto, Nil intentatum reliquit—'He left nothing untried'—serves as a fitting epitaph to this extraordinary man.*

CAPTAIN COOK

The second-oldest tale in Yorkshire cricket takes the form of a conundrum: 'Who is the only Yorkshire captain to go to Australia and never play in a Test match?' Answer: 'Captain Cook.' Yes, it's an old one, its antiquity exceeded only by the story of the Southerner who, for some reason that escapes everyone north of the Trent, went to a Roses match and, after applauding the play of men on both sides, was told by the Yorkshireman on his right and the Lancastrian on his left to mind his own bloody business because that game had nowt to do with him. But, Test-appearance conundrums apart, the story of Captain Cook is fascinating because his career, a major part of English history, had the most unlikely beginning.

James Cook was born on October 27, 1728, in a two-roomed thatched cottage in Marton, a hamlet just south of the dreary mud flats alongside the River Tees, where the great industrial complex of Middlesbrough later grew. A week later, at St Cuthbert's Church, 'James, ye son of James Cook, day labourer [was] baptised,' according to the register. That, at least, is a matter of record, but it is uncertain whether he was one of seven or eight children born to the unlettered labourer of Scottish descent and the former Grace Pace, a local girl. Their neighbours, the Walker family, were rather better off than the Cooks, and it is, perhaps, to them that we owe the deepest debt of gratitude, because, while doing odd jobs for Mr Walker, young James was taught to read and write by Mrs Walker, making him substantially more accomplished than most youngsters of his social standing.

Then the elder James Cook moved five miles down the road, towards the Cleveland Hills and to a better job as hind to Thomas Skottowe, of Airyholme Farm, Great Ayton. It is unlikely that young James had ever seen the sea when he moved to Great Ayton and it could well be that his first glimpse of the North Sea was from the summit of Roseberry Topping, the signal beacon hill that rises sharply behind Great Ayton as one of the northern outposts of the Clevelands. It was here that warning was given of the approach of the Norsemen and the danger signals shone out from one beacon top to the next, deep into the country-side. And it was from here, if the prevailing mist was not clinging to the steep, upper slopes, that James Cook could look out to sea, far to the northeast.

Who knows whether he dreamed then of exploring the southern seas, charting new coastlines, discovering new outposts of Empire? It seems impossible that such thoughts could ever spring to the mind of a boy who lived with so many brothers and sisters—many destined to die young—in a cottage of modest dimensions. Yet young James stood out in the Cook brood. He was not sickly like most of the others; he was quick to learn; and, building upon the rudiments taught him by Mrs Walker back in Marton, he made further progress at the Michael Postgate School in Great Ayton.

The rest of his time was spent helping on the farm, so that by his early teens, James Cook was very much a country boy. He was, however, a well-educated teenager by 18th-century standards—certainly for the son of a farmworker—and so impressed Squire Skottowe with his quick wits and his ability with 'his letters', that he sent him off to apprenticeship with William Sanderson, haberdasher and grocer in the fishing village of Staithes, one of the many attractive coastal villages that still exist, despite greedy erosion, at the foot of the great cliffs of northeast Yorkshire.

Staithes must have seemed wonderful to James Cook—a place of locally built fishing cobles (pronounced 'cobbles'), of smugglers, of towering cliffs fighting an incessant, losing battle against irresistible tides, of damp, clinging sea mists. There would be around a hundred fishing cobles based at Staithes in Cook's day and their sturdy, clinker-built hulls impressed the young Cook by their stout resistance to the cruel seas. He watched them being built in Staithes, and he remembered them… And it was here that he met another family called Walker who, in turn, were to have a powerful influence upon his life.

The Walkers, a Quaker family, were the owners of a fleet of colliers in Whitby, where James Cook now began an apprenticeship of a very different kind from the haberdasher's of Staithes. If the fishing port of Staithes had seemed huge and romantic to him, Whitby must have looked like the centre of the universe. Again,

ABOVE *Postcard-perfect Staithes, where James Cook first fell prey to the allure of the high seas.*

YORKSHIRE'S CHANGING COASTLINE

As SCARBOROUGH's Holbeck Hall Hotel teetered above a new landslip in June 1993, it performed one last public service. It brought home to the British public, watching the drama on television, just how fragile the country's eastern coastline is. Long stretches, from Kent up to Cleveland, suffer constant erosion, with Yorkshire being particularly vulnerable. Tides and currents gnaw at the flimsy seaside terrain of chalk and clay cliffs. The Holderness coast, north of the Humber Estuary, has been called the most rapidly decaying shoreline in Europe. In some areas, it retreats before the waves by as much as 15 feet a year.

The erosion is nothing new, dating back at least to Roman times. Old markers, maps, paintings and registers, including the Domesday Book, indicate that in some regions a strip of land as much as a mile wide has been eaten away. The Holderness coast alone has lost more than 30 villages to the sea since Roman times.

Defensive measures traditionally include sea walls and revetments (long stone barriers), to protect cliffs at risk, and breakwaters and groynes (solid fences projecting into the sea), to deflect the force of the waters. But the expense is enormous. And the diverting of currents and drifting sand results in unforeseen erosion of beaches, and hence cliffs, further down the coast. Newer techniques, such as the dumping of boulders or concrete blocks on beaches or in harbours, have aroused controversy, too. Some experts in shoreline management now favour a policy of minimal intervention, at least in thinly populated areas, as if to let nature take its course. Like King Canute, they realise that trying to hold back the sea is sometimes a futile exercise.

RIGHT *Going, going, gone: Scarborough's Holbeck Hall Hotel stares into the abyss after the devastating landslip that ultimately destroyed it in 1993.*

great cliffs loomed high above the harbour, but whereas at Staithes they seem to be locked in eternal and futile combat with the ocean, at Whitby they somehow give an impression of solid protection, clasping the anchored shipping in affectionate embrace. In 1746, Whitby was one of England's leading seaports, with great, ocean-going sailing ships in the harbour as well as the fishing fleet. It was here that the forerunners of the poet John Masefield's dirty British coasters were built—no 'salt-caked smoke stacks', but 300- to 500-ton sailing ships that carried cargoes of Tyne coal down the east coast to London.

His first voyage was in a ship of 450 tons called the *Freelove* and when, years later, he laid down to their Lordships of the Admiralty his specifications of the ship he wanted for his voyages of exploration, Cook plainly had the east-coast collier in mind. He wanted 'a ship not of great draught of water, yet of sufficient capacity to carry a proper quantity of provisions and necessaries for her complement of men, and for the term requisite to perform the voyage. She must also be of a construction that will bear to take the ground and of a size which, in case of necessity, may be safely and conveniently laid on shore to repair any accidental damage or defect.' Something between a fishing coble and a collier, perhaps? Certainly Cook could not find all the characteristics he thought desirable among 'ships-of-war of forty guns, frigates, East India Company ships, three-decked West India ships'.

By the time he was twenty-six, Cook was ready for command of one of the Walker ships. Instead, he decided to join the Royal Navy. England was at war with France, and while the crews were largely made up of reluctantly 'pressed' men, promotion prospects were good for enthusiastic and skilful officers. Cook was both enthusiastic and skilled, and during the Seven Years' War between England and France he had ample opportunity to improve his skills.

Cook was in the sixty-four-gun *Pembroke* when she convoyed the troops of General Wolfe to Canada. He was in charge of navigation and was encouraged by the *Pembroke*'s captain to further his studies in mathematics, astronomy and hydrographic survey. All these—plus his experience in sailing colliers up and down the east coast of England—were now put to use in charting a difficult stretch of the St Lawrence River that was especially hazardous to vessels trying to move upriver to Quebec. Cook's skills helped Wolfe to land his men in position to scale the high, jagged cliffs protecting Quebec and capture the city in 1759.

Three years later Cook married twenty-one-year-old Elizabeth Batts at Barking, but that young lady was destined to see very little of her husband. Within months he was away surveying the Newfoundland coast and during the course of this voyage his knowledge of astronomy was enriched by observing and recording an eclipse of the sun. This was recalled by the Lords of the Admiralty when, six years later, they were asked to provide a ship to take members of the Royal Society to Tahiti to observe the transit of Venus across the sun. James Cook was given the rank of lieutenant and command of the *Endeavour* over the heads of many more senior officers. Three years were allowed for the voyage, which was perhaps as well since *Endeavour* could manage, flat out, about seven or eight knots. She displaced 366 tons, had a length of 106 feet and a beam of 29 feet.

In this little cockleshell, Cook, with his crew and a group of scientists, set out round the Horn for the largely unexplored and completely uncharted waters of the South Pacific. Once the scientific work had been completed in Tahiti, Cook then broke open his sealed orders from the Admiralty and found himself commissioned to establish the existence (or not) of a 'continent or land of great extent' in the southern oceans. Cook discovered no land filled with gold and spices, as European folklore suggested, but he did find New Zealand, the land of the long white cloud, which had been mistakenly identified as part of Australia a century earlier by the Dutchman, Abel Tasman. Meticulously, Cook charted the coastline to show that, quite apart from being separated from Australia by more than 1,000 miles of sea, New Zealand consisted of two quite distinct islands separated by—what else?—the Cook Strait. And he logged his opinion that the islands were admirably suited for settlement 'should this ever be thought an object worthy of the attention of Englishmen'. Well, that proved prophetic enough, not only for Englishmen but for Scotsmen as well, especially in South Island.

Cook charted the eastern coastline of Australia, returned to England in mid-1771, and the following year was off on his travels again. Poor Elizabeth! This time Cook was commanded to 'complete the discovery of the southern hemisphere'—a pretty tall order, but at least he had the help of improved equipment, including a chronometer devised by another Yorkshireman, John Harrison. And this time he had two ships, *Resolution* and *Adventure*, which probed beyond the Antarctic Circle, landed domestic animals on New Zealand and planted a number of vegetables. Most important of all, he found a way to combat scurvy by feeding his crew a diet of sauerkraut and lemons among their rations. Cook's third voyage, in 1776, took him among the pack ice of the North Pacific into the Bering Strait, then back to Hawaii where he died, speared in the back, on St Valentine's Day, 1779.

ABOVE *In 1713 the British government offered an award of £20,000 for the discovery of an accurate method of determining longitude. Horologist John Harrison, after many trials, was awarded first prize for his marine chronometer* (top).

ABOVE LEFT *Captain Cook's* Endeavour *crumbled away off the coast of Rhode Island at the end of the 18th century; this superbly crafted replica, pictured sailing into Whitby harbour in 1997, was built in Fremantle, Western Australia.*

During his charting of the Australian coast in 1770, the first landfall was a head-land which was given the name Point Hicks, because the sighting was first reported by the officer of the watch, Lieutenant Hicks, and Cook gave the country the name of New South Wales. Looking for a safe anchorage, Cook sailed past Point Hicks into the sheltered water of what now became Botany Bay. Just round the corner was a marvellous and beautiful natural harbour where Sydney, one of the greatest cities of the southern hemisphere, would rise over the next two centuries. Australia is a wonderful country—young in outlook, vigorous, vibrant, challenging. I look forward to every trip there with the eagerness of a schoolkid awaiting his first trip to the seaside, and I am delighted to think that it was a Yorkshireman who brought it into the Commonwealth's family of nations.

THE KINGDOM OF RIBBLESDALE

There is a tendency to think of the Ribble as a Lancashire river because it arrives at Preston and meets the Irish Sea through a wide estuary where there was once a flourishing port. Yet the truth is that it rises very close to the Wharfe

EXPLORING THE THREE PEAKS

THE THREE PEAKS of the Yorkshire Dales, all within a few miles of each other, perhaps owe some of their popularity to the fact that they are like three brothers: Ingleborough, Whernside and Pen-y-Ghent —'the highest hills 'twixt Tweed and Trent'—all sprang from the same stock, but have turned out rather differently. The tallest is Whernside (2,414 feet), followed by Ingleborough (2,373 feet), and last but not least is the brooding Pen-y-Ghent

(2,273 feet). Walking all three in the same day is one of the Dales' stiffest challenges.

The Celtic provenance of the name Pen-y-Ghent is unclear. Some say it means 'hill of the border', and that the mountain is so called because it once marked the border of a Welsh kingdom. Another explanation has this exposed peak as 'hill of the winds'—for obvious reasons. The Pennine Way marches across its summit, where walkers are rewarded with views over Pendle Hill to the south and the moors of Langstrothdale to the north. Like the other peaks here, Pen-y-Ghent is punctured with caves and potholes. The hills are made of limestone rock, which in places has been dissolved by centuries of rainfall. Beneath

LEFT *Walk the Three Peaks from Horton-in-Ribblesdale, and Ingleborough will be your third and final ascent.*

those peaks are great holes, in which another world exists. Potholers are constantly exploring this vast network of underground caverns and tunnels. The less daring can gain an idea of the thrills and challenges involved—not to mention the dangers—by visiting one of the region's show caves. Here one need do nothing more strenuous than take a guided tour. The best are the White Scar Caves in the belly of Ingleborough, whose underground waterfalls and rivers might be found in the pages of a Jules Verne adventure classic.

Below Ingleborough is Gaping Gill, one of the best-known potholes in Britain. It is said to be large enough to contain York Minster, a claim anyone can check by visiting on the spring or summer bank holidays, when local caving clubs erect a bosun's chair above the chamber and lower visitors down the straight drop of around 350 feet. The descent is free—but you must make a donation of a few pounds in order to be taken back up again!

and at least half its journey to the sea is from north to south in Yorkshire. North Ribblesdale (between Ingleborough and Pen-y-Ghent) and Chapel-le-Dale (between Whernside and Ingleborough) are of some importance to our Yorkshire story because they form a vast, natural outdoor-pursuits centre for dwellers of the industrial West Riding and, indeed, beyond. This is the land of the climber, the fellwalker and the potholer.

There is a whole kingdom still to be explored under the great triangular landmass of the Three Peaks, even though miles of caves have already been discovered, explored and mapped. Speleology is not a science to attract the claustrophobic, but for adventurous souls who do not mind close, dark and often wet confinement, it holds an endless fascination. There are not many parts of the earth that have not been explored by man, but here there are caves and caverns and lakes just two or three hundred feet beneath the surface of these Craven peaks still awaiting their first visit.

Ribblesdale, in its upper reaches, is inviting, with its grey villages clustered around areas of greenery and pleasant pubs to refresh the traveller. Chapel-le-Dale,

ABOVE *Their wealth of potholes mean it's possible, quite literally, to get under the skin of the Three Peaks, if merely scaling them isn't challenging enough for you.*

LEFT *A snow-covered Pen-y-Ghent rises above a limestone lattice at Sulber.*

by contrast, is stark and forbidding. Here, with an average annual rainfall of around seventy inches, the wind keens through gaps in the hills to the south-west at seventy knots on occasion. Small wonder then that vegetation is largely restricted to bracken and ling, and the ground is a mess of peat bogs.

The few farms cling to the bare fellsides; even the sheep seem to wonder what they are doing there as the wind howls and the rain sheets across the valley, turning trickling streams in a matter of minutes into roaring torrents tumbling angrily down the slopes. Some disappear underground to chase through the honeycomb of limestone passages, trapping the novice potholer. Others swell the main waters of the two rivers that emerge from opposite sides of Whernside, Yorkshire's highest peak, at 2,414 feet. The Doe runs the shorter course, from the east of Whernside; Kingsdale Beck sweeps from the west and the two meet in Ingleton, 'the land of woodland and waterfall' to form the Greta. From a point a couple of miles above the town, the rivers plunge over a series of limestone shelves in miniature valleys flanked by trees to provide a network of glorious woodland walks. Colonies of dippers splash merrily in the upper reaches; families of red squirrels once frolicked among the trees, but may now have been driven to more cloistered territories. Ingleton is a haven for the day-tripper and the caravan fraternity and it is easy to see why.

In the parallel valley to the east, the Ribble flows serenely through Settle, that lovely old halfway house of a town between the industrial West Riding and the Lakes, or the Lancashire coast. The great limestone mass of Castleberg towers so sheerly over the marketplace that at times it seems to be hovering suspended in the air, and on market day the stalls of farm produce stand side by side with those of Indian traders from Bradford, selling 'seconds' from the textile mills of two counties. Now the Ribble moves out onto the more fertile plains of Bowland before it crosses the border into Lancashire and is lost to us.

THE SETTLE–CARLISLE RAILWAY

Let us go back to the bogs and the fells of Ribblehead, where, over a hundred and twenty years ago, the old Midland Railway Company conceived the idea of building a line over country so difficult that its ultimate construction ranks as one of the most ambitious concepts of engineering ever carried out. Certainly the hold this line exercises on the minds of railway enthusiasts is stronger than any other in the British system. And when, in 1981, engineering prudence and caution prompted a suggestion that the line should be closed, there was an immediate and impassioned outcry, led by John Watson, MP for the area, who probably summed up the feelings of the romantics when he declared: 'The Settle–Carlisle reflects some of the most heroic achievements of Britain's railway age. Many men and women died to build the line. It properly occupies a position of immense importance in our history.' All that is undoubtedly true, but it has to be weighed against warnings that the great Ribblehead Viaduct, spanning one of the most difficult and bleakest parts of the route, is deteriorating. The cost of replacing it runs into millions of pounds.

ABOVE *Remarkably, the elegant dipper seeks out much of its food by walking under water on shallow riverbeds.*

OPPOSITE *The awesome Ribblehead Viaduct bestrides Batty Moss, its sheer scale reducing trains and cars to mere children's toys. Regular passenger services and occasional 'steam specials' still run on the Settle–Carlisle line.*

It was the cutthroat competition of the railway companies in Victorian Britain that led to the construction of the line in the first place. As W. R. Mitchell and David Joy recount, in their admirable *Settle to Carlisle*, the Midland Company could transport passengers and freight as far as Ingleton but anyone or anything requiring to travel further north had then to transfer to trains of the London and North-Western Company—a serious competitor! So if the passenger coaches or freight cars travelling on from that point were overburdened, who would be left at the wayside to wait for the next train but those whose bookings originated with the rival Midland Company? That was not exactly the most pleasant fate for a passenger in the 1860s. Apart from barges, there were no alternative forms of transport. Everything has progressed so quickly in the 20th century that it's a little difficult for us to realise that just over a hundred years ago you might find yourself utterly stranded in the middle of the Yorkshire Dales. So there was little alternative for the Midland Railway Company but to build its own line.

It almost certainly could not be done today; it couldn't have been all that easy at a time when Karl Marx was publishing his treatise *Das Kapital*, John Stuart Mill his *Subjection of Women* and the Suez Canal was just being opened. The cost of building the seventy-two miles of railway from Settle to Carlisle was £3,500,000—a mind-boggling sum at that time and utterly unthinkable in today's terms. And from an engineering point of view the project was just as formidable. If you remember that locomotives were limited in their pulling power 110 years ago, then consider that the line had to climb to one of the highest parts of the Pennines and go right through the range at 1,169 feet above sea level, you begin to see that one of the first problems was achieving an acceptable gradient. Only when that had been worked out could the engineers think about tunnelling and drilling through immensely hard rock. After that came comparatively minor matters like housing a work force of thousands far from any town or village; getting supplies and materials to them by horsedrawn transport; filling in the bogs to provide a sound base for bridges and viaducts; and working with equipment that must seem to us to have been primitive. And all this had to be done in whatever weather one of the most inhospitable parts of Britain decided to serve up.

The Settle–Carlisle railway is an engineering marvel. It has no sharp bends, the result of a brilliantly ambitious concept of driving it in an almost straight line to link the valleys of the Ribble and the Eden, even though that meant cutting through a wilderness of almost impossible country between the two. There are fourteen tunnels—the longest, Blea Moor, 2,629 yards long—and twenty major viaducts, of which the masterpiece is Ribblehead, 1,328 feet long and supported by twenty-four arches. As it is the only construction larger than an isolated farmhouse in this wild part of the dale, it seems, at first glimpse, totally incongruous, especially when it appears out of swirling mist or low cloud. But if you stand and look at it, its severe lines gradually begin to blend into the whole austere scene.

Here, in the squelching treachery of Batty Moss, picture this forbidding land in 1870, the hutted homes of a thousand masons and engineers and navvies, with their imported 'wives', their drunken sprees, their Sunday services conducted by travelling preachers, their fights, their deaths. This was England's Klondike, without the rich rewards. The masons got 6s 3d for a nine-hour day, which would have made them well-to-do workmen of their times, but they must have earned every penny of it, as did the miners working, incongruously, above the masons to drive their tunnel through the dripping dampness of Blea Moor. Every one of those 2,629 yards cost £45 to blast away, making use of the recent discovery of the Swedish chemist, Alfred Nobel. His dynamite cost £200 a ton, largely because it had to be transported from Newcastle to Carlisle by road before starting another fifty-mile trip into the Pennines. The first surveys were carried out in 1869; not until May 1876 was the line open for regular passenger traffic.

Ribblehead's station then provided a new focus for the slight social life of the dale. The vicar of Ingleton drove in pony and trap to conduct services in the passengers' waiting room and a harmonium was brought in to accompany the hymn singing. Years later it became a weather station for the Air Ministry.

ABOVE *Dent's splendid isolation has kept it delightfully free from many of the trappings of late 20th-century life.*

At the other end of the Blea Moor tunnel the little valley of Dentdale shoots away to the west to what must be one of the remotest townships in England, even today. Dent has a fascination all of its own, perhaps because of its remoteness, but it achieved an odd fame during the First World War because of the abundance of knitted woollen comforters produced by its womenfolk for the men in the cold and muddy trenches of Flanders. So it's perhaps right that Dent should have been given a unique station, far from the town itself and, at over 1,100 feet, the highest on English railways. The station clings dizzily to the hillside, reached by a road that climbs, from the valley bottom, 450 feet in about half a mile. I don't really see it as the ideal start to a holiday, lugging a suitcase three miles up the valley before climbing that last hill to the train.

The line grinds on, still climbing, burrowing through Rise Hill to the highest point of the line at Aisgill Summit, and now it has to cross the desolation of Mallerstang Common, the roof of this part of the Pennines, before starting the descent into the broad and lovely valley of the River Eden and on to Carlisle.

The Midland Railway made its point: it got its mainline passenger and freight route into Scotland. The cost, in every way, was staggering but the legacy was a piece of engineering and communications history. A whole generation has grown up taking Britain's railway system for granted as something sleek and streamlined—and diesel-electric powered. But when steam-train enthusiasts arrange one of their nostalgic 'steam specials' and one of those wonderful engines hauls its train gingerly across the venerable Ribblehead Viaduct, you will see hundreds of romantics with their cameras, capturing the scene on film. They know that each occasion may now be their last opportunity to do so.

CHAPTER SIX

CULINARY TRADITIONS

FIVE TIMES ALMOST EVERY WEEK for the past twenty-five years, Mrs Peggy Jones has eaten fish and chips for lunch. This information may alarm dieticians and heart specialists but it will cause no great surprise to Yorkshiremen and women when I explain that Mrs Jones is the restaurant manageress at Harry Ramsden's, the world's greatest fish-and-chip shop. What else would they expect her to eat? No, if there is anything calculated to cause remark it is possibly the fact that the lady's weight is closer to seven stones than seventeen. There will, of course, be a minor outcry in certain quarters at the claim of 'the world's greatest', but it is difficult to see any rival claim that will stand close scrutiny.

A YORKSHIRE INSTITUTION

Harry Ramsden's is no longer the largest fish-and-chip shop in area or seating capacity but it was certainly the first of the large-scale establishments; its reputation had gone round the world before newer, and perhaps even more salubrious, emporia had even laid their foundation stones; and the sentimental attachment to it felt by Yorkshire people has never faltered. If it is not absolutely the biggest, its operational figures, overall, make impressive reading: one and a half million fish-and-chip meals are served there every year involving 697,000lb of fish—mostly haddock, but with a fair demand for the two alternatives, plaice and halibut; to go with the fish, 1,010,000lb of potatoes are chopped up into chips; and to fry it all, 230,000lb of beef dripping are melted in the frying ranges. In the chandeliered dining room, decorated in cream, orange and brown, 31,000 bottles of sauce are emptied onto the plates of fish and chips, and the sideplates of bread and butter take up 39,400 loaves a year and 19,000lb of butter. The teapots take 10,000lbs of teabags, to be served with 19,000lb of sugar and

BELOW *Harry Ramsden was already a successful fish fryer in Bradford, when his wife's TB forced him to shift his business out to the cleaner air of the countryside, and set up shop at Guiseley.*

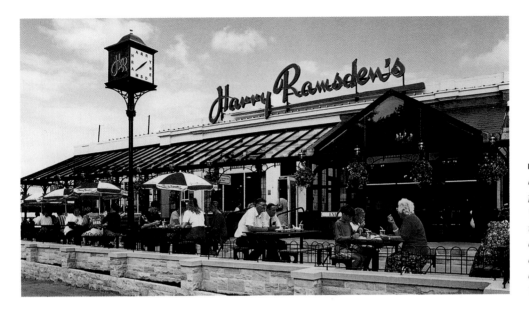

LEFT *Alfresco dining at Harry Ramsden's flagship branch at White Cross in Guiseley; today, there are outlets of this legendary fish-and-chip shop as far afield as Hong Kong, Tenerife and Melbourne.*

120,000 pints of milk. Over the meals are sprinkled and shaken 3,000lb of salt and 13,000 pints of vinegar.

Those are the bald, but impressive statistics. What makes Harry Ramsden's so different from a growing band of rivals is the sheer romance of its story. It was in the 1920s that Harry set up his first shop in a wooden hut beside the junction of the A65 and the A6038 at White Cross in Guiseley. There would not have been much trade from the motoring community in those days and the spot was not, at that time, particularly heavily populated. But if Harry had his eye on the future and could see the development of the car-owning family and the motorcoach outing, then it was an utterly inspired choice because travellers between Bradford and Otley or Ilkley, or between Leeds and Ilkley (and on to the Dales), or in reverse direction, were all going to pass his front door.

After three years Harry's business had developed to such an extent that he moved, just thirty yards, to the other side of the road where new, stone-built premises, with a restaurant, were opened in 1931. It was called, quite simply, 'T'Biggest Chip 'Oile i' Yorkshire'. The terminology is interesting because it is usually only in Lancashire that the titular emphasis is placed on the sale of chips. In Yorkshire, it is usually the 'fish shop' or 'fish 'oile' (a corruption of fish hole).

In 1972, with Harry now gone to the great frying range in the sky and a multi-corporation running the business, it was extended again, given a complete face-lift and redesignated 'T'Biggest Chip 'Oile i' t'World'. But if the restaurant is today a glittering tabernacle to heavy-calorie ingestion, with acres of parking space, a children's playground, with a beautiful arrangement of potted plants inside, it was Harry Ramsden whose foresight made it all possible. Rightly, it is his name that blazes over the entrance, his name by which the place will always be known.

It cost him £150 to start his first business, on the western side of the road; he arranged to sell it for £35,000 in July 1952, and a great gala occasion was arranged. Packages of fish and chips were sold at the price Harry originally charged in his first wooden hut: 1d for a fish and 1/2d for chips. With the Yorkies' taste for a bargain, my countrymen queued for a mile down the Otley road. There was a firework display and a cocktail party, of formidable proportions, for the press.

Amid all these festivities, old Harry found he just couldn't bear to part with his baby and the sale was called off! He died in 1963 and left £44,177, a notable triumph for private enterprise.

Harry Ramsden's, then, is a Yorkshire institution and one that has sent away visitors from just about every part of the world with lingering memories of the quality of West Riding fish and chips. It would be wrong, however, to regard Harry Ramsden's as the be-all and end-all of that particular trade in Yorkshire. For a hundred years, fish and chips have been a staple diet of the working class and it is a little difficult to explain just why the dish should have become a special favourite in the North of England generally, in Yorkshire especially, and in the West Riding specifically. Friday lunchtime has long been established as that part of the week when housewives contemplate no cooking—every fish 'oile in the area will be frying from 11.30 onwards. But the trend started by old Harry was followed by a number of businessmen, setting out not only to cater for the day-long trade but to establish a dining-out tradition.

Mother Hubbard's started up on the Bradford ring road, not far from the city centre, and claimed for its stylish, 200-seat restaurant a Civic Trust award for good design. I'd give the firm a special award of my own, for branching out to open another place in Oldham, Lancashire. That is missionary work of the highest order because Lancastrians have long been starved of quality fish and chips. They sell hake, principally, rather than the Yorkshire staple of haddock; they cook theirs in vegetable oil while we use beef dripping; their batter seems to have been thrown together while ours is carefully blended—in some cases to a recipe that is guarded as closely as the Crown Jewels.

Fish, in 19th-century England, was a cheap commodity and thus had a great appeal to the poor, who were numerous. It was cooked, with no great regard for hygiene, or the disposal of waste, in premises that would have caused the modern health inspector to faint on the spot. Such malodorous sites were not difficult to find! The marriage of fish with chips at the end of the 19th century became an established and popular meal.

The trade has become more cosmopolitan in Yorkshire in recent times. There are Chinese takeaways selling fish and chips, and Indian and Pakistani immigrants have got in on the act. Shops have begun to sell a wider variety of food—curry sauce, pies, sausages in batter, fritters of various kinds. But to the purist, haddock and chips remains the fish 'oile's *raison d'être*.

THE CRICKETERS' CHOICE

It's a pretty safe bet that you can stop at any fish 'oile in Yorkshire and rely on the quality of the food you buy. The gilded emporia are the showpieces, but it's the little shops you will find in every other street that feed the workers—and some of the pleasure seekers as well. Just five minutes' walk from the Test match ground

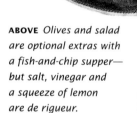

ABOVE *Olives and salad are optional extras with a fish-and-chip supper— but salt, vinegar and a squeeze of lemon are de rigueur.*

at Headingley is Brett's, where there is usually a queue for the 'outpatients' end of the business and a full house in the café, both of which are accommodated in an ivy-covered cottage fronted by a rose garden. Of all the small fish shops in the county, this is a prime favourite with cricket lovers, and during a Yorkshire match or a Test, the hum of conversation is strongly cricket tinged.

It took quite a time to persuade the great BBC commentator, John Arlott, to taste the delights of Brett's, despite its popularity with his friends among the London-based cricket writers. It was Peter Laker, the *Daily Mirror*'s cricket correspondent, who finally coaxed John to the ivy-covered-cottage-in-the-rose-garden early in the 1970s and, from then on, no Test match was played at Headingley without John dining there on one evening during the match with a string of England cricketers who have gone, over the years, as his guests. As John went through his last season as a commentator, there was a farewell dinner to him at every Test venue, but for Headingley John threw his own party. He took over Brett's for the evening with a guest list including almost the whole of the Test Match Special commentary team and the English press corps. It was quite an occasion.

YORKSHIRE'S FISHING INDUSTRY

FOR CENTURIES, FISHING formed the mainstay of life for thousands of Yorkshire folk. It provided them with food and income; more profoundly, it set them apart, culturally, from their relatives in the hinterland.

Today, a combination of overfishing, foreign competition and changing tastes has blighted this once-flourishing enterprise. Hull, for example, a major commercial city, in 1958 boasted a fleet of 146 ships and a work force of some 3,500; today just a dozen or so ships remain, served by a few hundred active fishermen. Light industry and services are now the chief employers in the region.

When did this collapse begin? In the mid-1970s, Britain lost the 'cod war' when new restrictions excluded its deep-sea fishing fleets from the greater part of its traditional grounds. The 1980s brought further blows: cheap imported frozen fish swamped the market, while soaring insurance, fuel and tackle costs meant that

fishermen had to spend increasingly long periods at sea, just to break even.

In spite of the decline of Yorkshire's fishing industry, its heritage lives on, in the form of picturesque attractions and recreational fishing. And, at the eleventh hour, Hull's own residents have woken up to the uniqueness of their fishing heritage, and are uniting to preserve the historic remains of the dock.

ABOVE RIGHT *Wearing protective gloves, a worker sorts frozen fish at Hull's Albert Dock. Freezing usually takes place at sea in factory freezer vessels based at Hull, home of the UK's only such fleet.*

ABOVE LEFT *The Albert Fish Dock is situated in close proximity to Hull's fish market, facilitating the speedy transfer of fish to auction or cold storage. The market originated at a nearby site over 100 years ago.*

John was the wine correspondent of *The Guardian*, as well as its chief cricket writer, and he devoted that week's wine column to his visit to Brett's. It was prepared with many a chuckle in the commentary box and the cutting, now yellowed with age, is framed and hangs on the wall of the restaurant:

Brett's was founded in 1919 by Arthur Brett as a sideline to his carriage business. He stabled the wagons and horses on the other side of their semirural lane. It is now run by his son Charlie ('Charles on Sunday') whose wife and their daughter Jane run the dining room. Special haddock and chips, with tea and bread and butter, costs 60p—with a double portion of haddock, 82p. Soup as a first course is 15p; cheese salad and a sweet are available but these are not the serious matters; the fish and chips are, and the claim that Brett's is the best fish-and-chip shop in England, and therefore the world, must be taken seriously. The South does not know what this dish means. The haddock is full and fleshy with a splendid depth of flavour, utterly clean with no hint of overcooked fat which so often taints the dish elsewhere. It is delivered straight from Grimsby into the cold cupboard at the back of the shop during the night and eaten within the day.

ABOVE *Ivy-covered Brett's Fish Restaurant may have changed hands, but it still serves fish and chips and is a favourite haunt of hungry cricketers.*

The chips are flowery, dry and biteable ('I never jib at paying over the odds to get right potatoes'). A sophisticated variant may be plaice (65p) but the haddock is the soul of the matter.

What to drink with this splendid plate? At Safeway, just over the main road, there is a fine, rounded, *appellation contrôlée*, French-bottled Mâcon Blanc, at £1.20, which is good enough for any man. Mr Brett will allow you to bring in your bottle and will supply glasses free from corkage charges if you come, stay and leave in an orderly fashion. He may even store your bottle in his icebox so that it is chilled for your meal.

Well, the prices quoted there—both fish and chips and wine—will date the article to the early seventies, but as each new season comes round, there is a comforting air about the prospect of the lunchtime pilgrimage up to North Lane to taste once again the excellence of Charlie's culinary art. Charlie Brett's is not only a part of Yorkshire's fish-and-chip tradition—it's part of cricket's story as well.

THEAKSTON'S BREWERY

The Norsemen of a thousand years ago sailed their longships into the Humber and up the Ouse and from there fanned out into the smaller river valleys leading up to the High Pennines. Everywhere they left their mark with their topographical terms. Their becks run down their gills from their fells; they wander over mosses, through the heath and ling, skirting hamlets and villages that were Norse setts, seats and sides.

With them, around AD 950, came a man who settled near the North Yorkshire village that was to become Masham (pronounced 'Massam') to the locals of today. His name, Anglicised over ten centuries, was Theakston. Through the aftermath of the Norman Conquest, through the Middle Ages, the Tudors, the Stuarts and the Hanoverians, the Theakstons led a quiet, unremarkable existence on their farms and smallholdings where Wensleydale gently subsides into the Vale of York. It was not until the reign of George IV that a Theakston broke with family tradition and left the land to ply a new trade, and even then it was scarcely a spectacular plunge into the unknown. Young Robert Theakston moved just two miles across the fields from his father's farm at Warthermaske into the village of Masham to set up a brewery—or rather to take over the Black Bull and its brewhouse. His partner was John Wood, his friend and brother-in-law.

This was scarcely an era when a small brewery in North Yorkshire was likely to make a dramatic impact upon the commerce of Britain, but quietly, steadily, the business of the Black Bull prospered until its brewhouse could no longer cope with the demand for its ale. A new brewhouse and maltings were built a few hundred yards away, and the founding Robert lived just long enough to see it go into production. By now John Wood was long since dead and old Robert saw the brewery they had created together pass into the hands of his two sons, Robert and Thomas. More than a hundred years later it is old Robert's great-great-grandson, Paul, who is chairman of the limited company that, in the last two decades, has seen a massive explosion of success.

It all came about because of two factors. First, the family business's standards have been maintained with great care over many years. The brewing formula evolved just under a century ago by Edwin, grandson of old Robert, is still basically that which gives us Theakston's excellent best bitter and the more renowned Old Peculier (note that 'e', by the way). The second factor, ironically, was the policy of the giant combines which, through the 1950s and 1960s, gobbled up so many of the small brewers of traditional English ale. The Big Six, as these huge conglomerates became, developed a policy of supplying their countless thousands of pubs with refined beer in metal kegs—'pasteurised' beer, as it was contemptuously dismissed by the traditionalists.

As always in times of social revolution, there was a resistance movement lurking in the shadows, seeking the chance to counterattack. CAMRA, the Campaign for Real Ale, was born; this beer-drinking Maquis combed the countryside, shunning pubs that served only the despised 'pasteurised' beer, and pointing the way to the Real Ale dispensaries. It became a cult form of drinking, and nearly a hundred and fifty years after the brothers-in-law Robert and John had started up their business, Theakston hit the jackpot. Today their beer goes around the world—to the USA and the Middle East, and to the Dutch, who have spent centuries learning how to recognise a good pint when they taste one. And it is still sold to pubs and clubs throughout the length of our own land.

In just over ten years the output of best bitter and Old Peculier has increased twentyfold. From twenty-three employees in 1969, the brewery now has a payroll

ABOVE *Theakston's Old Peculier derives its name from Masham's Peculier Court, an independent court established in medieval days so that the Archbishop of York wouldn't have to travel to this distant parish to administer the laws ecclesiastical.*

ABOVE *A stained-glass image of a polar bear decorates the new White Bear in Masham. The original White Bear was destroyed by a stray German bomb in 1941.*

of more than a hundred and fifty and the 'new' brewhouse of 1875 cannot cope with the demand. It's still there and it's still working, homely and mellowed, looking rather like a film set for a Dickens novel, and to real-ale-drinking purists it is very much a place of pilgrimage.

Like all success stories, this was not achieved without one or two problems on the way. Indeed, looking at the records of the Old Peculier (ah! now we have it) Court of Masham, it seems that the Theakstons were lucky to stay in existence for old Robert to start his brewery in 1827—brawling and failing to attend church got them into trouble from time to time. And what about 'Being rude to the Vicar— fined Six Pence'? Now that made me think; it would have cost me a bob or two, if that had been a 20th-century offence, to play in the same Test side as the Reverend David Sheppard.

Generations of Theakstons served with distinction in two world wars and in between found time to buy up the local opposition, the Lightfoot Brewery. But as old Robert's mother had been a Lightfoot, perhaps it wasn't so much a takeover as a family merger. And the company records show that it brought Theakston

BREWERIES OF YORKSHIRE

FANCY A PINT? Yorkshire folk certainly do, and across the region there are scores of breweries catering for them. Large or small, their brewing methods are similar: steeping malted barley in hot water produces a sweet liquid of fermentable sugars, called wort, which is mixed with hops to imbue it with the bitterness and aroma of beer; finally, a yeast is added, converting the sugars into alcohol.

Established in 1758, John Smith's of Tadcaster is Yorkshire's oldest brewery— though in fact the Smith family's interest dates back only to 1847. Upon John Smith's death in 1879, his company's Old Brewery passed to one Samuel Smith, while the mother company moved into its own premises. Today, John Smith's is part of the Scottish Courage brewing group; but Samuel Smith's remains independent, and, bearing the White Rose as its emblem, is proud of its Yorkshire heritage.

The only family with a rival claim to be the first family of Yorkshire beer is

Masham's venerable Theakston dynasty, brewers since 1827. Since Fred Trueman wrote his book, Paul Theakston, unhappy with the sale of Theakston's parent company to Scottish & Newcastle Breweries, has flown the family nest and set up independently. The beers produced by his aptly named Black Sheep Brewery receive many plaudits.

As one might expect, Yorkshire's main settlements boast their own breweries.

LEFT *A brewer at the Malton Brewery checks the temperature of his wort.*

BELOW *When a sheep is stuck on its back, it is said to have 'riggwelted', from the Old Norse,* rygg, *or 'back', and* velte, *'to overturn'—hence the name of this ale.*

William Stones opened the Cannon Brewery, in Sheffield, in 1865; today, it's said that one in eight pints of ale consumed in Yorkshire is a pint of malty, straw-coloured Stones Bitter. In Leeds, meanwhile, Tetley's have been supplying the city's hostelries since 1822. To this day, the company maintains a stable of shire horses, providing a quaint link with the times when beer barrels were delivered on the back of a cart.

not only the brewery but 'nine pubs and an excellent cricket team'. Nice to see they got their priorities right in 1919!

The flagship of the Lightfoot fleet of nine pubs was the White Bear, but it went for a burton (to mix my metaphors) in 1941. It's difficult to think of a quiet village pub in rural North Yorkshire as a primary target for German bombers, but that's how Theakston lost the old White Bear—demolished by a lone bomb. Maybe it was the fumes of the maturing Old Peculier, borne up into the night sky, that befuddled the Heinkel bomb aimer. Or perhaps he was just trying to get rid of his load after being driven away by the ack-ack defences of Teesside.

However, the new White Bear rose from the rubble after the war by the expedient of transferring the licence to a row of cottages near the former Lightfoot Brewery, knocking the houses' insides out and creating a brand-new pub with an old-world atmosphere. It is here that pilgrims from a remarkable number of countries try their first pint of Old Peculier after visiting the shrine of old Robert, the founder—the 1875 brewery about a quarter of a mile away.

ABOVE *It's a hard job, but someone has to do it: a Theakston brewer undertakes a little quality control.*

So there you have a happy ending to the story. I'm not a great beer man myself these days, but I do like a story with a happy ending. I wonder what old Robert would make of it all if he could come back today. His Black Bull is now shops and offices. But his great-great-grandson sits in the chairman's seat just across the yard from the new White Bear.

KIT CALVERT AND WENSLEYDALE CHEESE

When I met Kit Calvert, the blue eyes twinkling under the sparse white brows, the brown trilby hat set firmly on his head, even indoors, it was difficult to remember that this man waged a series of boardroom battles worthy of one of those dynastic serials on television, and that the business Kit Calvert revived in 1935 with a working capital of £1,085 was sold thirty-one years later for £487,000. A more unlikely tycoon is difficult to envisage, but then who would think of tycoonery in terms of Wensleydale cheese? Far more important to Kit Calvert than making money was the work of saving a foundering business that was a lifeline for the valley farmers, and after retiring from business he bought not a string of race-horses, but a three-year-old black and white pony, Dolly, and then a donkey, Jack.

Dolly, a sprightly if venerable old lady of eighteen, is something of a star. She leads the annual gala procession, and has appeared on television in episodes of James Herriot's *All Creatures Great and Small*. Dolly and Jack share a paddock behind Kit's bungalow, and until Kit died, mourned by a whole valley, in 1983, no day passed without an affectionate exchange of views between the three of them.

Kit Calvert told me he was born on April 26, 1903, at Burtersett, a mile and a half up the fellside above Hawes, the son and grandson of quarrymen. For just under eight years—starting when he was five!—he walked the round trip of three miles to school in Hawes five days a week winter and summer, carrying lunch in a waterproof satchel strapped to his back. The menu never varied—with his father, even on the top rate, earning 18s a week, there was little scope for a varied diet. It was two slices of buttered bread with either treacle, marmalade or jam between them, and half a round bannock with currants in it. Spending money was 1/2d a week, ritually handed out on Tuesday (market day), which bought a handful of sweets at Mrs Metcalfe's general grocery store. Kit left school shortly before his thirteenth birthday, but he had already earned his first wage—4d—from the proprietress of a boarding house, plus a lunch, for one working day—Saturday. He was then ten years old and his duties were: wash the flagged footpath and sweep the cobbled yard; polish the brass and steel fire irons; clean the brass taps in the bathroom and then any other jobs about the house that could be found for him. His employer was imaginative in this respect.

At thirteen, Kit was earning 5s a week plus full board, working for a lead miner-turned-farmer who was crippled by a cough from his mining days, but when Kit asked for 1s a week rise, the farmer could not afford to pay it. So off went young Calvert to exercise the farm hand's time-honoured right to stand in the marketplace and hire himself to anyone who would pay the best wages. Kit was staggered to learn that a cattle dealer in Bainbridge, three miles from home, valued his services at £1 a week plus full board. He soon discovered the reason for this: his new boss was fond of drink and Kit earned his £1 the hard way.

Five years passed and then an accident ended Kit's working days on the land. A spell of part-time work at the auction mart taught him the value of livestock and he began to invest his savings in calves and lambs until he had his first £100—an enormous sum for a working man, especially in the acutely depressed agricultural industry. Then a farmer he had helped in his spare time died and left Kit around £300. He rented a piece of land at £70 a year and sold milk over the kitchen table to neighbours, taking what was left over to the local cheese factory, only 200 yards away.

The story of Wensleydale cheesemaking is a long one, going back to the great Norman Earl Alan, who was concerned about the spiritual welfare of his troops garrisoned at Richmond and so asked for monks to be sent from Normandy. The Cistercians were practical men and the shrewd old abbot agreed only on condition that land was granted to his monks so that they could be self-sufficient. The land they were given was on the northern side of the Ure Valley, between Askrigg and the break in the Pennines beyond Hawes, and today it is still known as Abbotside Common. That is where Wensleydale cheese was first made—from the milk of the monks' ewes grazing on the land where the forest and scrub had been

BELOW By printing a portrait of Kit Calvert lighting his pipe on one of their labels, the Wensleydale Creamery doffs its cap to this entrepreneur and his pivotal role in its history.

painstakingly cleared—but the monks couldn't grow corn there, so they asked for more fertile land and were given the area further down the valley where they built their abbey of Jervaulx. However, they were thrifty souls and retained the land at Abbotside, so it was their tenants who now produced the cheese to be taken to the abbey either for the monks to eat or to be sold.

The business continued in just the same way until the Dissolution of the Monasteries, after which it was discovered that the cheese could be made just as well, and with less trouble, from cows' milk. For the next three and a half centuries Wensleydale cheese continued to be made, still to the monks' recipe, using a process known as 'pickling'. This involved running the cheese into tins coated with brine, leaving it there for three days, but turning it every day. It was not until 1874 that a visitor to the area—the head of an agricultural college in Buckinghamshire—pointed out that this was a laborious way of making cheese. He experimented, and discovered that entirely satisfactory results could be achieved by introducing dry salt directly into the cheese at an earlier stage. Overnight, the stage was set for mass production.

BELOW *Rolling green hills crisscrossed by dry-stone walls are typical of the area surrounding Burtersett, birthplace of Kit Calvert.*

FLEECES AND FRIARS: YORKSHIRE'S CISTERCIANS

LEFT *The ruins of Jervaulx Abbey display the chill dusting of a winter frost. Rain or shine, its monks attended seven services daily. In winter, matins was celebrated at 2am—in an unheated church.*

BELOW *An artist's impression of Rievaulx Abbey in its prime. So narrow is the Rye Valley, in which the abbey stands, that its architects had to forgo the standard east–west alignment of the nave, and the abbey was built at an angle.*

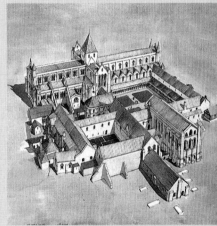

WITH ITS REMOTE wooded valleys and vast tracts of wild, uncultivated but fertile land, Yorkshire must have seemed like 'God's own country' to the monks who went there to seek refuge from the world. This was particularly true of the Cistercians, a reform movement within the Benedictine order, who began to found religious houses in England during the first half of the 12th century. Although other orders such as the Cluniacs and Augustinians were active in Yorkshire at this time, none could match the Cistercians' spiritual drive and, eventually, their wealth—

to which the magnificent ruins of abbeys such as Fountains, Rievaulx, Byland and Jervaulx still testify.

Formed in 1098 at Cîteaux, France, the Cistercian order founded its first English monastery around 1130 and its first in Yorkshire—at Rievaulx—a few years later. Known as the White Monks from their undyed woollen habits, the Cistercians strove to revive the simplicity and integrity of the early Church. Their austerity showed itself in their strict observance of monastic rules; and in their grand but plain Gothic architecture. At the same time, aided by 'lay brothers'— peasant farmers and labourers—they helped to develop Yorkshire by creating arable land, mining lead, smelting iron ore, and farming cattle and sheep.

LEFT *A detail from a medieval manuscript depicts monks chopping wood. Living in self-sufficient communities, monks, assisted by lay brothers, undertook a range of manual tasks.*

Yorkshire's Cistercian abbeys quickly increased in size, prestige and wealth. The richest was Fountains, founded around 1133 beside the River Skell. With the help of 200 lay brothers, the monks of Fountains cultivated enormous tracts of land—even, in their zeal, enforcing the clearance of peasants' homes and hamlets. Their acreage was huge, and their flocks yielded as much as 13 tons of wool a year—a commodity sold to English clothiers, and to Italian traders from Venice, Siena and Florence.

Monastic life in England came to an abrupt end between 1536 and 1540, when Henry VIII ordered the dissolution of the monasteries. In Yorkshire, over 100 religious houses were closed. Monastic lands were sold off, bells were melted down and religious icons were destroyed. With their roofing lead stripped, abbey churches soon fell into ruin, yet today their weathered traceries and arches still point to a former age of spiritual glory.

By 1930, however, every branch of agriculture, including cheesemaking, was in a desperate state. Kit Calvert, now married, could get only £2 each for his lambs in 1931; the following year the price was 31s, and in 1933 it was down to 17s 3d! His wife sold milk at 1½d a pint and whatever was unsold was sent to the dairy, to be made into cheese or butter, at 5d a gallon in summer, 8d in winter. Then, in 1933, the owner of the dairy became insolvent and, although the business was revived briefly, it collapsed again in little more than a year. Gone was the cheesemaking industry in Hawes.

ABOVE *Wensleydale's many waterways and limestone-rich soil make for fertile pastures; the area is consequently prime dairy country.*

The old blue eyes saddened for a moment as Kit Calvert reflected on the next part of the story. He puffed in silent recollection on his pipe. 'We had all been selling milk at uneconomic prices. Many farmers had gone bankrupt; some had been driven to suicide. It was a dark, forbidding world for the farmer in the 1930s and no one could see how it was ever going to get any better.'

It rankled with Kit Calvert that a small but vital local industry had been allowed to die. He thought and thought. Then he called a meeting of local milk producers and tried to persuade them to reopen the local dairy and to buy shares in the new company. No one offered to risk a single penny. He tried again: 'I'll show my own faith in the idea by investing a hundred pounds myself.'

His bank had just told him he was £234 overdrawn and unless this was reduced to £200 in one week it would foreclose on his stock of sheep and cattle. The bank also demanded the deeds of the Calvert house as security for the overdraft. Kit refused to hand them over and, instead, used the house to secure a loan with which he reduced the overdraft by £35 leaving him £100 to buy twenty £5 shares in the new dairy business he was trying to promote! Still the local farmers were unwilling to support the venture. So Kit now turned to local tradesmen and persuaded a few to buy small blocks of shares. Then he turned again to the farmers—with just the faintest hint of blackmail.

The dairy depot in Appleby and the recently formed Milk Marketing Board took about five hundred gallons of milk a day from the Hawes area, but that was less than half the local production and the only other outlet for the producers (apart from over-the-table sales) would be the Wensleydale creamery—if it was reopened. Kit told the farmers they couldn't expect help from a business they were unwilling to support themselves—at least to the extent of two £5 shares. So a little more money trickled in.

Arrangements were made to form a company, with the board of directors made up of shareholders with an investment of not less than £25 (five shares) and this persuaded a few reluctant farmers to shell out another £15 apiece. If they were going to have any brass at all in this new company, they wanted to know what was happening to it! And so Kit Calvert set out on his great financial adventure with a company capital of £1,085.

He ran into his first snag straightaway. The man who held the creamery building on a £950 mortgage refused either to lease or rent the building to the new company. So Kit's board bought it for £800 and promptly remortgaged it for £600. The first £200 of capital had gone but at least they had somewhere to make cheese, even if they hadn't yet the apparatus. Next came the discovery that they had to provide £500 security to the Milk Marketing Board to cover one month's milk prices and they got round this by buying £500 worth of government stock, which the Milk Board held as their security. That left £385 to buy vats and shelves to store the cheese, a one-ton Ford truck to collect the milk (few farmers had their own motorised transport and still fewer had anything big enough to carry a cargo of milk churns) and then 200–300 pigs to drink the whey—the by-product of cheesemaking. There were one or two other problems, too, but Kit Calvert pressed on. A licence was obtained to make cheese and butter, and arrangements were made for 500 gallons of milk a day to be processed.

On May 20, 1935, Wensleydale Dairy Products Ltd went into production with a board of nine directors, a cheesemaker at 35s a week (to go up to £2 as soon as the company could afford it), an assistant cheesemaker at 25s and a fourteen-year-old general help at 7s 6d. The company secretary was Kit Calvert. He agreed to work for one year without salary and the board was to decide what to pay him after he had produced his first balance sheet. A buttermaker joined the staff a few months later at 45s a week and the staff was completed by a lorry driver who doubled up as milk collector and as the-man-who-looked-after-the-pigs (35s a week).

Again, problems. A month's supply of milk had to be paid for not later than the 20th of the following month, so cash flow was vital. Yet such is the nature of cheesemaking that, once the milk is bought, the cheese is not ready for sale for some time. Reserve capital is necessary and the company had none.

Cheeses from the factory were normally great big sixteen-pound whoppers that had to be carved up and weighed by shopkeepers into saleable portions. Kit hit upon the idea of producing one-pound cheeses (which were ready for sale in four days) and talked farmers' wives, and their children, into selling them at farm gates or local beauty spots like Aysgarth Falls, to the day-trippers. Even at 6s a dozen, the price at which these miniature cheeses left the creamery, they solved the cash-flow problem. They probably saved the life of the company, and by the end of the first year's trading, Wensleydale Dairy Products Ltd showed a profit of just over one thousand five hundred pounds—nearly half as much again as the capital sum that had seen them start up the business.

Then he encountered difficulties much closer to home. His board was composed of hard-headed Yorkshiremen, essentially conservative in all business matters, concerned about the spending of every penny, with a horror of 'speculation'. And the most conservative of them all was the chairman, Jimmy Dinsdale. Dinsdale was a retired farmer and therefore had time on his hands to watch young Calvert, his thirty-two-year-old company secretary. He didn't like, and was highly suspicious of, anything that broke traditional patterns—like making miniature Wensleydales and flogging them at farm gates.

So when the time came for the board to decide on Kit's salary, although he was a director and, indeed, the principal shareholder, he was asked to step outside while the matter was discussed. When he was recalled, he was told that his wage was to be £1, payable from the time the company had started trading. His reward for turning a bankrupt company into one making a £1,500 profit in his first year was about £50.

'I was deeply upset and offended,' he recalled, 'but I didn't complain.'

After thinking it over, he told the chairman that while he accepted the first year's wages, he was not prepared to carry on at those rates, and when Mr Dinsdale called another meeting of the directors, they increased the offer to 25s a week! Kit refused and was asked what he thought he ought to be paid. He replied, 'At least three pounds a week.' I can just see the expression on the faces of those tight old blighters. One of them choked on his words. 'No workman in Hawes is worth three pounds a week,' he spluttered. It must have been a boardroom battle to beat anything ever seen in the City of London because these were fellows who wouldn't dress anything up in smooth phrases. They were used to conducting their business deals over sheep-pen rails down at the auction mart.

ABOVE *The Wensleydale sheep's dreadlocked coat keeps it warm during the cold Dales winter; huddling behind the nearest dry-stone wall provides further shelter from the elements.*

Kit sailed into them. 'And what about t'cheesemaker? He's due for a rise. He agreed to take thirty-five shillings a week until we could afford to pay him two pounds. We can afford to do it now.' And then came a bit of real Yorkshire—a classic case of looking after t'brass. 'He's not asked for a rise,' said the chairman. 'We don't give money to anyone until he's asked for it.' Kit was told to say 'nowt' to the cheesemaker, but he went off and put the point that a five-bob-a-week rise was due to him. And what did he reply? Need you ask? 'It's mine by right and I'm damned if I'll ask for it.'

Kit decided it was now all becoming too daft for words, so back he went to the board and said, 'If he doesn't get his five shillings, I'm resigning here and now.' The cheesemaker got his rise, but the old chairman hadn't finished with Kit. No young upstart was going to get the better of Jimmy Dinsdale. Ten days after that board meeting, Kit read an advertisement in the local paper: 'Secretary wanted for Wensleydale Dairy Products Ltd. Applications to the Chairman. Salary to be negotiated.'

The power struggle was now in full cry in that unlikely setting beside the slow, lazy waters of the Ure. Kit Calvert took stock of the situation. He went to see the owner of an old mill at Bainbridge, five miles down the valley and asked, if he got a licence, could he lease the property to start his own creamery. The landlord said yes and within an hour the story was back in Hawes, where it circulated through the town like a forest fire. With this little plot simmering nicely, Kit went along to the Wensleydale Products meeting held to sift the applications for a new secretary.

The chairman's welcome was not exactly cordial. 'You can't sit in this meeting,' he said. 'The only business is to find your successor as secretary.' 'That's right,' agreed Kit amiably. 'I'm a director so I thought I'd drop in and help you.' A short list of three was drawn up from seventeen applicants and the meeting was adjourned.

THE PLOT THICKENS

The following morning, Chairman Dinsdale steamed into Kit's office to announce with heavy satisfaction that he had it 'on good authority' that Kit wouldn't get a licence to run his own business in Bainbridge so he was wasting his time. The plot was thickening quickly. Next, Kit rang up a senior Milk Marketing Board official in Newcastle and asked if he would come over to see him in Hawes. The following Thursday, Mr Pepperall from the MMB arrived in town. He had a cup of tea at the Calvert residence and his arrival did not pass unnoticed. Word drifted round town: 'Kit Calvert's got a bigwig with him from t'Milk Board.' The pair of them walked

MAKING CHEESE THE TRADITIONAL WAY

THOSE CELEBRATED Wensleydale cheese aficionados, Wallace and Gromit, would surely approve of the Wensleydale Creamery in Hawes. Though most cheese is nowadays bulk-produced in factories, at Hawes they prefer using traditional methods to make their Wensleydale.

It takes eight pints of milk to produce one pound of Wensleydale cheese. Originally, the cheese was made from ewes' milk, but cows' milk is mostly favoured today. After a quick blast of heat to destroy harmful bacteria, milk is pumped into vats, and a souring bacterial culture or 'starter' added. Traditionally, an enzyme called rennet, taken from calves' stomachs, was stirred in at this point, to curdle or thicken the mix; but today a vegetarian-friendly fungal substitute is added. A little later, rotating knives and stirrers cut the semisolid mix into small pieces, a process that separates the curds, or solids, from the yellowy-green liquid called whey. The stirring done, the curd is left to settle at the bottom of the vat, then salted, shredded, packed

into moulds and lightly pressed to expel any remaining whey.

The cheesemaker is now on his last lap: the individual cheeses are wrapped in muslin and placed in a drying room, and are turned upside-down daily for four or five days to ensure even drying. Bagging and labelling follow, after which the cheeses are stored in a cool place. Four to six months later, they are ready to take their place on the cheese board.

LEFT *A tester plunges a cheese iron into a maturing Wensleydale. Checking the colour, texture and aroma of the core extracted enables him to monitor the cheese's progress.*

BELOW *Blades shaped like a garden rake cut and stir the mix, in order to release the unwanted liquid, or 'whey'.*

down the main street where Kit casually introduced Mr Pepperall to Mr Chapman the grocer—who just happened to be a director of Wensleydale Products. No business was discussed; it was just a friendly social call on a fellow director, but the mere fact of who Mr Pepperall was had now begun to take on a sinister significance to the other directors. After all, it had been Kit's idea to revive the cheesemaking industry; he was the one who had done all the talking to the Milk Board; he was the one who knew the men in high places; and he did seem pretty friendly with this chap Pepperall who had come a long way just to see him. Jimmy Dinsdale had only got his tale—that Kit wouldn't get a licence for his own business—from the local secretary of the National Farmers' Union. It could be wrong. In fact it was beginning to look as though it was wrong.

Kit drifted into the Board Hotel with the big man from Newcastle and they 'just happened' to run into Mr Blenkinsop, another director of Wensleydale Products. Again it was a friendly, social chat—but the seeds of doubt were now growing to full bloom. Next, the Calvert–Pepperall duo strolled across the river to the local beauty spot, Hardraw Force, passed a pleasant hour there and then walked back into Hawes for a meal before Mr Pepperall set off home to Newcastle. Not a word of business had been discussed, and Mr P. must have been mightily intrigued about what was going on. He told Kit, 'I've had a very pleasant afternoon, but I'm sorry I haven't been able to help you at all.' 'Don't worry, sir,' said the arch plotter, 'I'm sure it has been a useful afternoon.'

And indeed it had. While they had been savouring the rural delights of Hardraw Force, a hurriedly convened meeting of six of the nine directors had been taking place in the Board Hotel. Lounging outside the pub was one Joss Hutchinson, ostensibly carrying out his duties as the market tolls collector, but also half a crown better off for reporting to Kit the comings and goings of his fellow directors. Kit went home well satisfied with his day's work.

We shall never know what was said in that unofficial board meeting but the atmosphere at the next official meeting was distinctly more cordial towards the company secretary. They were sorry, said the other directors, that he had not applied for his own job because he would certainly have been on the short list— or maybe a short list would not even have been necessary. Would he not now reconsider his position and apply for the post? 'No,' replied Kit, 'but if this meeting is in order I'll do my best to help pick a new secretary.'

Well, some of the directors might have changed their views but not the chairman, not old Jimmy Dinsdale. He still wasn't going to have a thirty-two-year-old upstart getting his own way. He leapt to his feet now and thundered, 'Of course the meeting is in order. I convened it.'

It was obviously a situation that impressed itself on Kit Calvert to a marked degree because more than forty years later his memory of the dialogue which followed was very clear:

Calvert: I know you convened the meeting but what is the business?

Chairman: To select a secretary from the three candidates that we are about to interview.

Calvert: How did these men know we needed a secretary?

Chairman: From an advert in the *Stockton and Darlington Times*.

Calvert: Who sent the advert to the paper?

Chairman: I did—because you resigned.

Calvert (turning to the other directors): Did I? And did you authorise the advert being published?

Confusion. Then muttered debate. A request (again) for Kit to apply for the job himself.

Calvert: No. Not with those three chaps out there. Not until the chairman goes out to tell them they are not required.

Chairman: Never.

Calvert: Then I'll not have my name considered.

They seemed to have reached deadlock until one of the other directors offered to go out and tell the waiting candidates that they were no longer required. Kit wouldn't allow this. The chairman had to do it himself. And after a lot of snarling and teeth-grinding, Jimmy Dinsdale went out to see the three applicants. What it must have cost him in lost pride, only the good Lord knows.

But Kit Calvert still hadn't finished with him. When the chairman came back into the room, Mr Blenkinsop (whose 'chance' meeting with Kit and the man from the Milk Board must have contributed to giving the directors cold feet) moved that the company engage Mr Calvert as secretary at a wage of £3 a week. Before the motion could be put, Kit intervened: 'Wait a bit. I'm not taking three pounds a week.'

What?

'Yes. I would have taken three pounds and given you of my best, but now it's all different. I want four pounds a week, to be recognized as manager and not be harried by the chairman in things I believe to be in the best interests of the company.'

There was a long, long debate. It must have been just one pill too many for Jimmy Dinsdale to swallow and some of the directors must have felt that Kit had gone a bit too far. But the threat of the man who had worked miracles in the past year now starting up a rival business only five miles away was enough to sway the waverers. One by one the directors ranged themselves against the chairman and Kit Calvert was appointed secretary and manager at £4 a week. Trying to salvage something from the total wreckage of his pride, the chairman obtained from every director a solemn pledge that nothing of the boardroom business would ever be disclosed outside the room.

Kit Calvert went home to supper, well pleased with his day's work but with no thought of communicating the cause of his satisfaction to anyone else. A promise is a promise. Before he had finished eating, the local joiner called at his house. 'Isn't thy ears burning?' he asked. 'No. What for?' replied Kit. 'For what thoo's done t'owd Jim Dinsdale…and torn a wage o' fower pund a week out o' t'company.' There are no secrets in a community like that.

I suppose Kit Calvert can be thought of as just another awkward old Yorkshireman, as many of us have been termed over the years, but to me he is a bit of a hero. I wish we produced a lot more like Kit Calvert, the Complete Dalesman. ■

OPPOSITE *It is possible to walk behind the curtain of water of Hardraw Force—though shoes with good grips will be needed to cope with the shingly path. The lip of the waterfall had to be reconstructed late in the 19th century to repair terrible flood damage.*

HIGHLIGHTS

The best that Yorkshire has to offer

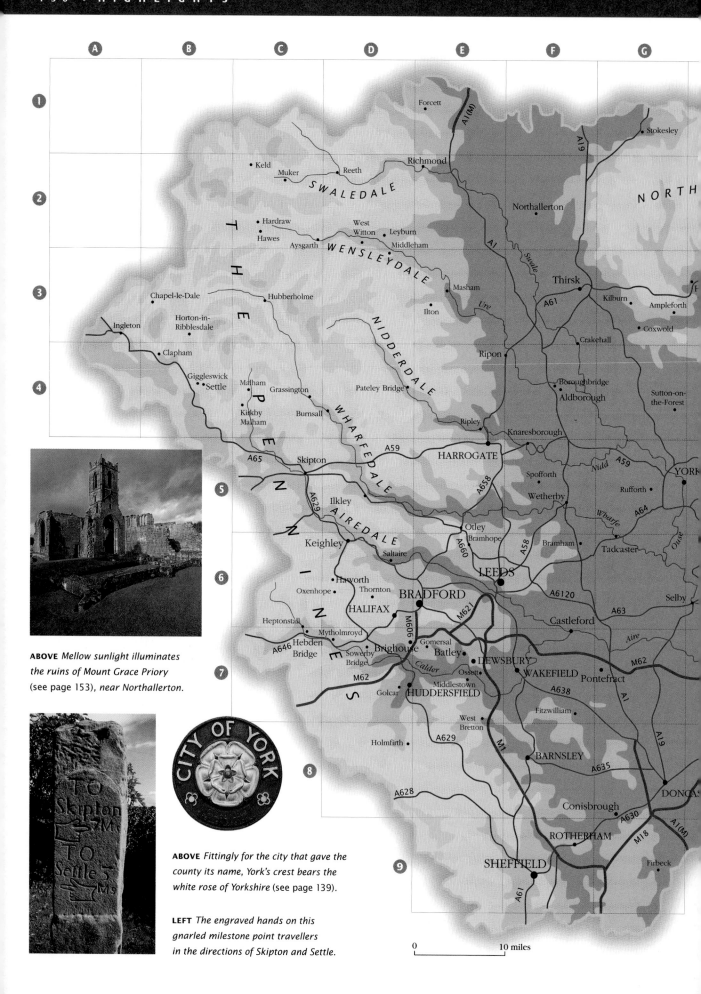

A B C D E F G

1
Forcett
A1(M)
A19
Stokesley

2
Keld
Muker
Reeth
Richmond
SWALEDALE
Northallerton
NORTH

3
Hardraw
West Witton
Leyburn
Hawes
Aysgarth
Middleham
WENSLEYDALE
Masham
Ilton
Ure
Studo
A1
Thirsk
A61
Kilburn
Ampleforth
Coxwold
Chapel-le-Dale
Hubberholme
Horton-in-Ribblesdale
Ingleton
NIDDERDALE
Crakehall
Ripon

4
Clapham
Giggleswick
Settle
Malham
Grassington
Pateley Bridge
Boroughbridge
Aldborough
Sutton-on-the-Forest
Kirkby Malham
Burnsall
WHARFEDALE
Ripley
Knaresborough

5
A65
Skipton
A59
HARROGATE
Spofforth
Wetherby
Nidd
A59
YORK
Rufforth
A64
Ilkley
AIREDALE
A629
A658
Wharfe

6
Keighley
Saltaire
Otley
Bramhope
A660
Bramham
Tadcaster
Ouse
Haworth
Oxenhope
Thornton
BRADFORD
LEEDS
A6120
Selby

7
Heptonstall
Mytholmroyd
HALIFAX
Brighouse
Batley
M606
M621
M62
Castleford
A63
Aire
A646
Hebden Bridge
Sowerby Bridge
Gomersal
DEWSBURY
WAKEFIELD
Pontefract
M62
Golcar
HUDDERSFIELD
Ossett
Middlestown
Calder
A638
A1

8
Holmfirth
West Bretton
A629
Fitzwilliam
M1
BARNSLEY
A635
A628
DONCA
Conisbrough
A630
A1(M)

9
ROTHERHAM
M18
SHEFFIELD
Firbeck
A61

ABOVE *Mellow sunlight illuminates the ruins of Mount Grace Priory (see page 153), near Northallerton.*

CITY OF YORK

ABOVE *Fittingly for the city that gave the county its name, York's crest bears the white rose of Yorkshire (see page 139).*

LEFT *The engraved hands on this gnarled milestone point travellers in the directions of Skipton and Settle.*

0 —— 10 miles

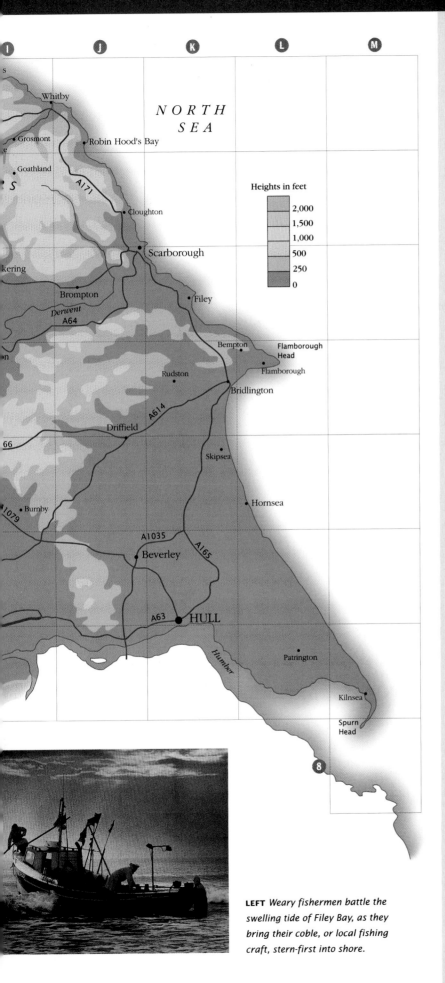

I   J   K   L   M

Whitby

NORTH SEA

Grosmont   Robin Hood's Bay

Goathland

S   A171

Cloughton

Heights in feet

2,000
1,500
1,000
500
250
0

kering

Scarborough

Brompton   Filey

Derwent
A64

Bempton   Flamborough Head

Rudston   Flamborough

Bridlington

A614

Driffield

66   Skipsea

1079   Burnby   Hornsea

A1035

Beverley   A165

A63   HULL

Humber   Patrington

Kilnsea

Spurn Head

8

CONTENTS

ABOUT THIS SECTION

IF READING *Fred Trueman's Yorkshire* has left you longing to pay a visit to the area, then you'll want to spend some time browsing the pages that follow.

In 'Highlights' we showcase a selection of the wide range of attractions Yorkshire has to offer. Its most historic cities and greatest houses, its venerable religious sites and unique natural features—all these are covered and more. We also introduce you to some of the region's famous sons and daughters, and provide a calendar of its more noteworthy festivals and events.

There is so much one could see and do in Yorkshire that this section cannot pretend to be an exhaustive guide, and readers should consult local tourist offices (see page 169 for details) for further information, opening times, entry fees and so on.

Where appropriate, our 'Highlights' entries contain grid references for the map opposite.

LEFT *Weary fishermen battle the swelling tide of Filey Bay, as they bring their coble, or local fishing craft, stern-first into shore.*

CITIES, TOWNS AND VILLAGES

Aldborough F4
This pleasant Georgian village stands on the site of the capital of the Brigantes, the largest tribe in Roman Britain. Beside a small museum explaining the site is a section of the Roman town wall, and a path that leads to two mosaic pavements, preserved in their original positions. Close by are the huge Devil's Arrows menhirs and the attractive neighbouring town of Boroughbridge, with its large market cross.

Beverley J6
Two masterpieces of Gothic church architecture, the Minster and St Mary's Church (*see detail of carving below*), dominate the skyline of this remarkably well-preserved

market town, whose narrow streets and squares contain many Georgian and earlier buildings. Dating from 1409–10, and guarding the northern entrance to the town, the North Bar is the only survivor of five medieval gateways that originally stood in the city.

Bradford E6
The growth of Bradford, once one of the greatest of England's Victorian cities, parallelled that of its prosperous textile industry. Although much has since been demolished, numerous mills, a fine Gothic town hall and an area of converted warehouses known as Little Germany, survive. Saltaire, on the city outskirts, is an outstanding example of a 'model' community created by an industrial philanthropist—in this case, the alpaca manufacturer, Sir Titus Salt.

Coxwold G3
Grass verges line the sloping street of this unblemished village, south of the Hambleton Hills. The 18th-century novelist Laurence Sterne lived at Shandy Hall, named after his novel *The Life and Opinions of Tristram Shandy, Gent*, and open to the public. The church boasts fine monuments and box pews.

Filey K3
Two long-distance paths, the Cleveland Way and the Wolds Way, end at Filey Brigg, the rocky headland just outside this seaside resort, where fishermen haul traditional boats known as cobles up the beach. Within two medieval fishermen's cottages, a small museum remembers the town's yesteryears.

Halifax D6
Squeezed into a dramatic location in Calderdale, Halifax has survived as one of the most rewarding of Yorkshire's textile-making towns. At its heart is the Piece Hall of 1779, where merchants used to sell homespun cloth in 315 galleried rooms round a piazza. Built of the golden limestone that characterises much of Halifax, the town hall was designed by Charles Barry, architect of the Houses of Parliament. On the edge of town, the 253-foot-tall Wainhouse Tower, erected in 1875 as a dyeworks chimney, has a viewing balcony accessed by some 400 steps.

Harrogate E5
Victorian hotels flank the great swath of grass, known as the Stray, at the heart of this elegant spa town. Although Harrogate now functions as a conference and exhibition centre, the sulphurous waters, discovered by William Slingsby in 1571, may still be sampled at the Royal Pump Room, now a museum. There are also Turkish baths, and string trios perform to the clinking of coffee cups within the palm-court atmosphere of the Assembly Rooms.

Haworth D6
Literary pilgrims make their way up the steep cobbled village street to the Parsonage, now a museum, where the Brontë sisters spent their tragically brief lives (*see feature on page 52*). Steam trains on the Keighley and Worth Valley Railway stop at the village.

Hebden Bridge C7
The mainly Victorian mill town is stacked up terrace by terrace at the confluence of Hebden Water and the River Calder. Beyond the stone bridge (1508) that gave the town its name, a steep cobbled lane known as the Buttress leads up to Heptonstall.

Helmsley H3
A stream cuts through this small stone-built town on the threshold of the North York Moors. Just behind the spacious marketplace lie the jagged ruins of the castle and the landscaped estate of Duncombe Park.

Heptonstall C6
Heptonstall predates nearby Hebden Bridge as a textile centre. Tucked behind the cobbled main street of this hilltop village is a hexagonal Methodist chapel and a ruined church, which contains the grave of the notorious 18th-century coin forger 'King David' Hartley of nearby Cragg Vale; the poet and novelist Sylvia Plath was laid to rest in the new churchyard.

Hull K6
Officially known as 'Kingston upon Hull', this large port on the Humber Estuary has recently undergone a renaissance following substantial bomb damage in the Second World War. The attractive waterfront area of the old docks, with its yacht marina, is a refreshing marriage of Georgian dock walls and Victorian and modern architecture. The historic old town has a host of museums with some fine old buildings standing on and around the high street.

Ilkley D5
In 1756 White Wells bathhouse was opened nearby, heralding Ilkley's emergence as a spa town. In its Victorian heyday it developed steadily, and the wooded ravine of Heber's Ghyll was laid out with walkways. Earlier relics abound in the neighbourhood: All Saints Church contains three Saxon crosses; the 16th-century Manor House Museum stands on a Roman fort site; while nearby Ilkley Moor features rocks bearing enigmatic 'cup and ring' markings dating back some 3,000 years.

YORK: THE LIVING MUSEUM

LEFT *A flagstoned medieval thoroughfare, and originally the site of York's meat market, the Shambles usually throngs with tourists eager to explore its souvenir shops and boutiques.*

RIGHT *The Pilgrimage of Grace's ringleader, Robert Aske, is said to have been hanged in Clifford's Tower in 1537.*

YORK IS VIRTUALLY its own museum, its buildings, city walls and ancient streets all doubling as exhibits of a rich history. Remnants of Roman fortifications, for example—most notably the Multangular Tower—are still visible, harking back to the city's origins in AD 71 as Eboracum, a Roman garrison and later a provincial capital of the Roman Empire. Several Roman emperors visited the city, and Constantine I was actually proclaimed Emperor while on a visit here in AD 306.

Under Saxon rule, the city, now called Eoforwic, became capital of the Kingdom of Northumbria, and in the 7th century it acquired a new role when it became the northern centre of Christianity and learning. Next, under Danish rule in the 9th and 10th centuries, the city—now Jorvik—became capital of the Danelaw, the Vikings' territory in northeastern England, and developed into a flourishing riverine trading centre. This is celebrated at the Jorvik Viking Centre.

It was after the Norman takeover that York really began to assume its familiar layout and skyline. Though little survives of its two original Norman castles, their site remains a prominent one, accommodating both Clifford's Tower and the York Castle Museum. During the medieval period, York flourished commercially, largely thanks to wool. In the 13th and 14th centuries, the city was encircled with strong stone walls, now restored as a popular promenade. Of the myriad buildings that were springing up at this time, many still stand today: half-timbered inns and guildhalls; bustling shops and houses, such as those in the Shambles, an astonishingly narrow medieval street; and above all, religious buildings—most notably magnificent York Minster. Built and rebuilt between 1220 and 1470, it is the largest Gothic church in Britain, complete with the largest medieval stained-glass window in the world.

York suffered a decline in fortune in the 15th to 17th centuries, but re-emerged in the 18th century as a fashionable social centre. Although largely bypassed by the Industrial Revolution, the city benefited greatly from the expansion of the railways in the mid-19th century, and from its burgeoning confectionery industry. Today, York's intriguing historical heritage ensures that it benefits from another, more contemporary industry—that of tourism.

ABOVE *Unearthing artefacts such as this jet pendant dating from Roman times enables archaeologists to open a window upon old York.*

RIGHT *Light from York Minster's central tower coaxes a russet glow from its 15th-century choir screen, which features 15 statues of English kings, from William I to Henry VI.*

CITIES, TOWNS AND VILLAGES (CONTINUED)

Knaresborough F5

At the heart of the town (*below*), the River Nidd flows under an imposing railway viaduct and beneath crags where a house is carved

out of the rock. In the 12th century St Robert of Knaresborough occupied a hermit's cave by the river. The prophetess Mother Shipton was another troglodyte, living by the Petrifying Well, whose lime-rich waters seem to turn the everyday objects hung beneath them by tourists into stone, in a few weeks.

Leeds E6

Victorian architecture is a hallmark of the largely traffic-free centre of Leeds. Minarets, domes and a glass roof adorn the oriental-style covered market, Yorkshire's largest. The city's shopping areas include magnificent covered arcades (*below*) and the corn exchange, home to designer boutiques and specialist shops. Built as a grand statement of municipal confidence, the town hall hosts prestigious events like the Leeds International Pianoforte Competition finals. The Waterfront area houses the Royal Armouries Museum and Tetley's Brewery Wharf.

Pickering I3

Red roof tiles and yellow limestone walls characterise this busy tourist centre, southern terminus to the North Yorkshire Moors Railway, and boasting a fine medieval church. The ruins of Pickering Castle stand on the northern edge of town.

Pontefract G7

Horse-racing and liquorice lozenges, known as Pontefract cakes, have put this town on the map, but its history predates both of these. The ruins of Pontefract Castle harboured such prisoners as Richard II and James I of Scotland, and below the hospital in Southgate is a tiny 14th-century hermit's retreat, carved into the rock by Brother Adam de Laythorpe. Among the town's 18th-century features are the town hall and the butter cross, both in the marketplace.

Richmond E2

Set above the wooded banks of the fast-flowing River Swale, the massive keep of the castle rises high above cobbled Market Square, reputedly the largest marketplace in England. Richmond's well-preserved streets contain many Georgian and earlier houses, as well as the late 18th-century Theatre Royal, Britain's oldest theatrical interior in its original form. Cornforth Hill, one of a number of wynds, or alleys, leads through one of Richmond's two surviving town-wall gateways.

Ripon F4

Georgian and earlier buildings line the marketplace, where stalls are set up on Thursdays and Saturdays, and the Wakeman (*see page 35*) nightly fulfils a centuries-old tradition by blowing a buffalo horn at 9pm. Dominating the town's narrow streets is the superb Early English façade of its cathedral.

Robin Hood's Bay J1

Huddled together round a labyrinth of stepped passages and narrow streets, the red-roofed cottages of this fishing village were once the haunt of smugglers. Cars must be left at the top of the village.

Scarborough J3

Sea-bathing has long drawn people to this lively resort and former spa (*pictured at top*), set in two bays divided by a promontory on which the castle ruins stand. South Bay contains the earlier part of the town, with cliff lifts connecting the beach to the hotels and parks of the upper town. Anne Brontë came

ABOVE *Fairy lights, ferris wheels and fishing boats seem to sum up the coastal town and beach resort of Scarborough.*

here several times and died here in 1849; her grave is at St Mary's Church. Premieres of works by local playwright Alan Ayckbourn are performed at the Stephen Joseph Theatre. Among the town's numerous attractions are the Sea Life Centre and Peasholm Park, where miniature sea battles are staged on the duck lake.

Settle B4

In the market square of this compact Ribblesdale town stands the two-storey Shambles, once the town's slaughterhouse. Settle gained its market charter in 1249 and still bursts into life every Tuesday. A short stroll reveals small squares, terraced cottages and several dated 17th-century door heads.

Sheffield F9

A sprawling industrial city and lively cultural centre, Sheffield occupies a hilly setting and boasts some fine countryside on its Pennine threshold; the 10-mile Sheffield Round Walk takes in many of its green spaces. Much of the city centre has been redeveloped since the Second World War, and there are numerous museums and attractions—among them the Abbeydale Industrial Hamlet—commemorating the city's steel-making heritage. The town hall bears a statue of Vulcan and a frieze depicting steel craftsmen. Three galleries are of interest: the Graves, the Ruskin and the Mappin.

MUSEUMS

kipton C5
larket Street, with its Georgian houses and
aturday market stalls, rises to the imposing
ulk of the castle, the former Clifford
ronghold; the Leeds and Liverpool Canal
uts through the heart of the town, where
ie church contains Clifford tombs and a
5th-century screen.

taithes I1
his atmospheric coastal village lies some
ight miles northwest of Whitby. Tightly
acked cottages and tiny chapels, separated
y narrow alleys with names such as Gun
utter and Slippery Hill, flank a sinuous main
reet running along a narrow valley to the
eafront. Its fishing industry has declined
ince the 19th century, although a few fishing
obles can still be seen here. As a boy in the
740s, Captain Cook had his first job in
taithes, as a haberdasher's apprentice—the
own's bracing North Sea winds may have
een instrumental in luring him onto the sea.

Vhitby I1
A whalebone arch, commemorating the
mportance of the town's erstwhile whaling
ndustry, stands close to a statue of Captain
Cook, whose great ships of exploration were
ll locally made 'Whitby cats'. From here, the
iew extends across the mouth of the Esk,
luttered with fishing boats and yachts, to the
ast Cliff, on which stands the ruined abbey,
eached by a flight of 199 steps. In the 19th
century the railway brought holidaymakers in
great numbers, and the West Cliff was
leveloped as a resort to cater for them.

ARC York G5
The emphasis at the Archaeological
Resource Centre is on 'hands-on'
archaeology. With the assistance of
professional archaeologists, visitors attempt
to identify ancient pottery, make Roman
shoes, and so on. Mosaics, animal bones
and Viking locks are displayed.

Bagshaw Museum Batley E7
A miscellany of items collected by Walter
Bagshaw, a local alderman, fill one of the
rooms in this imposing Gothic revival
mansion, set in attractive parkland. Other
attractions include an Egyptian gallery
and the Enchanted Forest, a walk-through
rain forest.

Bar Convent Museum York G5
During the 17th century Mary Ward fought
against her incarceration in a convent
here; the museum tells the story of her
success in setting up Roman Catholic
girls' schools throughout Europe, and
charts the story of Christianity in the city
of York.

Beck Isle Museum of Rural Life
Pickering I3
A varied collection in a 17th-century house,
where the highlights include shop interiors,
carts and bygone implements.

Bishop's House Sheffield F9
Life in Sheffield in Tudor and Stuart times
is recorded in this attractive timber-framed
16th-century farmhouse.

Brontë Parsonage Museum
Haworth D6
The home of the Brontës from 1820 to
1861 (*below*) has been restored to its
former character. The handwritten miniature
books the siblings produced during
their childhood are displayed, along with
other personal items and much of the
family furniture. (*See also feature on the
Brontë sisters, page 52.*)

Cannon Hall Barnsley F8
This late 17th-century house, remodelled
in 1760, contains decorative arts including
furniture and pottery. Among a wide range
of displays devoted to the local 13/18th
Hussars, there is a laser video portraying
the Charge of the Light Brigade. The
museum is set in 70 acres of parkland,
with gardens and lakes which are home
to water birds.

Captain Cook Memorial Museum
Whitby I1
While apprenticed to John Walker, Cook lived
at this house with his master's Quaker family.
Two rooms are furnished as they may have
been at the time, and elsewhere are boat
models and explanations of the scientific
advances made during Cook's great voyages
of discovery.

Clifton Park Museum Rotherham F9
An internationally renowned display of
Rockingham pottery is the highlight of this
collection, which also features period
furniture, social history exhibits and a
Victorian kitchen. It is housed in an 18th-
century iron magnate's mansion.

Colour Museum Bradford E6
This unusual museum investigates how
colours are used and how we perceive
them, focusing in particular on dyeing and
textile printing.

Cusworth Hall (Museum of South
Yorkshire Life) Doncaster G8
Displays of mining, childhood memorabilia,
costume, entertainment, domestic items
and transport chart over 200 years of life in
South Yorkshire. Additions to this Grade I
listed building were made by James Paine
and the mid-18th-century hall has fine
plasterwork by Joseph Rose.

Dales Countryside Museum Hawes C2
Expect a wide range of artefacts relating
to past life in the Dales—both at home and
in the workplace—including Wensleydale
cheesemaking equipment and items relating
to lead mining and knitting.

Eden Camp near Malton I4
Scenes from the Second World War, including
the Blitz and the interior of a bomber
command operation room, are re-created
in this former prisoner-of-war camp. Children
can let off steam by tackling a commando
assault course.

MUSEUMS (CONTINUED)

THE DAWNING OF VIKING YORKSHIRE

DURING THE EARLY 9th century AD, clergymen across Western Europe coined a new prayer in response to seaborne raids by fierce pagans: 'Deliver us, O God', they chanted, 'from the wrath of the Northmen!' Originating from Norway, Denmark and Sweden, these 'Northmen', or Norsemen or Vikings, attacked, plundered and settled in parts of Europe for nearly three centuries. Their wanderlust has never been fully explained, but overpopulation at home, coupled with the lure of the booty awaiting them in undefended towns and monasteries overseas, were probably major factors.

England's Viking age began in 793, when a war party raided Lindisfarne Monastery. From the 830s, incursions grew more frequent, and in 865 a large Danish army began its conquest of the ancient kingdoms of Northumbria, Mercia and East Anglia. Wessex, under Alfred the Great, stood firm, and an 886

treaty between Alfred and the Vikings divided the country roughly in two, with the Vikings confined to an area (later called the Danelaw) north of a line stretching roughly from the Thames to Liverpool.

The Norsemen were not simply bloodthirsty warriors. Many set down roots in the Danelaw, married local women and accepted the Christian religion. Energetic explorer-traders, they brought new economic vigour to their settlements. This was especially true of York, which the Danes took in 867 and renamed Jorvik. Excavations at York's Coppergate site have revealed that Viking artisans made wooden cups, bowls and plates, jewellery, worked leather, iron and other goods, which they traded for Irish brooches, German wine and the like. Of course, the Vikings' influence in Yorkshire was felt beyond York. The county's three Ridings were probably formed in Viking times, and the presence of Viking words in place names—for example '-by' ('village' or 'farm'), 'thorpe' ('village') and 'beck' ('brook')—earmark communities settled or renamed by them.

After the death of Alfred the Great in 899, his successors continued to win back

territory for the English throughout the 10th century. Yet these gains were quickly reversed in the early 11th century, following renewed Viking invasions, and in 1016 Canute became the first Viking to govern the whole country. English rule was restored under Edward the Confessor in 1042, but his death in 1066 triggered the invasion of the Normans—who were themselves of Viking stock.

TOP LEFT *Battered and gnarled, this unembellished iron bowl was found on York's Coppergate dig, where the Jorvik Viking Centre now stands.*

LEFT *Workers at Coppergate painstakingly scraped away centuries of silt to learn more about the ways of the Vikings.*

TOP RIGHT *Viking longships were for many centuries powered by oars; square sails, thought to have been an 8th-century adaptation, lent considerable impetus to their overseas conquests.*

LEFT *This cross from Middleton bears a carving of a dead Viking warrior, with his shield and weapons about him.*

...reka! Halifax **D6**
...ned directly at 3- to 12-year-olds, this is
... of Britain's liveliest museums. Themed
...leries allow visitors to save a yacht in peril,
...mine the senses and the way the body
...rks, and learn about activities like cooking
...he kitchen and working in a bank.

...irfax House York **G5**
...scued from a period of neglect, when
... house was used as a cinema and a dance
...ll, this fine 18th-century building is richly
...corated and features superb plasterwork.
... collections include clocks, 18th-century
...glish furniture, silver and porcelain.

...nds On History Hull **K6**
...is schools resource centre records Hull's
...cial history and is housed in the city's
...lest secular building, which dates from
...e 1580s.

...ornsea Museum Hornsea **L5**
...emories of village life from yesteryear fill
...s former farmhouse, with its period rooms,
...cal history displays, agricultural implements
...d other rustic mementos.

...ll and East Riding Museum Hull **K6**
...n exploration of the archaeology and
...ology of Hull and the East Riding. Roman
...osaics and the 2,000-year-old Hasholme
...oat are among the museum's exhibits.

...ull Maritime Museum Hull **K6**
...haling, model ships, figureheads, nautical
...struments and trawling exhibits illustrate
...ull's long and fascinating maritime history.

...orvik Viking Centre York **G5**
...rvik—York as it was known 1,000 years
...go—is imaginatively brought to life as
...sitors sit in Time Cars and travel back to
... reconstruction of a Viking street, complete
...ith the sights, sounds and smells of the
...aily life of the time. The tour brings you
...ack to the present by affording a glimpse
... the archaeological work carried out here.

...useum of Army Transport Beverley **J6**
...ll manner of military vehicles for air, sea and
...nd are displayed; there is also a junior
...ssault course.

...useum of Badges and Battledress
...rakehall **F3**
...niforms ranging from the days of spiked
...elmets to the latest military gear are
...isplayed, as well as badges and photographs.

ABOVE *Visitors to the Royal Armouries Museum in Leeds—viewed here from across Clarence Dock—get to see an awe-inspiring array of pikes, breastplates, helmets and other apparatus of war.*

**National Coal Mining Museum
for England** Middlestown **E7**
(See **YORKSHIRE'S INDUSTRIAL
HERITAGE**, *page 147.)*

**National Museum of Photography,
Film and Television** Bradford **E6**
After its 1997–9 refurbishment, the National
Museum of Photography, Film and Television
should again blend audiovisual, and hands-on
exhibits to fascinating effect.

Red House Gomersal **E7**
Charlotte Brontë visited her friend Mary
Taylor at this 1830s house—the Taylors
inspired the fictional Yorke family in
Charlotte's novel *Shirley*.

Richard III Museum York **G5**
Monk Bar, the best-preserved gateway in
the city wall, is home to the Richard III
Museum. Here, visitors can ponder the
evidence of the monarch's reputed murder
of Edward V and his brother, and record
their own verdict.

Ripon Prison and Police Museum
Ripon **F4**
Bygone prisons and methods of punishment
are illustrated in the former jail. The old
police station beneath has displays relating
to law and order.

Rotunda Museum Scarborough **J3**
Dating from 1829, this museum is noted
for being one of the finest purpose-built

museums of its age in the country—original
mahogany display cabinets, a gallery and
spiral staircases evoke a strong period
atmosphere. Within the museum, there are
finds from the Mesolithic camp of Star Carr
and a Bronze Age tree-trunk burial.

Royal Armouries Museum Leeds **E6**
The centrepiece of this museum (*pictured
above*) is its magnificent collection of arms
and armour, previously housed in the
Tower of London. High-tech displays
explain the manufacture and use of
weapons, and there are live performances
of duelling and jousting.

Royal Pump Room Museum Harrogate **E5**
A chance to sample the sulphur water at
the original spa counter; the octagonal
pump-room building (*pictured below*) has

MUSEUMS (CONTINUED)

ABOVE *A mainly 17th-century phenomenon, witch posts like this one at the Ryedale Folk Museum were carved with talismanic designs, intended to keep evil spirits from the hearth of a house.*

displays of items dating from Harrogate's heyday as a spa town.

Ruskin Gallery Sheffield F9
Social reformer, writer, artist and admirer of Sheffield craftsmanship, John Ruskin founded this wide-ranging collection and library in 1875, as a philanthropic gesture to the people of the city. Themes include minerals, medieval illuminated manuscripts and watercolours.

Ryedale Folk Museum Hutton-le-Hole H2
Vanished and vanishing rural lifestyles have been frozen in time by the re-creation of 13 historic buildings, among them village shops and an Elizabethan manor house, in this award-winning museum (*pictured above*), covering over 4,000 years of civilisation.

Sheffield City Museum and Mappin Art Gallery Sheffield F9
Fittingly, Sheffield's major museum reflects the city's rich heritage by housing the world's largest collection of Sheffield plate, as well as ceramics, clocks and natural history exhibits. There are also displays of archaeology, metalwork, geology and meteorology. The Mappin Art Gallery features 18th- and 19th-

century English art, and other rolling exhibitions of contemporary works.

Shibden Hall and Folk Museum Halifax D6
Various periods in the history of this half-timbered 15th-century house are evoked within its rooms. In the grounds is a folk museum, with displays of horse-drawn vehicles and reconstructions of 19th-century workshops.

South Yorkshire Aircraft Museum Firbeck G9
Aviation history is remembered in this former RAF officers' mess, where displays of uniforms, planes, relics from crashes and other aviation memorabilia are on show.

Tetley's Brewery Wharf Leeds E6
Tours of the brewery are available, and there is a small museum area—plus a team of shire horses—to check out.

Thackray Medical Museum Leeds E6
An interactive overview of how medicine has developed in Britain, proceeding from the days of sawbones, right through to the contemporary picture.

Thirsk Museum Thirsk F3
Occupying the birthplace of Thomas Lord, founder of Lord's cricket ground, this muse contains cricketing memorabilia and items o local interest. Among the latter is the infame Busby Stoop chair, cursed by local ne'er-do well Thomas Busby before he was hanged murder in 1708, and said to have caused the deaths of many who sat in it subsequently, in the Busby Stoop Inn.

Victorian Reed Organ Museum Saltaire D6
The country's sole harmonium museum boa 95 eye-catching pedal-powered reed organs and harmoniums, one of them as small as a family Bible.

Whitby Museum and Pannett Art Gallery Whitby I1
The catholic miscellany that has been amassed in this old-fashioned museum includes Whitby jet ornaments, fossils, model ships, costumes and a surviving part of James Cook's journal. Local scenes hang in the art gallery.

Wilberforce House Hull K6
Birthplace of the abolitionist William Wilberforce, in 1759, this 17th-century house contains displays on the slave trade and the long battle for its abolition.

Wood End Museum Scarborough J3
The family home of the literary Sitwell family for some 60 years—Edith Sitwell was born here in 1887—contains a virtually complete library of their works. Much of the museum is given over to exhibits from the natural world, including local wildlife, rocks and fossils.

Wordsworth Gallery Brompton J3
Situated at the erstwhile home of Mary Hutchinson, whom William Wordsworth married at Brompton church, near Scarborough, in 1802, this exhibition invites visitors to enter the world of Wordsworth and his fellow Romantic poet and long-time friend, Samuel Taylor Coleridge.

York Castle Museum York G5
A full day is needed to see the Castle Museum's displays of social history, military and costume collections. This huge assortment was begun by a Dr John Kirk, who gathered everyday objects that, together with such items as early radios, form the hub of the 'Every Home Should

THE SURVIVING CRAFTS OF YORKSHIRE

THE QUICK MARCH of modern technology may have trounced many of Yorkshire's older crafts underfoot, but opportunities still exist for visitors to peer into the region's creative past.

Visitors to Robert Thompson's Craftsmen Ltd of Kilburn, for instance, will see demonstrations illuminating traditional woodworking and carving skills. Eccentricity, tenacity and a profound attention to detail were combined in the work of master craftsman Robert Thompson (1876–1955). Almost single-handedly, Thompson revived Yorkshire's tradition of authentic English oak carpentry, and today his family firm's famous mouse trademark adorns cupboards, chairs, tables, crucifixes and plaques in public buildings, hotels and churches across the country. Perhaps his finest legacy is the Benedictine Abbey School at Ampleforth, which he refurbished in loving detail. Thompson's descendants continue his craft, working only in naturally seasoned oak, and finishing their surfaces with a medieval tool called an adze—traditionally used to shape ships' timbers. As to the mice, Thompson himself always claimed that

RIGHT An employee twists a new length of rope at W. R. Outhwaite & Son of Hawes. With plans afoot for all the church bells in the land to ring in the new millennium, this is a very busy period for the company.

BELOW Though jet is a form of coal, it is hard enough to take a lustrous polish.

he was first spurred to carve them into his handiwork when, working up in the roof of a church, one of his craftsmen grumbled that they were as poor as church mice.

Clogs were once the norm as workaday footwear around Northern factories and farms. Clogmakers, or 'cloggers', were a common sight in the forests of the region, carving soles which they would sell on to clogging factories for finishing. Clogging is a dying art today, but workers at Walkley's of Hebden Bridge continue to turn out the genuine article, often for clog-dancing troupes. Their clogs have wooden soles, like their more famous Dutch cousins, but leather uppers. The best clogs are crafted from alder wood and finished with a razor-sharp knife called a 'stock'.

Traditional ropemaking is another industry that has all but died out. Most rope is now machine-made, using man-made fibres, but not so at W. R. Outhwaite & Son, Ropemakers, of Hawes. Here, they still keep the faith, producing cattle halters, dog leads, leading reins for horses,

RIGHT Hickory, dickory, dock...Robert Thompson's eccentric trademark earned him the nickname 'the mouseman of Kilburn'.

LEFT Rubber boots may have superseded clogs, but the art of clogmaking is still demonstrated at agricultural shows like the Kilnsey Show.

candlewicks and church bell ropes, in a painstaking process that involves careful handling of slender strands of yarn, and miles of walking up and down a purpose-made rope-walk building. Visitors to their Hawes workshop can witness this process at first hand.

In Whitby, meanwhile, several firms still work jet, a hard coal formed from the fossilised wood of coniferous trees, and found locally on the seashore. Though it has been crafted since the Bronze Age, its stock increased in the last century after Queen Victoria wore jet jewellery while in mourning for her Albert. At its height the industry employed a tenth of Whitby's population. Drop by at the Victorian Jet Works, and you'll see craftsmen working jet jewellery, and get to see an 1867 jet workshop that was discovered sealed into an attic.

MUSEUMS (CONTINUED)

Have One' gallery. A complete re-creation of a cobbled Victorian street, Kirkgate, is named after him, and visitors can step inside the cell in which Dick Turpin spent his final night before his execution. Discovered nearby in 1982, the York Helmet is one of only three Anglo-Saxon helmets yet unearthed.

York Dungeon York G5
Scenes of gore, torture and punishment await visitors who are brave enough to come to these musty cellars and eerie passages. The Guy Fawkes Experience tells the story of the Gunpowder Plot, while in the Dick Turpin Story, England's most famous highwayman gets to recount his many adventures before he is executed.

York & Lancaster Regimental Museum Rotherham F9
The history of the York & Lancaster Regiment from 1758 to 1968 is told with the aid of campaign relics, military insignia, uniforms and medals.

York Story York G5
Set in an 11th-century church, the York Story chronicles 1,000 years of this important city's history, with the help of an audiovisual display and a three-dimensional model of the city.

Yorkshire Air Museum & Allied Air Forces Memorial Elvington H5
Preserved as a memorial to those who served in Yorkshire in the Second World War, the Yorkshire Air Museum occupies a wartime bomber command station, complete with restored buildings and some 20 aircraft. Among the exhibits is a replica Halifax Second World War bomber called *Friday the 13th*.

Yorkshire Museum York G5
A county chronicle, commencing with the Romans' arrival in northern England, and including items from the Viking period. Exhibits from medieval times include the superb Middleham Jewel, discovered in Middleham in 1985.

Yorkshire Museum of Farming Murton H5
Farmyard animals and bygone implements provide the focus of this museum. It is set in Murton Park, which contains a reconstructed village of the Dark Ages, and the Derwent Valley Light Railway.

GALLERIES

1853 Gallery Saltaire D6
Housed in a former textile mill dating from 1853, the gallery features some 300 works by the Bradford-born artist David Hockney (*see* **THE FAME OF YORKSHIRE**, *page 166*).

Cartwright Hall Art Gallery Bradford E6
Joshua Reynolds's painting *The Brown Boy* hangs in the Baroque-style 1904 building. Victorian and Edwardian art, photography and crafts are exhibited, and a transcultural South Asia collection is also on display.

Graves Art Gallery Sheffield F9
The top floor of the City Library houses British and French art and the Grice Collection of Chinese Ivories. There are temporary shows British and European 20th-century modern art.

The Henry Moore Institute Leeds E6
Sited beside the City Art Gallery, the Henry Moore Institute devotes itself to the exhibiti understanding and promotion of works of sculpture (*pictured below, David Nash's Sphere, Pyramid, Cube*).

HENRY MOORE

FEW ARTISTS HAVE left as indelible a mark on the iconography of the 20th century as the sculptor Henry Moore, born the seventh child of a Castleford coal miner in 1898.

As a youngster, Moore showed great academic promise and no little interest in sculpture, but war interrupted his studies in 1917. Wounded in France, he returned to England and used a rehabilitation grant to enrol at the Leeds School of Art in 1919. In Leeds, Moore encountered modern abstract art for the first time, an experience that was to shape his life; in 1921 he left for London's Royal College of Art to study sculpture. London afforded imagery denied him in Yorkshire, particularly the pan-global works of art in the British Museum. Moore was also much influenced by Surrealism. In 1928 he held his first one-man exhibition, and in 1933 he co-founded the Unit One group, conceived expressly to popularise new directions in modern art. Meanwhile, his own works had become increasingly daring and abstract—to the

BELOW The reclining figure was a theme to which Henry Moore returned regularly through his career; this piece, from 1929, reflects Moore's fascination with primitive art.

extent that he was harried out of his position at the Royal College. Hewn from various stones and metals, Moore's sculptures typically represent fluidly abstract human forms, either reclining or standing, and sometimes hollowed or even pierced.

Yet his work never displays the aggression typical of most Surrealists. Indeed, as an official war artist in the forties, his drawings of Londoners huddling in underground stations show great dignity and compassion.

After the war, a retrospective exhibition in New York's Museum of Modern Art cemented Moore's reputation, and a host of prestigious commissions ensued. In 1965 he moved to north Italy, but he returned to live a quiet life in England, where he died in 1986.

YORKSHIRE'S INDUSTRIAL HERITAGE

eds City Art Gallery Leeds E6
rticularly strong on 19th- and 20th-century
tish art, the gallery includes English
tercolours (*see* Turner's The Washburn
ley, *below*) and sculptures by Henry Moore.

nley Spencer, Graham Sutherland, Alison
lding, Paula Rego and Francis Bacon are
o represented.

arborough Art Gallery Scarborough J3
e Victorian painter Atkinson Grimshaw,
rticularly known for his moonlight scenes,
among the artists represented in this
gaging gallery, set within an impressive
ted building dating from the first half of
e 19th century.

akefield Art Gallery Wakefield F7
a acclaimed collection of 20th-century
inting and sculpture from Britain and
rope, which includes works by such
portant British modern artists as Barbara
epworth and Henry Moore; touring
hibitions also feature periodically in the
llery's programme of events.

**hitby Museum and Pannett
rt Gallery** Whitby I1
ee **MUSEUMS**, page 144.)

rk City Art Gallery York G5
e romantic nudes of local artist William
ty—who was responsible for saving the
y walls from demolition in the early 19th
ntury—hang among works by Lely, Lowry
d Reynolds. Also on-site is an excellent
llection of studio pottery.

rkshire Sculpture Park West Bretton E7
ontemporary and modern sculpture graces
0 acres of 18th-century parkland and
rdens, just a few miles southwest of
akefield. Works by Henry Moore and
rbara Hepworth are displayed, and
siting exhibitions hosted.

THE RESIDUES *of Yorkshire's industrial
past are visible across the length and
breadth of the region. And what a range
of industry has existed here through the
years! Since time immemorial, natural
deposits have been hacked and hewn from
the region's soils—among them lead, long
plentiful in the Dales; alum and ironstone,
worked from the North York Moors; and
coal, still mined to this day from the rock
shelf to the west of the Humber Estuary.
In Sheffield, a flourishing steel industry
was developing by the 16th century; while
at grassroots level, the sheep that graze
on hill and dale have fed a textiles industry
for many centuries. The dawning of the
Industrial Revolution had a profound effect
upon Yorkshire: mills and factories replaced
cottage industries; towns grew out of all
recognition; and newer, more efficient
means of transport appeared. Vestiges of
all these features of Yorkshire's past are
plain to see on a tour of the region.*

Lead Mining
Within the Yorkshire Dales are striking
legacies of lead mining, which prospered
from about 1720 to 1840. Many of the villages
of Wharfedale, Wensleydale, Arkengarthdale,
Swaledale and elsewhere comprise former
miners' cottages, and the moors and pastures
harbour such reminders as the abandoned

mine buildings, shafts and water courses north
of Hebden in Wharfedale (*pictured above*).
Gunnerside Gill, in Swaledale, can claim to
harbour the most spectacular relic: a walk
northwards from Gunnerside village enters
the gorge where the Old Gang Mines
operated up to 1900. In this eerie landscape,
ruins of smelting and crushing mills perch
among a moonscape of spoil heaps. There's
a walk-through reconstruction of a lead mine
at the **Dales Countryside Museum** (*see page
141*) in Hawes (C2).

Coal Mining
Barnsley, Dewsbury, Featherstone, Batley,
Rotherham and Castleford lie at the hub
of what was once a major coal-mining
area. Sadly, few of the area's pits are still
operational. In the 19th century, colliery
owners erected model pit villages and
furnaces in the area. Within the former
Caphouse Colliery at Middlestown (E7),
near Wakefield, the **National Coal Mining
Museum for England** gives visitors
the chance to experience the working
conditions of miners from the 19th
century to the present day. Pit ponies
and 'paddy trains' are among the surface-
level attractions.

Textile Manufacture
The atmosphere of a small-scale textile-
making industry before the era of the
great Victorian mills is evoked at the **Colne
Valley Museum** in Golcar (D7), where
three weavers' cottages are filled with rag
rugs, looms and bobbins. The hilltop
village of **Heptonstall** (*see page 138*) with
its old cottages and Cloth Hall, where
dealing took place, survives as one of the
best-preserved examples of a former hand-
loom weaving centre, which prospered in
the 18th century. The grandest of the
cloth halls to have survived is the **Piece
Hall** (*pictured below*), built in Halifax (D6)
in 1779, rising in three colonnaded tiers
round a huge piazza, and still functioning
as a general marketplace.

BELOW *The elegant arcades of the Italianate
Piece Hall in Halifax, designed by Charles Barry
as a centre for cloth trading.*

YORKSHIRE'S INDUSTRIAL HERITAGE (CONTINUED)

The Great Mill Age

Manningham Mills in Bradford (**E6**) and Titus Salt's mill (*right*) at **Saltaire** are among the numerous mills that appeared in the era of mass production, when such medieval weaving centres as Wakefield, Dewsbury, Huddersfield and Halifax became factory towns and imposing town halls and other gestures of civic pride were erected. The area of Bradford known as **Little Germany,** after the German traders who settled there, has some fine 19th-century warehouses used in the cloth trade. Many mills have closed, been demolished or converted, and some of these have been redeveloped as attractions. Occupying what was once the world's largest woollen mill, the **Armley Mills** in Leeds (**E6**) tells the story of textile-making,

with a working water wheel, demonstrations of static engines and reconstructions of a clothing factory and a tailor's shop; other showcases include the story of cinema projection, and a gallery that examines the printing trade. Within another venerable woollen mill, the **Bradford Industrial Museum and Horses at Work** (**E6**) recalls Victorian Yorkshire, with rebuilt 'back-to-back' houses and a ponderously furnished mill-owner's house. There are demonstrations of shire horses at work and machines in operation. A wool baron's mansion is now home to the **Tolson Museum**, in Huddersfield (**D7**), with displays embracing the textile industry, local and natural history, archaeology and a very fine collection of horse-drawn vehicles.

MINING THE SEAM: YORKSHIRE'S COAL INDUSTRY

ABOVE *Things have come a long way since the days of child labour in the mines: here, a miner at the Selby coalfield uses a remote-controlled shearer to shave off coal from the face.*

BELOW *In wintertime, children working shifts from before dawn until after dusk could go days without seeing daylight.*

COAL HAS BEEN MINED in Yorkshire since at least the 13th century, and quite probably even since Roman times. Today, fellwalkers in the Dales still encounter the remains of shallow bell pits or open-cast quarries.

Yorkshire's coal industry long relied upon child labour to effect certain tasks. Children as young as four worked as 'trappers', opening and closing ventilation doors, often in total darkness; while young men and women hauled half-ton coal tubs deep underground. Happily, the Royal Commission Report of 1842 revealed the

hidden horrors of the collieries, and Parliament banned women, and children under 10, from working underground. But this did not remove the hazards of firedamp explosions or tunnels collapsing. In 1866, some 360 coal miners died at Oaks Colliery.

As technology improved and the demand for coal increased, companies built larger, deeper mines around major urban centres like Sheffield, Leeds and Doncaster. A new 'coal rush' broke out in the early 20th century, with shafts sunk in Castleford, Pontefract and Ingleton. Soon, almost half of Britain's coal came from one giant coalfield, the East Pennine shelf, which lies under the West Riding of Yorkshire, Nottinghamshire and North Derbyshire. Another field links South Yorkshire with East Midlands collieries.

Advanced remote-control technology at collieries like Kellingley led the world in the 1960s. Yet by the 1970s and 1980s, British coal mining was on the wane, not least in Yorkshire itself. Now that subsidised coal can be imported so cheaply from abroad, and oil and gas have largely replaced coal in Britain's power stations, pits based around narrower seams have been deemed too expensive to mine—though 'super-pits' like the one at Selby are still worked profitably.

teel Manufacture

he manufacture of steel in Sheffield (F9) an industry that far predates the dawning f the Industrial Revolution. A cutlery-rinding works—where blades would have een sharpened—was established in 1584 nd later named after an 18th-century mployer: the **Shepherd Wheel** is now a useum, and its aged water wheel is still in orking order. Left intact in the mossy eaf valley when the last workers were aid off, **Abbeydale Industrial Hamlet** Sheffield is a water-powered scythe-akers' forge, dating from the 18th century, d also now a museum. The restored orkers' cottages, manager's house and orkshops—the latter complete with rnaces for melting steel—huddle round quadrangle; skilled craftsmen show how e scythes would have been forged. effield's **Kelham Island Museum** has splays outlining the industrial development Sheffield. Attractions at the museum clude workshops, demonstrations of tlery-making, and the most powerful nctioning steam engine in Europe.

ind and Water Power

me of Yorkshire's once-numerous atermills and windmills are now open to e visiting public. Erected in 1821 at a cation where milling has been carried out r many centuries, and an imposing Wolds ndmark, **Skidby Windmill**, near Hull (K6), ntinues to grind flour for sale, and houses museum of agricultural bygones. **Thwaite ills** in Leeds (E6) stand beside a Georgian ll-owner's house on an island between the ver Aire and the Aire and Calder Navigation; eir two water wheels were previously used r crushing stone for putty- and paint-aking. Barnsley's (F8) **Worsborough Mill** oduces stoneground flour to this day, and set in a country park where paths lead to her early industrial sites, among them the ckley Engine House and Museum and Darwin Ironworks.

e Growth of Transport Systems

rkshire's early industrialisation went hand hand with the emergence and development its transport system, which included the rld's first steam-hauled trains and the liest passenger trolley buses. Ancient ckhorse routes over the Pennines, some which survive as flagstoned moorland ths, are evocative reminders of an age fore railway lines skeined the landscape our country.

SHEFFIELD CUTLERY

LEFT *This selection of cutlery from Osborne Silversmiths of Sheffield includes such dinner-party must-haves as fruit fork, tart lifter and grapefruit spoon.*

SHEFFIELD IS VIRTUALLY synonymous with cutlery, and has been since the 16th century, when its abundant local sandstone proved ideal for grinding, and its five fast-flowing rivers were harnessed to pump furnaces. By the time steam replaced water power, Sheffield's cutlers bestrode their industry, and by the mid-19th century the city is thought to have boasted 10,000 cutlers—ten times as many as London.

Technological innovation has kept Sheffield ahead of its competitors. First came table knives with hollow handles filled with pitch—an ingenious economy which enabled humbler folk to afford quality silverware. Then, in 1742, Benjamin Huntsman pioneered the use of ferociously hot furnaces to create a new, purer and stronger material, called crucible, or cast, steel. And, in 1913, a young metallurgist named Harry Brearley accidentally discovered stainless steel while working on rifle barrels. He added chromium to iron and produced a metal which did not rust.

The cutlery industry afforded jobs, but not always health. 'Grinder's lung', a condition caused by inhaling metal dust, meant that few cutlers survived till the age of 30 until the mandatory introduction of extraction fans in 1867 began significantly to improve working conditions.

Nevertheless, cutlery has served Sheffield well and, despite the cheaper foreign imports flooding the market, a 'Made in Sheffield' label remains a hallmark of quality worldwide.

Canals

The need to convey increasing quantities of cargo led to the opening in the 18th century of a network of canals. In 1700 the River Aire was made more navigable up to Leeds, and in 1704 the Calder to Wakefield, a project forming in its entirety the new **Aire and Calder Navigation**. Other canals followed. In 1804 the 33-mile **Rochdale Canal** became the first to cross the Pennines, linking Calderdale with Manchester; restoration is currently under way, thanks to a Lottery award, after which its towpaths should make for fine walking in the vicinity of Hebden Bridge. A later waterway, the 127-mile **Leeds and Liverpool Canal** (*pictured right*) passes Saltaire and includes a staircase of locks at Bingley; used today by leisure craft, it becomes increasingly rural as it proceeds westwards through Airedale and past Skipton. The **Huddersfield Narrow Canal** was the third to cross the Pennines when it opened in 1811, and runs through the three-mile Standedge Tunnel; following a successful Millennium Fund bid, the entire length of the 20-mile canal is currently being made navigable once again.

YORKSHIRE'S INDUSTRIAL HERITAGE | CASTLES

ABOVE *In 1938, its sleek, streamlined design helped the* Mallard *set a world speed record for a steam locomotive of 126 miles per hour, on the London–Edinburgh route. Visitors can marvel at its gleaming curves at York's National Railway Museum.*

Railways

Colliery lines launched Yorkshire's **railway age**. Operated by enthusiasts since 1960, the **Middleton Colliery Railway** in Leeds was, in 1758, the first line to be authorised by Parliament, and in 1812 became the earliest railway to run steam locomotives successfully. The **Lake Lock Railway**, just north of Wakefield, marked the birth of public railways in 1796, and over the next century the engineers took on the challenge of the difficult terrain of industrial Yorkshire, constructing cuttings, embankments, viaducts and tunnels, and showpiece stations such as Huddersfield. Among the most spectacular of the lines on the national network to have survived is the **Leeds to Manchester** route. Completed in 1841, it included five miles of tunnel as well as fine viaducts at Huddersfield and Lockwood. Another is the scenic **Settle to Carlisle** line of 1876, which crosses the high moors of the Yorkshire Dales, passing over the mighty 24-arch Ribblehead Viaduct; the route occasionally hosts steam trains.

Of the many lines that have closed, a few have reopened as tourist attractions. The **North Yorkshire Moors Railway** makes an 18-mile trip from Pickering to Grosmont, which has a viewing window in its locomotive shed. Opened in 1836 as the Whitby and Pickering Railway, it served for its first 11 years as a horse-drawn tramway; the course of the route was altered to avoid a steep incline at Beck Hole, and the original course now forms a **Historic Rail Trail** for walkers. Built to serve the local mills, and in recent years used as a period setting for numerous films, the **Keighley and Worth Valley Railway** passes through the heart of Brontë country, running from Keighley via Haworth to Oxenhope, where the station includes a museum. Near Skipton, the **Embsay Steam Railway** runs for a couple of miles along the former Skipton to Ilkley line.

The premier collection of its kind in the world, the **National Railway Museum** in York (**G5**) has all manner of exhibits relating to the history of railways and rail travel, from Stephenson's Rocket to the Eurostar. Among the best-known trains and carriages on display are Queen Victoria's sumptuous royal coach and the *Mallard* (*pictured above*), which in 1938 reached 126 miles per hour, the record speed for a steam locomotive. Nearby, beside York station, the **York Model Railway** is an ambitious layout, running 20 trains at a time.

Other Transport Collections

The **Streetlife: Hull Museum of Transport** (**K6**) covers public transport—including Britain's oldest tram—as well as bicycles and cars. Housed in a former water mill by Aysgarth Falls, near Leyburn (**D2**), the **Yorkshire Carriage Museum** looks back to the pre-petrol age with its collection of horse-drawn vehicles, including a milk float, a hearse and a fire engine.

CASTLES

Bolton Castle near Leyburn **D2**

Massive and remarkably well preserved, this fortified manor house looms over Castle Bolton, the earliest estate village in the Dales. Built in rectangular plan round a central courtyard, the structure has four corner towers, three of which stand to their original height. Mary, Queen of Scots was held captive from 1568 to 1569 within its warren of rooms. There are fine rooftop views of Wensleydale.

Clifford's Tower York **G5**

This 13th-century tower, shaped like a four-leafed clover, stands on one of two mottes erected by William the Conqueror to guard the Ouse and hold York. It replaced a wooden keep that was burned down by a rampaging mob as Jews took refuge within and perished in the ensuing inferno. Roger de Clifford and other local opponents of Edward II were hanged by chains from its walls in 1322. Behind the nearby Castle Museum (*see page 141*) are remains of the curtain wall, and of two towers.

Conisbrough **G8**

Erected about 1180 by Hamelin Plantagenet, this impressive structure was notable for having a circular keep at a time when keeps were generally rectangular in plan. Support is given by solid buttresses, each projecting above roof level. Sited over its hall, the hexagonal chapel is another rarity. There are remains of the curtain wall and the foundations of the living quarters.

Helmsley **H3**

For six months in 1644, during the Civil War, the 12th-century castle (*below*), set within two rings of banks and ditches on the River Rye, withstood a siege by Parliamentary forces under Thomas Fairfax, before being captured and then razed. It retains remnants of its keep, west tower and domestic buildings.

aresborough F5

gh de Morville, one of the four knights
o murdered Archbishop Thomas à Becket
Canterbury Cathedral in 1170, was the most
orious occupant of Knaresborough Castle.
hard II was held at Knaresborough on his
y to his death at Pontefract. Set above the
er Nidd and now in a park, the ruins
stly date from the early 14th century and
ude a four-storey keep as well as curtain
ls, an underground sally port, and a
rthouse building ranging in date from the
h to the 17th centuries. Parliamentarians
maged the stronghold during the Civil War.

Middleham D3

With its huge 12th-century keep, one of
the largest of the period, the castle fell
through marriage to the Neville family,
later to produce the powerful Earl of
Warwick, Richard Neville, the 'Kingmaker'.
Subsequently it passed to Richard, Duke of
Gloucester, later Richard III, and after his
defeat at Bosworth in 1485 became a Crown
property of the Tudor monarchs. Although
dismantled after the English Civil War, the
roofless keep is a formidable sight, and
there are remains of 14th- and 15th-century
domestic quarters.

Pickering I3

A fine example of a motte-and-bailey castle,
its motte, or mound, is crowned by a keep
known as the King's Tower. In medieval
times it was used as a royal hunting lodge
for expeditions into the Forest of Pickering.

Poachers and other
local wrongdoers
were brought to the
castle, tried and
imprisoned. Last
occupied around
1640, the castle had
much stonework
pilfered, though it
retains an early 14th-
century curtain wall
with three towers—
Rosamund's Tower,
Diate Hill Tower and Mill Tower—as well as
a chapel housing a small exhibition, and the
outlying foundations of two halls.

Pontefract G7

Now reduced to scant ruins in a public park,
Pontefract Castle once belonged to the
powerful Thomas, Earl of Lancaster, who was
beheaded there for treason, by order of his
cousin, Edward II. Richard II was imprisoned
here and met his death under mysterious
circumstances in 1400 when the castle was
in the hands of Henry Bolingbroke, the future
Henry IV. Remains include the 13th-century
keep, the postern gate of the Piper Tower,
and the curtain wall (both 12th century).

Richmond E2

Perched high above the Swale, Richmond
Castle (below) has decayed more from
neglect than from ill-use, for it has never seen
military action. Yet it is of great architectural
value: thick curtain walls erected as early as
the 11th century enclose a triangular site
holding what is thought to be Britain's oldest
castle hall. The magnificent 100-foot-tall keep
dates from the 12th century.

NORMAN SUPPRESSION OF YORKSHIRE

LEFT *Under William the Conqueror, the
Domesday Book, a written record of the
wealth of the nation, was compiled. It took
the skins of 800 sheep to provide the
parchment for the book.*

WHEN WILLIAM, Duke of Normandy,
defeated King Harold at Hastings,
in 1066, England became a Norman
kingdom. Many of the population, though,
remained unconvinced.

William's attempts to cooperate with the
Anglo-Saxon nobility proved fruitless, and
a countrywide series of rebellions blew up
that threatened to undermine his rule. Of
these, the one which developed in northern
Yorkshire, in 1068, was taken particularly
seriously. William marched to York himself,
and set up a garrison there. And when
trouble broke out again the following year,
he acted swiftly and brutally. After buying
off the Danes who had sailed across the
North Sea to aid the rebels, he then set
about a near-genocidal programme of
suppression known as the Harrying of the
North, during which the region north of
the Humber was laid waste, crops burnt and
cattle destroyed, in order to starve out the
insurgents. This was an apocalyptic time for

the region: contemporary chroniclers tell
of survivors reduced to eating dogs and
cats, and of corpses rotting where they fell.

With the people of Yorkshire duly cowed,
William consolidated his position by dotting
the region with castles, Richmond and
Skipsea both being early examples. Norman
castles typically topped a motte, or mound,
and were linked to a bailey, or fortified
enclosure—mottes can still be viewed at
Pickering, at Skipsea, and at Clifford's
Tower, in York.

Once their position was secure, the
Normans made a profound cultural impact
upon England; French and Latin superseded
vernacular English at court, in law and in
literature; English script, spelling and
pronunciation altered greatly; and grand
new churches in the Romanesque style
replaced smaller Anglo-Saxon structures.
In Yorkshire, though, the restoration of
the monastic tradition was their greatest
legacy. Under the Normans, orders like
the Benedictines, Cluniacs, Augustinians
and Cistercians all set down roots in the
region, and the awe-inspiring religious
houses they built—among them Fountains
Abbey, Rievaulx Abbey and Bolton Priory—
still impress today.

CASTLES (CONTINUED)

ABOVE *Scarborough Castle snakes around a hilltop above the town's harbour. From the Bronze Age until 1914, this precipitous and easily defendable headland was put to regular military use.*

Scarborough J3

Scarthi, a Viking chief, built his *burh*, or fortress, on the breezy headland on which the 12th-century castle (*above*) now stands, so giving Scarborough (Scarthi's *burh*) its name. This has long been an important point of defence: the site has yielded evidence of Bronze and Iron Age settlers and a 4th-century Roman signal station. Nothing remains of the original Norman castle erected in about 1130 by William le Gros, Earl of Albemarle and Holderness, but Henry II's slightly later rectangular keep still stands. Strengthened with a barbican, fortified bridge and renewed curtain walls in the 13th century, the castle was damaged in the Civil War, then further ruined when shelled by a German battleship in 1914. In 1557 Thomas Stafford seized Scarborough Castle in a vain attempt to effect a coup against Queen Mary.

Skipton C5

Held by the staunchly Royalist Clifford family since the early 14th century, Skipton was the last northern castle to yield to the Parliamentarians. It was restored as a residence in the 1650s by Lady Anne Clifford, who added the balustrade over the gatehouse, itself flanked by great towers, bearing the family motto 'Desormais' ('Henceforth'). Within are a banqueting hall, a kitchen,

a dungeon, a courtyard known as Conduit Court and shaded by a yew tree said to have been planted by Lady Anne, and an 18th-century room decorated with seashells.

Skipsea K5

Drogo de Bevrere, a niece of William the Conqueror, erected a castle here in 1086. All that survives is the circular motte on which it was built. Approached by a short walk across fields and rising 36 feet above the surrounding farmland, this mound affords extensive views across Bridlington Bay and towards Flamborough Head.

Spofforth F5

Fortified in the 14th century, this ruined hall was a possession of the Percy family and was wrecked by their enemies after Sir Henry Percy's death in 1461. It retains 15th-century window tracery.

Stanwick Fortifications Forcett E1

Constructed during several phases at a time of infighting among factions of the Brigantes at the time of the Roman conquest, the huge fort is believed to have functioned as a rallying point for the army of Venutius, who was defeated by the Romans in AD 74. A rampart and ditch with dry-stone facing protect the 850-acre site.

PLACES OF WORS

All Saints Church Rotherham F9

All Saints Church was built on a grand scale with fine tracery on the stalls and bench en and Perpendicular-style fan vaulting; its 19th century restorer, Sir Gilbert Scott, designed some of the stained glass. On the town's 15 century bridge over the River Don is one of only four bridge chapels in the country.

Beverley Minster Beverley J6

A cathedral-scale structure of strikingly unif design, dating from the 13th century, the Minster contains the delicate 14th-century Percy Tomb, which displays a richly decora canopy. It also has a set of 68 misericords carved from Sherwood Forest oak, which depict such whimsical scenes as a pig playi a harp. Nearby St Mary's Church possesses

15th-century ceiling with panels representin medieval English kings; among its carvings is the figure of a rabbit that is thought to have inspired Lewis Carroll's White Rabbit in *Alice's Adventures in Wonderland*.

Bolton Priory near Skipton C5

Set on the turfy banks of the Wharfe are the ruins of the priory in which Augustinian canons worshipped. The priory church was stylishly restored by the 19th-century architects Pugin and Street; Pugin added stained-glass windows depicting stories from the Gospel. Further up Wharfedale, Hubberholme church, with its 16th-century musicians' gallery, has great rustic charm.

Byland Abbey Coxwold G3

The site of what was England's largest Cistercian priory church is mostly reduced t its foundations, though it retains a fine west front with a raggedly broken rose window, and some of its original tiled floor.

urch of St Peter and St Paul
kering I3
e Church of St Peter and St Paul features
h-century wall paintings depicting scenes
m the lives of saints and of Christ. For
ny years these were covered over as
y were feared to be a distraction for
congregation.

sby Abbey near Richmond E2
on the Swale near Richmond, Easby
bey was a house of the Premonstratensian
ite canons'—so called because of the
our of their habits. Its ruins include a
ehouse, refectory and monks' dormitory.
e 12th- and 13th-century church was
tored in the 19th century but retains
dieval wall paintings (*see detail below*).

untains Abbey near Ripon F4
llically set in the pastoral valley of the
ver Skell, in the Vale of York, Fountains
bey is perhaps the finest monastic ruin in
e country. Founded in 1132 by Benedictines,
was taken over by Cistercians three years
er and blossomed into the richest
stercian house in England. The abbey
ains much of its church and of the lay
others' quarters, as well as elaborate
terworks and drainage systems. Further
velopments followed after the Dissolution,

with Fountains Hall built in the 16th century
from some of the abbey stones and now
containing displays about the history of
Fountains, and Studley Royal (*see 'Gardens',
page 158*) landscaped in the 18th century.
Within the park, St Mary's Church (*bottom left*)
is a highly ornate building by the Victorian
architect William Burges.

Heptonstall Methodist Chapel
Hebden Bridge C7
Heptonstall's Methodist chapel claims to
be the oldest in the world to have been in
continuous use. It dates from 1764, following
Wesley's visit to the village, and was built
in a hexagonal, rather than a conventional,
church plan.

Jervaulx Abbey near Middleham D3
Founded in 1156 by Cistercian monks from
nearby Aysgarth, this is the only major
Yorkshire abbey resting in private hands.
The owner has encouraged the growth of ivy
and wild flowers, giving the ruins a highly
romantic appearance.

Kirkham Priory near Malton I4
Set on the River Derwent, Kirkham Priory
is a scant Augustinian ruin. Its gatehouse
survives, however, and is richly carved with
heraldic designs.

Kirkstall Abbey Leeds E6
On the River Aire, Kirkstall Abbey is a
remarkably substantial ruin of a Cistercian
house founded in the 12th century by monks
from Fountains Abbey. Its church features a
collapsed Perpendicular-style tower, and its
chapter house is well preserved. Within the
gatehouse is a museum of social history, the
Abbey House Museum (temporarily closed).

Monk Bretton Priory near Barnsley F8
Now framed within a semi-industrial
landscape, Monk Bretton Priory was founded
by Cluniac monks in 1153, and its site still
holds remains of a gatehouse, west range and
other buildings.

Mount Grace Priory Northallerton F2
Mount Grace Priory survives as Britain's finest
example of a house of the Carthusian order
of monks, a strict order whose members kept
vows of silence and lived in separate two-
storey cells—each with walled gardens—
and where wrongdoers were locked up in
a prison. One cell has been reconstructed,
and there are substantial remains of the
cloister and church.

Rievaulx Abbey near Helmsley H3
Magnificently set in steep-sided Rye
Dale, immortalised in paintings by Turner
and Cotman, and standing three storeys
high, the abbey (*see detail of carving below*)
was founded in 1132 by
French Cistercian monks,
who owned the first sheep
flocks in the area. Rievaulx
(pronounced 'Reevo')
features a large-scale
Cistercian nave dating
from 1140 to 1145, as well
as remains of the 13th-
century choir and monastic
living quarters.

Ripon Cathedral Ripon F4
Ripon Cathedral displays a great range of
architectural styles, including a Saxon crypt
and a fine west façade in Early English style.

Roche Abbey near Rotherham F9
This Cistercian ruin stands in the valley of
the River Ryton amid 18th-century parkland
landscaped by Capability Brown. Its transepts
stand partly to its original height and the
entire layout of the monastic buildings has
been excavated.

Selby Abbey Selby H6
The abbey church of an 11th-century
Benedictine foundation, Selby survived
the Dissolution of the Monasteries. Despite
extensive fire damage in 1906, it has much
Norman work and a fine 14th-century
stained-glass Jesse window.

St Mary's Church Lastingham H2
St Mary's Church includes a remarkably
preserved Norman crypt dating from 1068.
Lit by a single tiny window and unique in
Britain for having side aisles and a nave,
this was part of an unfinished abbey.

St Michael's Church Kirkby Malham C4
One of the most generously proportioned
of the Dales churches, St Michael's has a
16th-century timber roof and 17th- and
18th-century box pews.

St Patrick's Church Patrington L7
A former retreat for archbishops of York, the
village is dominated by soaring St Patrick's
Church, known as the 'Queen of Holderness';
cruciform in plan with a central tower and
spire, it has fine Decorative-style tracery as
well as some 200 gargoyles and a 14th-
century font with carved angels.

PLACES OF WORSHIP (CONTINUED)

STATELY HOMES

St Peter's Church Howden H6

This is a superb cruciform structure with collegiate origins, and includes a fine tower, 14th-century west front, and a ruined octagonal chapter house. The Saltmarsh Chapel features family tombs spanning seven centuries.

Undercliffe Cemetery Bradford E6

Bradford boasts one of Britain's most spectacular Victorian burial grounds in Undercliffe Cemetery, where numerous wealthy magnates are laid to rest on a hill overlooking the city centre.

Wakefield Cathedral Wakefield F7

A bridge chapel, dating from the mid-14th century, stands on the river. Wakefield Cathedral gained its status only in 1888 and was heavily restored between 1858 and 1874 but contains a fine rood screen of 1635 and an organ case of 1743.

Whitby Abbey Whitby I1

Close to the clifftops, the abbey (*pictured below*) commands a view over the town and was valued after the Dissolution as a landmark for mariners, although bombardment from a German warship in 1914 destroyed some of the surviving fabric. Founded by St Hilda of Hartlepool in 657, the abbey was razed by marauding Danes in 867

but refounded by Benedictine monks in 1078. It retains stonework in the Early English and Decorated Gothic styles. Virtually adjacent, St Mary's Church contains a wealth of Georgian furnishings, with galleries, box pews and a triple-decker pulpit—to which is attached an ear trumpet used by a 19th-century vicar's wife. Eerily, the churchyard was the setting for an episode in Bram Stoker's 1897 horror novel, *Dracula*.

York Minster York G5

Foremost among Yorkshire's masterpieces of ecclesiastical architecture, York Minster dominates the walled medieval city. The site has its origins as a humble wooden chapel erected in AD 627, but the present structure dates from 1220 to 1470. Among many glories are its stained-glass windows, the oldest installed in 1150, and its polygonal chapter house, with a huge vault span unsupported by any central column. Elsewhere, a museum reveals the Roman masonry above which the Minster was built, and explains how the imminent collapse of the central tower was averted by engineers in the 1960s. York also contains a host of fine medieval churches, including the now redundant Holy Trinity Church, with its box pews and 15th-century stained glass. St Mary's Abbey, a mainly 13th-century Benedictine ruin, stands in Museum Gardens in the heart of the city.

Beningborough Hall near York G5

This imposing early Georgian hall contains one of the most impressive Baroque interior in England. Over 100 works from the Natio Portrait Gallery are displayed, heightening hall's period atmosphere. There is also a ful equipped Victorian laundry and an attractiv walled garden.

Bolling Hall Bradford E6

Now swallowed up by the suburbs of Bradford, this stone-built manor house was largely extended in the 17th century from a 16th-century tower. It houses part of the Bradford District Museum's collections, including paintings and Yorkshire furniture. The main hall, known locally as the 'housebody', boasts a fine heraldic stained-glass window.

Bramham Park near Wetherby F5

Versailles comes to Yorkshire: the early 18th century mansion of Bramham Park stands in a great park landscaped in the French manner, with ornamental lakes, temples, avenues and statuary. Badly damaged in a fire in 1828, and not repaired until nearly 80 years later, the austerely Baroque house contains 17th and 18th-century furniture and numerous pictures on sporting themes.

Brodsworth Hall near Doncaster G8

Few country houses in England are equippe with the architectural firepower to rival Brodsworth (*see entrance hall below*) as an evocation of Victorian magnificence, the wo of Italian architect Chevalier Casentini. That much has survived of the house's original contents is attributable to the fact that the family abandoned rooms and everything within them progressively as their fortune steadily declined.

BELOW *The Anglo-Saxon poet, Caedmon, whose gift was said to have been bestowed upon him when a voice in a dream ordered him to sing of the Creation, was an early resident of Whitby Abbey.*

LIFE AT CASTLE HOWARD

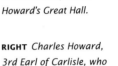

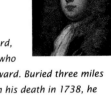

LEFT *The South Parterre's Atlas Fountain provides an impressive frontispiece to the dome of Castle Howard's Great Hall.*

RIGHT *Charles Howard, 3rd Earl of Carlisle, who conceived Castle Howard. Buried three miles away in Bulmer upon his death in 1738, he was later interred in the estate mausoleum, upon its completion in 1744.*

WHEN CASTLE HOWARD was first built, it sent a clarion call to the London elite that the Howard family was a dynasty worthy of esteem. In an age when display meant influence, and influence wealth, Charles Howard, 3rd Earl of Carlisle, deemed the original Howard family seat of Naworth in Cumberland too remote. In 1699 he set about building a new home more befitting for his upwardly mobile family. Choosing Henderskelfe, northeast of York, as its location, he then hired as chief architect the untested John Vanbrugh—wit, wag, playwright, soldier and spy, but never before an architect.

Vanbrugh proved equal to the challenge: laid out on an unorthodox north–south axis, his castle—a strange title, given the fact that it was never intended as a fortification —was based around a 70-foot-high Great Hall, topped by a lavish dome and flanked by two projecting wings. Howard filled the building with artworks commissioned from artists and craftsmen from the Continent. He then built the Temple of the Four Winds, and in 1729 began the impressive, Hawksmoor-designed Mausoleum, in the castle's vast estate. Horace Walpole, struck by the mausoleum's beauty, joked that it would 'tempt one to be buried alive'. By the early 18th century, the castle was a mainstay of the social circuit in the region.

Succeeding Howard generations added further embellishments to the original edifice: a Great Lake for boating in the 1790s; a private railway station in the 1840s; exquisite ornamental flowerbeds and fountains a decade later; and a chapel decorated in Pre-Raphaelite style in the 1870s. The talented 9th Earl contributed his own watercolours of Italy and Egypt to an art collection which by then included Canalettos, Gainsboroughs, Titians and priceless Roman antiquities.

In the 20th century, the castle fell on hard times: colossal maintenance costs were compounded when fire ravaged the southeast wing and Great Hall in 1940. Yet like a phoenix the castle rose again. In 1952 it opened to the paying public; and in 1981 starred in TV's *Brideshead Revisited*. Where once it hosted only an elite few, approaching 200,000 tourists a year now queue to experience the grandeur of Castle Howard.

Burton Agnes Hall near Driffield **J5**
Impressionist and Post-Impressionist paintings (including works by Renoir, Cézanne, Corot and Gauguin) hang in the Elizabethan house, wherein the Great Hall has a magnificently carved stone screen and period furnishings. The Old Hall, the original Norman manor house nearby, was remodelled in both the 17th and 18th centuries.

Burton Constable Hall near Hull **K6**
Set amid parkland laid out by Capability Brown, this Elizabethan mansion was embellished by a succession of architects, and houses an excellent collection of Chippendale furniture.

Castle Howard near Malton **I4**
(See feature above)

Duncombe Park near Helmsley **H3**
Work began on this imposing house in 1713, upon a site that slopes down to the River Rye. A grass terrace, with a Doric temple and Ionic rotunda at either end, makes the most of the setting. Although the house was badly damaged by fire and largely rebuilt in the 1890s, its entrance hall has changed very little since the early 18th century.

East Riddlesden Hall near Keighley **D6**
With its low gables and mullioned and transomed windows, East Riddlesden is a classic example of a West Yorkshire manor house. The hall was the home of the notorious Murgatroyds, whose villainous deeds reputedly caused the River Aire to change its course away from the house.

Locally crafted oak furniture fills the panelled rooms, and there is some fine plasterwork. A magnificent barn with a timbered roof contains agricultural implements from times gone by.

Harewood House near Leeds **E6**
Completed in 1772 by John Carr of York for Edwin Lascelles, the seat of the earls of Harewood occupies a park which was landscaped by Capability Brown with woodland and lakeside walks. The impressive interior includes delicate ceilings and plasterwork by Robert Adam, and one of Thomas Chippendale's most extensive commissions of furniture. There are paintings by old masters and quite beautiful collections of Sèvres and Chinese porcelain.

STATELY HOMES (CONTINUED)

Lotherton Hall Leeds E6

Essentially Edwardian in character, the hall contains collections of furniture, pottery and porcelain, costumes, paintings, silver and oriental art. Its grounds feature formal gardens, a bird garden and deer park.

Newby Hall near Ripon F4

The Compton family seat since the 18th century, and subsequently modified by Robert Adam. Classical statuary and Gobelins tapestries are hallmarks of the interior, while the grounds contain a woodland walk, children's adventure garden and a miniature railway.

Norton Conyers near Ripon F4

Although of medieval origin, Norton Conyers has many 17th- and 18th-century features. Heirloom paintings and furniture lend it the atmosphere of a family home. On a visit in 1839, Charlotte Brontë was told of a mad woman who was incarcerated in the attic, a story that inspired her to ascribe the same fate to the first Mrs Rochester in *Jane Eyre*.

Nostell Priory near Wakefield F7

A doll's house (*below*) of 1735 at the priory is thought to be Chippendale's earliest surviving work; certainly the great furniture maker made numerous pieces specially for this Palladian mansion. Begun by James Paine, it has additions by Robert Adam, assisted by the plasterer Joseph Rose and the painter Antonio Zucchi. The grounds offer visitors pleasing lakeside walks.

ABOVE *A haughty peacock patrols the well-manicured lawns of Nunnington Hall; the hall's walled garden is noted for its clematis collection.*

Nunnington Hall near Helmsley H3

A family home for four centuries, the manor house (*above*) stands on the banks of the River Rye. Beyond the oak-panelled hall lie a haunted room and a nursery. The attics contain a charming series of miniature rooms in a range of period styles, created over a 40-year period by Mrs F. M. Carlisle.

Oakwell Hall near Batley E7

Charlotte Brontë used this gritstone Elizabethan manor as the model for Fieldhead in her novel *Shirley*. The building is remarkable in that few modifications have occurred since its erection. It is furnished as a gentry home of the late 17th century, when the Batt family lived here.

Ripley Castle Ripley E4

The Ingilby family home since the 14th century, the spectacular crenellated house includes a priest's hole panelled over for many years before rediscovery in 1964.

The 16th-century tower houses Royalist armour and its grounds contain tropical plant and a greatly respected collection of hyacinth. In the 1820s the estate workers' village of Ripley was rebuilt in Gothic style.

Sledmere House near Driffield J5

Sheraton, Chippendale and French furniture grace the Georgian and Edwardian mansion situated in the lonely Wolds landscape. Highlights include the Adam-style library and a Turkish room dazzlingly decorated with tile from Damascus.

Temple Newsam Leeds E6

This 1,200-acre park, a landscape design of the indefatigable Capability Brown, forms a countrified oasis within suburban Leeds. The city's outstanding collection of decorative and fine art is displayed within the huge Tudor and Jacobean house, the inside of which was largely remodelled in Georgian times.

ARDENS

dby Park Buttercrambe H5

is early 18th-century house, standing on the
e of a 7th-century castle, is encompassed
a period garden that has been carefully
stored since 1964. Planting makes the most
contrasts and coloration, with pale shades
against dark trees. Day lilies and
apanthus flourish in the sunnier areas.

lton Percy Selby H6

e churchyard has been transformed from a
lderness into a highly unusual and colourful
ttage garden. Some 1,000 species grow
mi-wild.

rnby Hall I5

vo lakes beside the hall, now council
fices, boast Europe's largest collection of
ies (below), some 80 varieties, which bloom
m June to mid-September. Erstwhile hall

vner Major Stewart originally constructed
e lakes as fishing ponds in 1904. There are
rnamental carp in the ponds, and there's
so a fine rose garden.

onstable Burton near Middleham D3

leasantly set in Wensleydale, the romantic
rounds of a Palladian house of 1768 feature
ature trails and a rock garden. Cedars shade
e lawns, and lilies, ferns and hardy shrubs
re seen in the terraced woodland, beneath
hich an 18th-century bridge crosses a lake.

illing Castle near Helmsley H3

raditional flower borders backed by majestic
ees flourish on a south-facing terraced
illside overlooking a golf course at Gilling
astle. The castle itself is a boarding school,
me parts of which are also open to
e public.

Golden Acre Park Bramhope E6

Originally a private pleasure park, Golden
Acre is now a municipally owned public
space and botanic garden. Rhododendrons
make an eye-catching display in late spring,
and there are highly regarded collections of
heathers and houseleeks, as well as an alpine
house. Demonstration beds enable gardening
enthusiasts to stock up on new ideas.

Hackfall Woods near Ripon F4

Crumbling follies, now undergoing
restoration, peep out among the overgrown
woodlands in a deep gorge cut by the River
Ure near Grewelthorpe. The estate was the
18th-century creation of William Aislabie,
who, with his father, laid out the celebrated
grounds at Studley Royal. William Wordsworth
admired this site, which was also the subject
of a painting by Turner. It is owned by the
Woodland Trust.

Harlow Carr Harrogate E5

The Northern Horticultural Society began
these 68-acre botanical gardens (below)
in Harrogate in 1949 for garden plant trials.
Today the gardens at Harlow Carr include
rockeries, an arboretum, rhododendrons,

demonstration suburban gardens, scented
gardens and a long streamside garden noted
for its moisture-loving plants, as well as
national collections of hypericums, heathers,
rhubarb and ferns. A hide enables visitors to
observe the wildlife that resides on an
adjacent pond, and there is also a model
village to view.

Rievaulx Terrace near Helmsley H3

A gently curving lawn stretches half a mile
along an escarpment above the graceful ruins
of Rievaulx Abbey (see page 153). At one end
is the domed Tuscan temple—probably
modelled on the Temple of Vesta at Tivoli—
while at the other end is the Palladian-style
Ionic temple, formerly used as a banqueting
house and resplendent with ceiling paintings
and period furnishings. Created in the 1750s
by one Thomas Duncombe, the Terrace
mirrors a similar feature that had been laid
out by his father at nearby Duncombe Park,
and is a fine example of the 18th-century
fashion of incorporating picturesque ruins
into a landscape design.

Roundhay Park Leeds E6

Owned by Leeds City Council since 1871,
Roundhay Park features sweeping parkland
as well as magnificent horticultural displays,
among them impressive national collections
of dahlias and violas, within the Canal
Gardens. Stocked with exotic butterflies and
birds, the tropical houses boast the largest
collection of tropical plants in Britain outside
Kew; and various types of cacti are displayed
in an arid house. Reptiles, fish and insects
can be seen in naturalistic settings around
the park, which hosts numerous musical
and other events.

Sheffield Botanical Gardens F9

Supported by volunteers and gardening
societies, the Sheffield Botanical Gardens
harbour fine floral displays and are stocked
with some 5,000 plants. Their 18-acre site
already represents a natural haven close to
the city centre, and looks set to be greatly
improved following a recent and successful
Lottery application.

Sheriff Hutton Park near York G5

At the centre of the park is a Jacobean
hunting lodge, remodelled into a Queen
Anne mansion. Bluebell and lakeside
walks explore the grounds, which include
a sunken rose garden and a croquet lawn
lined with a herbaceous border on one
side and a shrubbery on the other.

GARDENS (CONTINUED)

ABOVE *The Temple of Piety stands reflected in glassy Crescent Pond, one of several bodies of water that define the serene gardens of Studley Royal; adjacent is the circular Moon Pond.*

Studley Royal near Ripon F4

Following his expulsion from Parliament for his involvement with the South Sea Bubble scandal of 1720, John Aislabie set about designing for his country house what was to become Britain's finest water garden (*pictured above*). He dammed the River Skell to form a lake, and adorned the estate with grottoes, cascades and a Moon Pond flanked by crescent-shaped pools. Gothic and classical temples evoke an Arcadian landscape; a gazebo known as Anne Boleyn's Seat looks down from a hillside, and above the park the avenue aligns with distant Ripon Cathedral.

Sutton Park Sutton-on-the-Forest G4

Percy Crane began this garden, a skilful use of Georgian terrace design, in 1962. His scheme includes ironwork gazebos, a temple and a woodland walk with notable cherry trees, and there is a water feature with exotic ducks.

Thorp Perrow Arboretum
near Middleham D3

Many regard Thorp Perrow as northern England's outstanding tree collection. Some woodland dates from the 16th century, and there is a Victorian pinetum in addition to lakeside trees and shrubs, ornamental cherries, fine oaks, willows and hazels. An ornamental lake lies between the arboretum and a lawn embellished with topiary.

Valley Gardens Harrogate E5

Harrogate's celebrated pleasure ground dates from the town's heyday as a spa. The 18-acre site boasts well-tended formal beds and an annual dahlia border. Period features include a cast-iron tea room and a 600-foot-long Sun Colonnade erected for the benefit of convalescents.

Wentworth Castle near Rotherham F9

The grounds of Wentworth Castle, which were laid out by William Wentworth in 1740, include national collections of rhododendrons and magnolias, and an excellent array of camellias.

York Gate near Leeds E6

This one-acre plantsman's garden (*below*), divided into eight individual gardens, each with different plants and its own unique

features, was created by the Spencer family and bequeathed to The Gardeners' Royal Benevolent Society.

York University Gardens G5

Laid out on the outskirts of the city in the 1950s, this ambitious garden marries the grounds of Elizabethan Heslington Hall to a serpentine lake. Covered walks and bridges make the most of the water features, and there is sculpture by Henry Moore.

Additionally, a number of Yorkshire's greatest gardens form the grounds of stately homes, such as Beningborough Hall, Burton Constable Hall, Castle Howard, Harewood House, Newby Hall, Nostell Priory, Ripley Castle and Sledmere House. See **STATELY HOMES** *on page 154.*

WILD PLACES

Blackstone Edge near Hebden Bridge C7

Sited north of the M62 on the Lancashire border on bleak, treeless moors that support red grouse, golden plover, redshank, skylark and meadow pipit. Ancient routes cross the moor, including a former packhorse road and a mysterious paved 'Roman road' of uncertain date. The crags rise to 1,475 feet.

Bridestones Cloughton J2

One of the most curious natural features of the North York Moors, these are a series of gritstone rocks weathered by the elements into top-heavy mushroom shapes (*below*). They can be reached by following the Dalby

Forest Drive, a road that passes mainly through conifer plantations. From the car park, the path to the Bridestones leads through Dovedale Wood, an ancient oak woodland harbouring greater spotted woodpeckers. The stones stand amid heather moorland, in a landscape slashed by miniature ravines, or griffs.

Brimham Rocks near Pateley Bridge D4

East of Pateley Bridge and on the fringes of the Yorkshire Dales, these natural outcrops have weathered into fantastic shapes, and bear such fanciful names as Anvil, Castle, Druid's Altar and Sphinx.

Burbage Rocks near Sheffield F9

A gritstone edge flanks a rim of a moorland valley in the northeast corner of the Peak National Park, close to the Derbyshire border. In the middle of the valley the remains of Carl Wark Iron Age hill-fort occupy a craggy hillock. There are walks in the National Trust's neighbouring Longshaw Estate.

ttertubs near Hawes **C2**

drive north from Wensleydale takes in
'26-foot-high Buttertubs Pass; the Buttertubs
emselves are a series of natural potholes
side the road, and earned their name after
mers used to lower butter into them for
oling on its way to market.

amborough Head near Flamborough **L4**

is headland (*right*) juts far out between
idlington Bay and Filey Brigg, gaining a
1g view of the coast. The relentless action
the sea has honeycombed the chalk cliffs
o pinnacles, pillars and caves. Kittiwakes
d other sea birds nest in great numbers
the cliffs, within view of two lighthouses.
arby, Bempton Cliffs RSPB Reserve is
me to some 200,000 birds in summer, and
a haunt for puffins and guillemots, as well
the only English breeding ground for
nnets. Summer cruises from North Landing
ve views of these sheer 400-foot cliffs.

ABOVE *Jutting some six miles out into the North Sea, the dramatic chalk headland at Flamborough is a popular first stopping-point for migrating birds.*

WALKING IN THE DALES

TWO OF BRITAIN'S most famous long-
distance footpaths—the Pennine Way
and the Coast-to-Coast Walk—meet in
the Yorkshire Dales. The paths cross
near Kisdon Force, a waterfall outside
Keld in Swaledale, one of the most
ruggedly attractive of the Dales. Add
to these the region's own long-distance
footpath, the Dales Way, and part of an
interloper from neighbouring Lancashire,
the Ribble Way, and it's clear that even
the toughest of walkers will face a
challenge in the Dales.

The ultimate challenge is to walk to
the summits of all of the Dales' Three
Peaks, a journey totalling some 25 miles.
Fell-runners can complete the distance
in about two and a half hours, but any
walker who manages it in less than 12
hours earns the right to join the Three
Peaks of Yorkshire Club. The appeal of
the Dales is just as great, though, for
weekend walkers who enjoy a short
stroll in the country without getting
lost on the way.

The landscape attracts walkers of all
kinds, during all seasons. Spring and
summer are perhaps best, when the grass

is lush, the lambs are in the pastures,
the birds are busy and there is a chance
to see the Dales at their absolute best—
beneath deep blue skies.

RIGHT *Official routes like the Pennine Way
are well signed—and at times too well walked.
Popular paths suffer erosion, and walkers
are asked to follow alternative routes where
indicated, to preserve the Dales' beauty.*

ABOVE *Weather this fine isn't guaranteed in
the Dales, so it's wise to pack your waterproof
and pull on sturdy hiking boots.*

WILD PLACES (CONTINUED)

YORKSHIRE'S NATIONAL PARKS AND SCENIC REGIONS

ABOVE *This tumbledown church is all that remains of the lost village of Wharram Percy.*

LEFT *Oddly, nothing more than half-remembered legend links Robin Hood's Bay with Robin of Sherwood.*

ENGLAND'S LARGEST uninterrupted expanse of heather moorland, a sea of purple in late summer, covers over a third of the North York Moors National Park's 554 square miles. Sparsely populated today, the moorlands harbour evidence of early settlers and travellers: prehistoric man left thousands of burial mounds; while the Romans are thought to have laid a length of road that crosses the moors between Pickering and Grosmont, of which a short stretch, the so-called Wade's Causeway, survives. From medieval times, a number of stone crosses, thought to have been waymarkers, were erected.

The moorland plateau is broken by lush, green dales of dry-stone-walled pastures, flecked with oak and ash woods. Red pantiled roofs and cottage walls of honey-hued limestone add further colour. To the east, conifer plantations are a notable feature. Beyond, the rugged coastline includes the highest cliffs on the east coast, at Boulby Cliff. The 108-mile Cleveland Way, a long-distance footpath from Helmsley to Filey Brigg, skirts the moors.

The Yorkshire Dales National Park is a land of corridor-like dales and hills, and pastures enclosed by dry-stone walls and dotted with sturdy barns. Much of the area sits on a base of white carboniferous limestone, which has in places weathered into waterfalls, gorges, caverns, scars, cliffs and pavements. The limestone bedrock and soils harbour oak and ash, sheep-grazed grasslands and profusions of wild flowers. Gritstone overlies much of the northerly dales, giving rise to starker moorland terrains of heather and cotton grass.

Dales villages are strikingly uniform, typically built of limestone blocks with gritstone lintels and mullions, rising to flagstone roofs. Some, like Burnsall, are grouped around greens. Many domestic buildings originate from the 18th and 19th centuries, when lead mining flourished here.

LEFT *Young Ralph Cross, the medieval cross adopted by the North York Moors National Park as its official emblem.*

RIGHT *A Swaledale sheep grazes contentedly, oblivious to the breathtaking Dales panorama behind it.*

Stretching from the Humber to the Vale of Pickering and from the Vale of York to the cliffs of Flamborough Head, the Wolds comprise gentle chalk hills cut by steep-sided dry valleys. Broad-verged roads— former drovers' routes—head along ridges hemmed by vast fields of corn and bright yellow prairies of oilseed rape. In the valleys are diminutive villages, typically boasting duckpond, green and Norman church. Elsewhere, grassy humps mark the sites of medieval villages abandoned after farmers turned labour-intensive arable holdings into sheep pastures. Wharram Percy, with its ruined church, is the most spectacular of these 'lost' settlements.

ardcastle and Hebden Crags
ear Hebden Bridge C7

hese gritstone outcrops rise up above
e wooded valleys of Hebden Dale and
rimsworth Dean. Waymarked paths lace
e woods, passing a disused textile mill
alled Gibson's Mill. Close by, and a target
r climbers, Heptonstall Crags command
izzying views out over the dry-stone-walled
lopes of Calderdale.

ornsea Mere L5

ocated about a half a mile inland from the
orth Sea, Hornsea Mere, Yorkshire's largest
eshwater lake, was hollowed out of the
arth by glacial action during the Ice Age.
'ith its two islands and its partly wooded
hores, the mere is a haven for wildlife: to
ate, more than 200 moth, 250 bird and 300
lant species have been recorded here. There
a waymarked walk that rings the lake, and
car park and vantage point near to the
djacent town of Hornsea.

ow Stean Gorge near Pateley Bridge D4

tched out by millennia of rushing waters, the
ow Stean Gorge is a well-hidden stretch of
he How Stean Beck, way up at the source
f Nidderdale. Fenced galleries, bridges and
alkways afford excellent views of caves and
'0-foot cliffs to visitors to the gorge.

ngleborough near Ingleton A3

he terrain around Ingleborough contains
wealth of caves, waterfalls and limestone
eatures. The flat, 2,372-foot summit of
ngleborough, capped by the remains of an
ron Age fort, affords views of the Forest of
owland, Morecambe Bay and the Lake
istrict fells. A fine approach to Ingleborough
s from Clapham and along the Reginald
arrer Nature Trail. Named after a botanist,
vho in the course of his early 20th-century
ravels in Asia found many new species to
ring back over to Europe, the trail passes
y Ingleborough Hall, where the Farrer family
ived and planted many trees. Beyond is
ngleborough Cave, where tours include the
irst 600 yards of a vast cave system that
xtends some seven and a half miles and
ncludes the pothole higher up Ingleborough
nown as Gaping Gill. This chamber is said to
e large enough to accommodate the entire
structure of York Minster, and it can be
ntered by means of a winched chair on bank
holidays. Some 200 feet across, and situated
n the eastern side of the mountain, Alum
ot is an even more spectacular hole in
the ground.

Ingleton Falls and White Scar Cavern A3

A major attraction since Victorian times, the
Falls Walk begins at Ingleton, and takes in
the rivers Twiss and Doe, where geological
faulting at the meeting-points of limestone,
slate and shale have spawned dramatic
waterfalls. Other waterfalls in the area include
Stainforth Force, set by a 17th-century
packhorse bridge; and Catrigg Force, reached
on foot from Stainforth village. Visitors to
nearby White Scar Cavern are led along an
underground river, past a waterfall to a huge
chamber, where formations include 'straw
stalactites' and calcite flowstone.

Kilnsey Crag near Grassington C4

Wharfedale's most prominent landform and
a magnet for rock climbers, Kilnsey Crag
towers some 165 feet high and its 40-foot
overhang is England's largest. Upper
Wharfedale has largely escaped agricultural
'improvement' and features lime-loving plants
such as oxeye daisies, orchids, yellow rattle
and betony, as well as many different grasses.

Kisdon Force near Keld C2

Located in Swaledale, Kisdon Force is a fine
waterfall, in a verdant setting beneath the
steep slopes of Kisdon Hill.

FOLLIES AND CURIOSITIES

LEFT *Locals swear 20 people can fit onto the
grass island that forms the eye of the White
Horse at Kilburn. Several tons of lime were
needed to create the horse, as the hill on
which it lies is not chalk.*

YORKSHIRE'S CLUTCH of curiosities
spans several millennia. Early settlers
left a host of enigmatic landmarks, the
tallest of which, the 25-foot standing
stone in Rudston churchyard, near
Bridlington, is estimated to be some
3–4,000 years old. The Devil also lends
his name to three giant gritstone
monoliths near Boroughbridge: the
Devil's Arrows, which date from a similar
period and may have been fertility
symbols. Henges of rather more modern
provenance have stood between Ilton
and Masham since the early 19th century,
when one William Danby paid local
jobless men a shilling a day to erect a
scaled-down replica of Stonehenge.

Indeed, moneyed landowners were
responsible for a host of eye-catching
sights. Wentworth Woodhouse, an 18th-
century house boasting England's longest

façade, sits in parkland embellished with
follies, one of which, the Needle's Eye,
is said to have been erected for a bet
that the landowner could drive his
coach through the eye of a needle.
A century later, Squire Barry of Fyling
Hall, near Whitby, built for his pampered
pigs a palatial sty, with Grecian and
Egyptian-style features.

So impressed was the grocer Thomas
Taylor by Oxfordshire's chalk white
horse that he hatched the idea of
duplicating it in his native Kilburn.
Decades later, Kilburn schoolmaster
John Hodgson and his pupils realised
Taylor's dream, marking out a 314
foot-by-228 foot horse which was
then cut out by the men of the village.
From horses to foxes: up on the
summit of Buckden Pike is a stone
cross with a fox's head set into its
base, erected by the sole survivor
of a Polish aircrew that came down
here in the snow in 1942. Working
on the assumption that the prints
of a fox, etched in the snow, might
be heading towards a food source, he
followed them, duly reaching a farm.

WILD PLACES (CONTINUED)

ABOVE *Yorkshire boasts several otherworldly limestone pavements such as this; their furrows, or grikes, seem to have been carved out by some vast, ancient plough.*

Malham C4

The Dales' most spectacular limestone landforms are near Malham, in Airedale. Malham Cove is a 250-foot, crescent-shaped cliff; it inspired Charles Kingsley's *The Water Babies* (1863) after the author jested that a chimney sweep might have made the black lichen marks on the rock while tumbling over the edge. Above the Cove is a natural limestone pavement, broken by deep fissures, which harbours limestone-loving wild flowers. Beyond a craggy dry valley lies Malham Tarn, England's highest freshwater lake, whose reedy shores are a habitat for damp-loving plants and nesting birds. A walk east from Malham along Gordale Beck passes Janet's Foss (where it drops over an 'apron' formed of tufa encrustation) before reaching Gordale Scar, a broad gorge formed from a collapsed cave system, where the beck somersaults spectacularly.

Mallyan Spout near Goathland I2

Approached on foot from Goathland, where sheep graze the verges of a mile-long village street, a tributary stream dribbles down this 60-foot column and into wooded West Beck. A riverside path meanders through ancient ash, elder, willow and oak woods that are thought to represent the last survivors of a natural forest that once covered this whole area.

Pen-y-Ghent near Horton-in-Ribblesdale B3

The lowest of the Three Peaks, Pen-y-Ghent (2,273 feet) forms the rockiest part of the long-distance Pennine Way, which on its approach from Horton-in-Ribblesdale passes close to the dramatic entrances to Hull Pot and Hunt Pot. Nearby Whernside—at 2,414 feet, Yorkshire's highest summit—boasts an awesome high-level walk running along its ridge.

Spurn Head near Kilnsea M7

Thrust out far across the mouth of the Humber, Spurn Head is one of the strangest features of the British coastline. Three miles long, in places no more than 30 feet wide, and traced along its entire length by a road, the curving spit is formed of material washed out from the rapidly eroding shores to the north. It is an excellent observation point for the huge autumn bird migration, featuring brent geese and arctic terns. Seals and porpoises are commonly sighted, too.

Strid Woods near Skipton C5

Near Bolton Abbey in Wharfedale, the Wharfe is forced through a narrow rock channel known as the Strid. A haunt of dippers, tits, jays, herons and great spotted woodpeckers, the surrounding Strid Woods form a nature reserve with waymarked trails; trees include sessile oak, beech, Scots pine, yew and ash, and in spring there are carpets of bluebells.

Stump Cross Cavern near Grassington C4

Set in the eastern Dales and graced with stalagmite and stalactite formations, Stump Cross was discovered by a 19th-century lead miner. It is now run as a show cave where, unusually, visitors can explore without a guide.

Sutton Bank near Thirsk F3

This 981-foot-high cliff bounds the western side of the North York Moors National Park and affords views encompassing the Pennines, York Minster and the Yorkshire Wolds. The long-distance Cleveland Way leads along the top of the escarpment, crossing the A170. Below, Gormire Lake was created when mud and rubble blocked a glacial overflow channel after the Ice Age some 10,000 years ago; a nature trail threads through Garbutt Wood by the lake's shore.

Wensleydale D3

Wensleydale lies at the the heart of the Dales' waterfall country. The best-known fall, Aysgarth Force, is a charming spot where the River Ure tumbles over rocks and ledges for half a mile. In summer the falls often become a gentle trickle, but in winter they can be a fierce, peaty torrent. Hardraw Force is within the grounds of the Green Dragon Inn, Hardraw; the 96-foot single drop is the greatest in England. Just off Wensleydale, Lake Semerwater, half a mile across, was formed by debris deposited when a glacier retreated, thus damming England's shortest river, the Bain.

A WEALTH OF BIRDLIFE

MORE THAN 420 SPECIES *of birds have been recorded across Yorkshire—that's quite some testament to the varied terrains of this beautiful region. All corners of Yorkshire have their particular fans in the avian world, making the place a rewarding base for a spot of 'twitching', or birdwatching.*

In the west are the Pennine moorlands, which contrast with the drier, more heathery North York Moors further east. The coastal cliffs and Humber Estuary bring their own salty drama to the mix; and inland are wooded valleys, farmland, bogs, reservoirs and other large bodies of water such as Malham Tarn and Lake Semerwater.

Spring, summer and autumn each bring passing migrants, and even winter will provide the twitcher with a wealth of sightings. In the list below, we've provided an appetiser for the sorts of species you might expect to see on a tour around the region. While obviously this cannot even pretend to be exhaustive, it does offer a representative cross-section of Yorkshire's airborne visitors, ranging from moorland birds to waders, and from birds of prey to sea birds.

Curlew

If the curlew's long, turned-down beak doesn't betray it, its 'cur-loo' call certainly will. The curlew breeds in damp grassland and moorland—nowadays, it is mainly confined to the upland regions of the Dales and Moors. The Humber Estuary is the best place to spot curlews in the winter.

Dunlin

Measuring six to seven inches long, this common wader winters on the coast, but prefers to breed on peatland at the tops of the Dales, where it is distinguishable by its black belly and rusty-brown upper parts. During the spring and autumn migration, the dunlin visits inland lakes, reservoirs and gravel pits; its whistling 'trrrreee' could have you reaching for your mobile phone!

Gannet

To say that someone eats like a gannet could literally be to imply that they plummet 100 feet into the sea, surfacing with a fish between their teeth! Alternatively, it could mean that they gobble down their food voraciously, as young gannets do, when fed in the nest. This large white bird has black-tipped wings of up to six feet in length, and nests in a cliff-based colony

ABOVE *The gannet colony at Bempton Cliffs is now reckoned to number at least 1,000 pairs.*

at Flamborough Head—home to the largest mainland colony in the whole of England.

Golden plover

Identifiable, in summertime, by its gold-speckled back and smart black bib and belly, this wader breeds in the Dales and the North York Moors. In wintertime, you'll see large flocks of golden plovers gathering in arable fields around the Humber Estuary and Lower Derwent Valley.

Hen harrier

To see this greyish harrier hunting for prey is a thrilling sight. Sadly, with locals persecuting them for their perceived role in the decline of the grouse on the moors, the sight is also an increasingly rare one. Hen harriers breed in small numbers in the Dales and North York Moors, and winter on the Humber Estuary, where they may be best spotted at the RSPB's Blacktoft Sands reserve. Females and young are darker, but with a noticeable white patch on the rump.

Kingfisher

You need to be quick or lucky to see a kingfisher: these birds are as shy as they are colourful. Check out rivers, canals, lakes and reed-beds near the coast, and scan sandy banks: nest entrance-holes with white droppings around are a dead giveaway.

Knot

A wading bird that winters, but never breeds, in Britain, the knot is, in wintertime, a stocky, greyish bird, with a short black bill. Though knots can occasionally be seen around inland reservoirs, you'll most likely see them on beaches around the Humber at high tide, when they gather in jostling flocks that can reach numbers of up to several thousand.

Lapwing

Yorkshire's wealth of arable land provides good summertime breeding habitats for the lapwing, easily identified by the dark crest on the back of its head. Its purple-green plumage and white underbelly are also distinctive, and so is the call which gives it its alternative moniker: the peewit.

Merlin

Looking not unlike the kestrel, and scarcely bigger than a blackbird, the merlin is Europe's smallest falcon, and is renowned for its fast, low hunting of smaller birds. There are good breeding populations of merlins to be found up on the North York Moors.

Peregrine falcon

A quite awesome flying and killing machine, the peregrine falcon has been known to reach top speeds approaching 200mph during its 'stoop', or near-vertical plunge towards unsuspecting prey. After breeding on the moors, the peregrine moves to lower estuarine areas in the winter, where it feeds on ducks and wading birds.

Pied flycatcher

Pied flycatchers—summer visitors to Britain—are wonderful fliers. They spring out from their perches, hover, pluck a fly from the air, and then return to their perch as if they were on an elastic band. You're likeliest to see pied flycatchers in wooded valleys around the edges of the Dales and North York Moors.

Puffin

Puffins spend winters on the open sea, but in summer many come to breed at

A WEALTH OF BIRDLIFE (CONTINUED)

Flamborough Head on the Yorkshire coast, choosing exactly the same nesting site every year, and usually the same mate. Puffins are sometimes called 'sea parrots', owing to their large red, blue and yellow bills. Despite these comical protuberances, however, they are anything but bigmouths, and their gloomy 'caw' is seldom heard.

Razorbill

The best way to view colonies of razorbills is from a boat. These hook-billed sea birds like to nest in remote crevices on cliff faces; 'nest' is putting it too strongly, perhaps, as they make no effort to furnish their rocky homes with twigs or leaves. Watch out for their synchronised surface-diving displays, designed to impress potential mates.

Red grouse

If you're yomping over the moorland and a plump, coppery-coloured bird shoots off from beneath your feet, wings whirring, and cackling loudly, it's most probably a red grouse. From the 'Glorious Twelfth' of August, for four months, grouse have to run the gauntlet of shooting parties on the moors.

Ring ouzel

This pretty member of the thrush family, distinguished by a white bar across its chest, may be seen on the high moors in spring and summer. But beware: if you venture too close to its nest, this otherwise shy bird is apt to swoop over and give you a sharp peck on the head.

Shelduck

The breeding plumage of these ducks, which may be found in winter on the coast or on inland waterways, is a striking mix of green, black, white and brown. The birds are also distinguished by their scarlet bills. Shelducks patter their webbed feet on muddy ground to bring food—including shellfish and worms—to the surface.

Whooper swan

A wild swan that winters in this country, the whooper swan carries its neck upright and sports a large black bill with yellow base. In flight, it makes a distinctive, trumpet-like call. Whooper swans live and graze in family herds, particularly in the Lower Derwent Valley.

ABOVE *Wheeling seabirds ride the thermals off the Bempton Cliffs RSPB Reserve, set high up on the the chalk knuckle of Flamborough Head. Gannets, puffins, guillemots, razorbills and kittiwakes all nest at the reserve.*

THE FAME OF YORKSHIRE

THEY'RE NOT GIVEN *to flattery in Yorkshire, nor to boasting. They don't believe in making a fuss. But they do take a quiet pride in their region, which extends to honouring its more celebrated sons and daughters—whether in the arts, politics or sport. The tributes may take concrete form—in Bradford, for instance, the diverse sculptures commemorating Frederick Delius and J. B. Priestley—or they may be less tangible honours, such as the honorary doctorates awarded by the University of Leeds to Dame Barbara Hepworth, Barbara Taylor Bradford and Alan Ayckbourn. Such Yorkshire notables are not necessarily lifelong Yorkshire-dwellers. They may be native-born fugitives, such as Delius or Charles Laughton, who chose to live abroad; or they may be adopted Yorkshire-folk, such as Ayckbourn or James Herriot. So long as their reputation is well earned, Yorkshire takes them to its heart.*

Alan Ayckbourn
Playwright and theatre director
(Born 1939 in London). His long association with the Stephen Joseph Theatre in Scarborough began in 1957, as actor and stage manager, then producer, and finally artistic director. It is here that he tends to premiere his own plays—polished domestic comedies, crafted as ingeniously as farces but poignant and insightful, and in recent years somewhat sombre and sceptical. He was awarded the CBE in 1987.

Sean Bean
Actor
(Born 1959 in Sheffield). He trained at RADA in London. Among his many stage roles was Romeo, for the Royal Shakespeare Company in 1986. On screen, his rugged blond good looks generate a compelling edge. The characters he plays, on TV in particular, duly tend to display an intense sexuality and sometimes villainy: Mellors in *Lady Chatterley's Lover*, for example; other appearances include roles in *Patriot Games* (1992), *Goldeneye* (1995), and *When Saturday Comes* (1995)—based on his home-town football team, Sheffield United.

Alan Bennett
Playwright and actor
(Born 1934 in Leeds). First displayed in the *Beyond the Fringe* (1960) review, his humour—both as actor and as writer—always bears a Yorkshire hallmark: understated,

quirky, reflective. His writings include stage plays, such as *Habeas Corpus* (1973), and masterly television scripts such as *An Englishman Abroad* (1983), about the exile in Moscow of British double agent Guy Burgess.

Geoffrey Boycott
Cricketer, writer and broadcaster
(Born 1940 in Fitzwilliam). Boycott (*below*) secured his first cap for Yorkshire in 1963, and went on to captain the county from 1970

to 1978. At international level, he represented England 108 times (1964–82), scoring more than 150 Test centuries and for a time holding the world record for Test runs scored. He was famously—or notoriously—dogged and painstaking at the crease, refusing to court popularity by flamboyant yet risky strokes. After retirement, he became a perceptive and valued cricket commentator.

Charlotte, Emily and Anne Brontë
Novelists
Born in Thornton, these three remarkable sisters—Charlotte (1816–55), Emily (1818–48) and Anne (1820–49)—grew up in remote Haworth, now part of Keighley, where their father was rector. The single year of 1847 saw the publication of *Agnes Grey* by Anne, *Jane Eyre* by Charlotte, and *Wuthering Heights* by Emily. (*For further details of their lives and careers, see feature on page 52.*)

Captain James Cook
Navigator and explorer
(1728–79, born near Middlesbrough, in Marton). Cook's three great Pacific expeditions, made in Whitby-based ships from 1768 to 1779, added many details to the contemporary 18th-century map of the world, and paved the way for British settlement of New Zealand and Australia. (*For further details of the life and career of Captain Cook, see page 105.*)

Frederick Delius
Composer
(1862–1934, born in Bradford). Though Yorkshire-born and bred (of German parentage), he lived and worked abroad throughout his adulthood, mainly in France. Still, his sensuous romantic music is often classified as 'English impressionism', and was championed and popularised by the English conductor Sir Thomas Beecham. His works include *On Hearing the First Cuckoo in Spring* (1912). Another Yorkshire link was forged during the last six years of his life. Blind and paralysed, he was able to continue with his work thanks to the assistance of a committed Yorkshire-born admirer Eric Fenby, to whom Delius would dictate his musical ideas.

Guy Fawkes
Would-be regicide
(1570–1606, born in York). Though he and his fellow Roman Catholic conspirators failed to blow up the Houses of Parliament and kill King James I, he is commemorated explosively by fireworks on Bonfire Night every year on November 5.

Dame Barbara Hepworth
Sculptor
(1903–75, born in Wakefield). She studied at the Leeds School of Art, alongside Henry Moore, and later in London and on the Continent, where she was influenced by Picasso and Brancusi. With her second husband, the distinguished painter Ben Nicholson, she made key contributions to flourishing artist groups in Hampstead, London, and then in St Ives, Cornwall. Her large abstract wood carvings and metal sculptures, sensuously shaped and finished, were exhibited around the world to great acclaim. Among her many commissions is the *Single Form* (1964), outside the United Nations Building in New York. She was made a CBE in 1958, and a DBE in 1965, and died in a fire in her studio in St Ives.

THE FAME OF YORKSHIRE (CONTINUED)

James Herriot, born James Alfred Wight
Vet and author

(1916–95, born in Sunderland). A rural vet based in Thirsk from 1939 to 1990, Herriot (*right*) decided to commit some of his work experiences to paper, and became a literary sensation in his fifties. Books such as *If Only They Could Talk* (1970) and *Vet in Harness* (1974)—humorous and heart-warming memoirs of working among eccentric farmers and farm animals, pets and pet-owners—have captivated millions of admirers from all over the world. So too have the TV adaptations. He was awarded the OBE in 1979.

David Hockney
Artist

(Born 1937 in Bradford). Hockney (*below*) studied at the Bradford College of Art, then the Royal College of Art in London. After experimenting with a variety of styles, he came to public prominence with his canvases of sunny swimming pools, among them *A Bigger Splash* (1967). These were inspired

ABOVE *Ironically for a man so inextricably linked with Yorkshire, the vet James Herriot was born in Sunderland and brought up in Scotland.*

by teaching and holiday trips to California, where he now lives. Common to most of his work—whether etchings, drawings, or painted portraits and cityscapes—are qualities of innocence, directness and accessibility. His more recent work has including photo collages and opera sets.

Philip Larkin
Poet and critic

(1922–85, born in Coventry). After studying at Oxford and publishing two early novels and some poetry, he became librarian of the Brynmor Jones Library at the University of Hull in 1955, and remained there until his death 30 years later. Among his best-known poems are 'Toads' and 'Church Going' (both 1954) and the notorious 'This Be the Verse' (1971). Larkin tended to adopt a disillusioned and curmudgeonly tone in his poetry, and a distinctive mix of bitterness and lyricism. He was a noted jazz-lover and critic.

Charles Laughton
Actor

(1899–1962, born in Scarborough). Trained at RADA in London, he made his stage debut in 1926 and became a noted Shakespearean performer. In 1932 he began acting in films, promptly winning an Oscar for his role as Henry VIII. His other famous roles include Captain Bligh in *Mutiny on the Bounty* (1935) and Quasimodo in *The Hunchback of Notre Dame* (1939). In 1937, he co-founded his own film company, which he named Mayflower Pictures. He became an American citizen in 1950 and died in Hollywood.

Henry Moore
Sculptor

(1898–1986, born in Castleford). Through his characteristic late sculptures—bulky semi-abstract shapes, powerful yet humane, based on landscape features and the human body—he became probably the best-known British sculptor of the century. (*For further details of his life and career, see feature on page 146.*)

John Boynton Priestley, known as J. B. Priestley
Author

(1894–1984, born in Bradford). Priestley began his writing career as a journalist and literary critic, and throughout his life continued to produce influential essays—in books, periodicals and broadcasts—on such subjects as war, travel, Englishness

and social decadence. But it is as a novelist and dramatist that he is best remembered.

His versatility was remarkable—grim realist fiction alongside cheerful novels such as *The Good Companions* (1929); light stage comedies alongside unsettling 'time plays' such as *Dangerous Corner* (1932). It would seem he declined both a knighthood and a peerage, but in 1977, as a grand old man of English letters, he decided to accept the Order of Merit.

Joseph Priestley
Scientist, clergyman and writer

(1733–1804, born in Fieldhead, near Leeds). He became a Presbyterian minister in 1755. As a distinguished amateur scientist, he is best known for isolating and identifying oxygen, in 1774. His other writings were very wide-ranging: psychology, education, grammar, theology and politics. On these last two subjects he was notoriously unorthodox. As a clergyman, he helped to launch the Unitarian movement in 1791. As a radical political commentator, he acclaimed the French Revolution and was publicly reviled—so much so that he left England in 1794 and spent the rest of his life in America.

...rence Sterne
...velist

...13–68, born in Clonmel, Ireland). After ...impoverished boyhood, he was sent to ...ifax Grammar School and then studied ...Cambridge. He returned to Yorkshire as ...lergyman, in a parish near York. His comic ...sterpiece *The Life and Opinions of Tristram ...andy, Gent* was published in nine thin ...umes between 1760 and 1767. He moved ...Coxwold, where 'Shandy Hall' still stands, ...ugh he lived mainly abroad, for the sake ...his health. In 1768 he duly published ...*Sentimental Journey Through France and ...ly*. His writing may have been eccentric ...d sentimental, but its comic techniques and ...axed structuring contributed to the ...bsequent development of English fiction.

...rbara Taylor Bradford
...velist

...orn 1933 in Leeds). Barbara Taylor Bradford ...rted out as a reporter on the *Yorkshire ...ening Post*, and later became a fashion ...itor and columnist on Fleet Street. Her early

books were mainly homemaking nonfiction; then in 1979 her career took a new turn when her novel *A Woman of Substance* appeared. A dozen equally accomplished romantic novels have followed, half of which have now been made into successful TV mini-series. Worldwide sales ...the books are approaching 60 million ...pies, in some 38 languages. With her ...usband and business partner Robert, she ...w lives mainly in New York.

...ederick Sewards Trueman, OBE,
...nown as Fred or Freddy Trueman
...ricketer, writer and broadcaster

...Born 1931 in Stainton, South Yorkshire). ...fter his long and record-breaking tenure ...s a county player for the Yorkshire County ...ricket Club (1949–68) and his 67 Tests ...presenting England, he remains a ...ouchstone for commitment and ferocity ...s a fast bowler, and a legendary figure ...n the game.

William Wilberforce
Philanthropist and social reformer

(1759–1833, born in Hull). A Yorkshire MP from 1780 to 1825, he adopted evangelical Christianity in the mid-1780s, becoming a leading light in the 'Clapham Sect', and promoting moral revival and welfare schemes. Above all, from 1788 to 1807 he led the struggle for the abolition of the British slave trade. That achieved, he began campaigning for the abolition of slavery itself, which duly came to pass in the year of his death.

Harold Wilson,
Baron Wilson of Rievaulx
Politician

(1916–95, born in Huddersfield). An Oxford-trained economist, he became a Labour MP in 1945, and party leader in 1963. He was Prime Minister from 1964 to 1970 and from 1974 to 1976. Through crises such as Northern Ireland, Rhodesia and entry into the Common Market, he maintained his deft political touch and dry wit. He resigned suddenly in 1976, and was made a life peer in 1983.

YORKSHIRE IN FILMS AND ON TV

ABOVE *The golden age of steam, as depicted in* The Railway Children.

LEFT *Quiet for now, Compo and his mates are sure to have some new scam afoot sooner rather than later.*

YORKSHIRE'S REMOTE stone villages, wind-blown moorlands, industrial towns and rugged coast have afforded rich pickings for TV producers and film-makers seeking decent locations, and have framed everything from light-hearted rural sagas to gritty tales of urban life.

Grand old Castle Howard was the opulent setting for 1981's acclaimed television adaptation of *Brideshead Revisited*, Evelyn Waugh's classic saga of prewar upper-class life. At the other end of the social scale, the BBC's long-running series *Last of the Summer Wine* has since 1973 familiarised viewers with the town of Holmfirth, setting for the whimsical antics of Compo, Foggy, Clegg and Nora Batty. Just as Holmfirth has now become a major tourist attraction, so the BBC series *All Creatures Great and Small*, based on former vet James Herriot's experiences in Yorkshire's farmland, has drawn tourists to the region in their droves. Yorkshire TV's police series *Heartbeat*

began similarly, as the reminiscences of a Yorkshire bobby in the 1960s.

Films set in Yorkshire have viewed life far less rosily. Typical of these are *Billy Liar* (1963), in which a young Tom Courtenay starred as a compulsive dreamer; and *Kes* (1969), the tale of a Barnsley schoolboy who escapes from his drab urban life by rescuing and training a young kestrel. *The Full Monty* (1997), in which unemployed Sheffield steel workers forge a new career as strippers, weaves comedy and social concern. Needless to say, Emily Brontë's *Wuthering Heights* has been filmed twice, in the thirties and again in the nineties.

Many other films have benefited from a Yorkshire backdrop, but none more so than *The Railway Children* (1970), worked from E. Nesbit's Edwardian tale of a family befriended by staff at a moorland station, in which the Keighley and Worth Valley Railway's beautiful Oakworth Station was as worthy of star billing as the leading actors.

HISTORIC HOTELS, INNS AND PUBS

The Black Bull Otley E5
Legend has it that during the Civil War a party of Cromwell's Ironsides descended upon this venerable hostelry and drank it dry on the eve of the Battle of Marston Moor—a tale recalled by the picture of Oliver Cromwell in the bar.

The Black Swan Helmsley H3
The Black Swan comprises three buildings: Tudor rectory, Elizabethan coaching inn and Georgian house. Long the venue for Helmsley's social engagements, and popular with visiting shooting parties, the Black Swan can count William and Dorothy Wordsworth among its many past guests. The stone that forms the rockery and the doorway to the cellar is thought to have been lifted from Helmsley Castle walls.

The Black Swan York G5
One of York's oldest inns, the Black Swan stands on the site of an early 15th-century manor house, some of whose timbers may still be in place within the present building.

It retains many of its original features, among them a secret chamber thought to have been used for cockfighting, and a secret passage linking it to nearby St Cuthbert's Church. Predictably, a ghost is said to wander the pub.

Coiners Halifax D6
Formerly a bank, after major refurbishment this century-old building opened as a smart pub in 1994—though the safe door in the cellar is a dead giveaway as to its former life.

The Dry Dock Leeds E6
Fronting the Dry Dock is a cheerily painted, 50-ton barge that traded on the Trent and Humber rivers and on the Aire and Calder Navigation canal, until its retirement in 1993.

The Fauconberg Arms Coxwold G3
Built on the site of a 12th-century Augustinian monastery, the Fauconberg is supposed to contain a tomb holding the headless body of Oliver Cromwell. Its name derives from the man who married Cromwell's daughter, Mary.

The George Hotel Hull K6
Hull's George Hotel claims to own the country's smallest window—staff leave customers to locate it for themselves—and to possess a ghost, which sets the hotel's ancient timbers creaking on the stroke of midnight.

The Old Hill Inn Chapel-le-Dale B3
Built in 1615, the isolated Hill Inn has serve up pints to such eminent guests as Winsto Churchill, Prince Charles, William Turner a John Buchan. If your visit coincides with a party of walkers and cavers, a cracking nig could lie in store.

The King's Arms York G5
The River Ouse overflows several times a year, yet although water levels sometimes reach the top of the King's Arms' bar count

its doors remain open, and patrons get to enjoy 'flood parties' at which beer that woul otherwise be ruined by the flooding is given away free.

The Tan Hill Inn Keld C2
Perched between the tops of Arkengarthdale and Swaledale, the Tan Hill is Great Britain's highest inn, at 1,732 feet. It is sited at an intersection of old drovers' roads, and every May a sheep show is held just outside.

The White Bear Masham E3
When Masham's original White Bear was destroyed by a German bomb in 1941, its licence was quickly transferred to some nearby brewery cottages, and today's version was born. A stuffed polar bear, shot by a local man in Alaska in 1901, sits behind the bar.

CULINARY YORKSHIRE

LEFT *Yorkshire pudding was first mentioned in a 1747 cookery book, Hannah Glasse's* Art of Cookery. *'It is an excellent good pudding', she wrote; 'the gravy of the meat eats well with it'.*

SOME FOODS WERE plainly made for each other: fish and chips, strawberries and cream, bangers and mash—and, of course, roast beef and Yorkshire pudding. Originally served either as a starter or as a side dish to mutton, Yorkshire's most famous delicacy is a fluffy baked batter pudding of eggs, flour and milk. The region's culinary output doesn't begin and end with its famous pud, however. If a full roast sounds like hard work, you may prefer a spot of Wensleydale soup, in which onions, potatoes, cider and walnuts are blended with Wensleydale cheese to ambrosial effect.

Yorkshire would seem to have harboured some exceedingly sweet tooths down through the years, judging by the region's lengthy checklist of sweets and cakes. Among them are parkin cake, a spicy ginger and black-treacle cake traditionally eaten to mark Guy Fawkes' Night; and the intriguingly named fat rascals—currant and raisin scones, originally known as turf cakes, after the turf fires over which they would have been cooked. Yorkshire curd tart is another local delight: sharper in taste than conventional cheesecake, it is said to have been first eaten by Wolds shepherds, and is delicious topped with fresh or stewed fruit. After any of these rich treats, you'll be glad of a couple of Pontefract (or 'Pomfret') cakes—actually soft, round and flat liquorice sweets—to clear your palate.

CALENDAR OF FESTIVALS AND EVENTS A SELECTION

YORKSHIRE OFFERS *an enormous variety of annual events, reflecting customs and culture both ancient and modern, of which a selection is presented below. For detailed listings contact the relevant tourist office (see below). They will also be able to provide exact dates for events, which vary from year to year.*

JANUARY

HUBBERHOLME LAND LETTING Ancient auction of letting of church pasture land at the George Inn.

FEBRUARY

YORK JORVIK VIKING FESTIVAL Crafts, boat-burning, combat and music at York's Viking museum.

MARCH

HALIFAX, HEBDEN BRIDGE, HEPTONSTALL AND MYTHOLMROYD PACE EGG PLAYS Local children enact the battle of St George and the dragon, every Good Friday.

KIPLINGCOTE DERBY (3rd Thursday) England's oldest horse race, first run in 1519.

APRIL

HARROGATE ROYAL HORTICULTURAL SOCIETY SPRING FLOWER SHOW

HORTON-IN-RIBBLESDALE THREE PEAKS RACE

OSSETT WORLD COAL-CARRYING CHAMPIONSHIP

MAY

BEVERLEY EARLY MUSIC FESTIVAL Venues include historic houses and medieval churches.

ILKLEY WHARFEDALE MUSIC FESTIVAL A week of competitive singing, playing and poetry.

LEEDS INTERNATIONAL MUSIC FESTIVAL

MYTHOLMROYD WORLD DOCK PUDDING CONTEST Contestants try to bake the best dock pudding, made of dock leaves and bacon fat.

SWALEDALE FESTIVAL Various locations in northern dales (May to June). Two-weeks of brass bands, classical music, folk, jazz, theatre and crafts.

WHITBY PLANTING OF THE PENNY HEDGE Originates from 1159 when hunters set about a monk who was guarding a boar pursued by the hunt; the hunters were ordered to erect a 'penance hedge'.

JUNE

BEVERLEY BEVERLEY & EAST RIDING FOLK FESTIVAL

BRADFORD FESTIVAL (June to July) One of Britain's largest community arts events, including the two-day Asian Mela festival (*pictured below*).

HARROGATE CRICKET FESTIVAL (June or July).

KNARESBOROUGH BED RACE Teams push a variety of beds through the town and across the river.

OTLEY CARNIVAL Floats, parades and stalls.

SCARBOROUGH SCARBOROUGH FAYRE MORRIS DANCE FESTIVAL

JULY

HARROGATE GREAT YORKSHIRE SHOW Largest and most famous of Yorkshire's agricultural shows. International Festival. Yorkshire's premier arts festival, with music, theatre and other events.

HELMSLEY GREATER YORKSHIRE TRACTION ENGINE CLUB STEAM FAIR AND RALLY At Duncombe Park.

HUDDERSFIELD CARIBBEAN CARNIVAL

MASHAM STEAM ENGINE AND FAIR ORGAN RALLY

OXENHOPE STRAW RACE Fancy-dress race, with contestants carrying bales of straw.

SHEFFIELD LORD MAYOR'S PARADE

YORK EARLY MUSIC FESTIVAL The largest event of its kind in Britain.

AUGUST

EGTON BRIDGE OLD GOOSEBERRY SHOW Contest to produce the heaviest gooseberry.

HARROGATE TRANS-PENNINE VINTAGE COMMERCIAL VEHICLES RUN FROM MANCHESTER TO HARROGATE

LEEDS CARNIVAL Bank Holiday spectacular, with parade, marching bands, crafts and stalls.

RIPON ST WILFRID'S PROCESSION A mitre-wearing 'St Wilfrid' on horseback in a procession to the cathedral for a service to mark the saint's return from exile in 686.

WEST WITTON BURNING OF BARTLE Ceremonial torching of the effigy of a legendary outlaw.

WHITBY FOLK WEEK Features some 600 events. Regatta and Carnival.

SEPTEMBER

HARDRAW BRASS BAND CONTEST

HARROGATE AUTUMN FLOWER SHOW Includes a contest to find the heaviest onion.

HULL INTERNATIONAL FESTIVAL Month-long cultural event including an Open House Weekend. International Sea Shanty Festival.

MASHAM SHEEP FAIR Morris dancing, tug of war, crafts, handbell ringers.

PATELEY BRIDGE NIDDERDALE SHOW Dry-stone walling, sheepdog trials and show jumping.

ROTHERHAM JAZZ AND FOLK FESTIVAL Marching bands, ceilidhs and numerous free events.

SOWERBY BRIDGE RUSHBEARING CEREMONY Cart bearing rushes to be strewn on church floors; street entertainment.

OCTOBER

HULL FAIR A venerable 700-year-old funfair.

LEEDS INTERNATIONAL FILM FESTIVAL

NOVEMBER

HULL LITERATURE FESTIVAL Readings and talks.

DECEMBER

YORK ST NICHOLAS FAYRE

USEFUL INFORMATION

Listed below are the details of Tourist Information Centres for a selection of Yorkshire's popular holiday areas. Please note that these details may be subject to change.

BRADFORD
Central Library, Prince's Way
Bradford, West Yorkshire
BD1 1NN
Tel: (01274) 753678

HARROGATE
Royal Bath Assembly Rooms
Crescent Road, Harrogate
HG1 2RP
Tel: (01423) 537300

HULL
1 Paragon Street, Hull
HU1 3NA
Tel: (01482) 223559

LEEDS
Leeds City Station, Leeds
LS1 1PL
Tel: (0113) 242 5242

PICKERING
Eastgate Car Park
Pickering, North Yorkshire
YO18 7DU
Tel: (01751) 473791

RICHMOND
Friary Gardens
Richmond, North Yorkshire
DL10 4AJ
Tel: (01748) 850252

SHEFFIELD
Peace Gardens
Sheffield,
South Yorkshire
S1 2HH
Tel: (0114) 273 4671

WHITBY
Langborne Road
Whitby,
North Yorkshire
YO21 1YN
Tel: (01947) 602674

YORK
The Grey Rooms
Exhibition Square,
York
YO1 2HB
Tel: (01904) 621756

For general information, contact:

YORKSHIRE TOURIST BOARD
312 Tadcaster Road, York
YO2 2HF
Tel: (01904) 707070

The following websites may also be of interest. Each one contains links to further Yorkshire sites.

Digital Yorkshire:
http://www.digital-yorkshire.co.uk/

Yorkshire Tourist Board:
http://www.ytb.org.uk/

Yorkshire Information Centre:
http://www.yorkshirenet.co.uk/

INDEX

Note: page numbers in **bold** refer to captions for illustrations

ACKNOWLEDGMENTS

The editors gratefully acknowledge the use of information taken from the following publications during the preparation of this volume:

AA Country Towns & Villages of Britain, Drive Publications Limited 1985
And The Glory by R. A. Edwards, Maney 1985
Around Island Britain, The Reader's Digest Association Limited 1996
Britain: a Lonely Planet Travel Survival Kit by Richard Everist, Bryn Thomas and Tony Wheeler, Lonely Planet Publications 1995
The Dales of Yorkshire: a Portrait by Richard Muir, Macmillan 1991
The Dictionary of Cricket by M. Rundell, Oxford University Press 1995
The Encyclopaedia Britannica
England: the Rough Guide, Rough Guides 1996
English Heritage Book of Roman York by Patrick Ottaway, Batsford/English Heritage 1993
Exploring England's Heritage—Yorkshire to Humberside by Jane Hatcher, HMSO 1994
History of World Religions by Katharine Savage, Bodley Head 1966
James Herriot's Yorkshire by James Herriot, Michael Joseph 1979
John Hillaby's Yorkshire by John Hillaby, Constable 1986
The Landscape of Roman Britain by Ken Dark and Petra Dark, Sutton 1997
Life in Roman Britain by Joan P. Alcock, Batsford/English Heritage 1996

The Mouseman of Kilburn by James Thompson, Dalesman 1984
The North York Moors National Park by Ian Carstairs, Webb & Bower 1987
Old Yorkshire by Richard Muir, Joseph 1987
Ordnance Survey Motoring Atlas: Britain, Ordnance Survey and Hamlyn 1996
Our Island Heritage, 3 vols, The Reader's Digest Association Limited 1988
The Oxford Illustrated History of Britain edited by Kenneth O. Morgan, Oxford University Press 1984
The Penguin Dictionary of English and European History, 1485– 1789 by E. N. Williams, Penguin 1980
The Reader's Digest Illustrated Guide to Britain's Coast, The Reader's Digest Association Limited 1996
The Reader's Digest Touring Guide to Britain, The Reader's Digest Association Limited 1992
The Story of Britain by Roy Strong, Hutchinson, 1996
The Story of Language by C. L. Barber, Pan Books 1972
Victorian Yorkshire by J. R. Thackrah, Dalesman 1979
Viking Expansion Westwards by M. Magnusson, Bodley Head 1973
Walking the Dales by Mike Harding, Michael Joseph 1986
The Yorkshire Dales by Geoffrey N. Wright, David & Charles 1986
The Yorkshire Dales by Marie Hartley and Joan Ingilby, J. M. Dent & Sons Ltd 1980
The Yorkshire Dales by Ron and Marlene Freethy, John Donald Publishers Ltd 1991
Yorkshire Dales National Park by Tony Waltham, Webb & Bower 1987
Yorkshire from AD 1000 by David Hey, Longman 1986

PICTURE ACKNOWLEDGMENTS

T = top; *C* = centre; *B* = bottom; *L* = left; *R* = right

Front Cover Michael Busselle **Back Cover** *T* Paul Ridsdale *B* Northern Picture Library **2** Getty Images/Rob Talbot **4** Joe Cornish **6-7** David Tarn **10–11** Joe Cornish **12** *TL* David Tarn *TR* Tim Woodcock/TWP **13** Mike Kipling Photography **14** Paul Ridsdale **17** Harewood House Trust Ltd/Open mid March to end of October annually **18** *T* Bruce Coleman Ltd *CL* The National Trust Photo Library/Matthew Antrobus **20** Ardea, London/Richard Vaughan **21** Images Colour Library Ltd **22** Tim Smith **24–5** David Tarn **26** ALLSPORT/Clive Mason **27** Images Colour Library Ltd **28** *T* Frank Graham/Painting by Ronald Embleton from *Landscape of Roman Britain BC* English Heritage *BR* English Heritage **30** *TL* Milepost Ninety-Two and a Half *C* Woodfall Wild Images/John Morrison **31** Woodfall Wild Images/David Woodfall **33** *T* Roger Scruton *CR* Collections/ John & Eliza Forder **34** *TL* The Bridgeman Art Library/Victoria and Albert Museum, London *TR* John Cleare/Mountain Camera **35** Harrogate International Centre **36** *BL* National Museums & Galleries of Wales *BC* The Bridgeman Art Library/Thyssen-Bornemisza Collection *BR* York Minster Archives/MS.XVI.K.6 fol.25V/Reproduced by kind permission of the Dean and Chapter of York **38–9** Paul Ridsdale **39** RSPB Images **40** *TR* Cephas Picture Library/ Mike Herringshaw *C* Guzelian Photography *BR* Guzelian Photography **41** The Bridgeman Art Library/Harrogate Museums and Art Gallery, North Yorkshire **42** John Cleare/Mountain Camera **43** Images Colour Library Ltd **44** Paul Ridsdale **45** *C* Collections/Roger Scruton *BR* Telegraph Colour Library/Denise Binks **46** Andy Williams **47** Jim Winkley **48–9** NHPA/David Woodfall **49** *T* Collections/ Robert Hallmann *B* The Bridgeman Art Library/Towner Art Gallery, Eastbourne/ Laurence Pollinger Limited on behalf of the Estate of Mrs J. C. Robinson **50** *TL* The Bridgeman Art Library/Towneley Hall Art Gallery & Museum, Burnley *BL* David Goble LRPS/Sealed Knot Photographic Unit *BR* The Bridgeman Art Library/Philip Mould, Historical Portraits Ltd, London **52** By courtesy of the National Portrait Gallery, London **53** Reader's Digest **54** *TL* Paul Ridsdale *TR* Collections/Mike Kipling *BL* Robert Harding Picture Library/Brian Harrison *BR* Woodfall Wild Images/David Woodfall **56** Trevor Jones Thoroughbred Photography/Trevor Jones **58** *TL* W. R. Mitchell *TR* Woodfall Wild Images/John Morrison *CL* University of Bradford/ Donated by Bill Mitchell **60** Collections/ David M. Hughes **61** *L* Jim Winkley *R* Mary Evans Picture Library **62** The Huddersfield Daily Examiner **63** *TL* Yorkshire Television *TR* Guzelian Photography/John Houlihan **64** *TL* Guzelian Photography/John Houlihan *CL* Guzelian Photography/John Houlihan **66** Thames & Hudson, London/from John James, *The History of Bradford*, 1841 **67** The Lebrecht Collection/Chris Stock **68** *T* Black Dyke Band Promotions Ltd *L* Jim Winkley **69** Getty Images **70** Collections/Dorothy Burrows **72–3** Ted Bottle **73** BBC Picture Archives **74** BBC Picture Archives **75** Performing Arts Library/Michael Diamond **76** *BL* York Early Music Festival *BR* Hull Tourism **77** BBC Picture Archives **78** Getty Images/Rosemary Weller **79** *TR* The Bridgeman Art Library/Marylebone Cricket Club, London *CR* The Bridgeman Art Library/Marylebone Cricket Club, London **80** The Bridgeman Art Library/Marylebone Cricket Club, London **81** The Tate Gallery, London/Louise Philippe Boitard **82** Reader's Digest/Colin Tatham/ Cricket Memorabilia Society **83** Punch Limited **84** *BL* John Wyand *BC* ALLSPORT/ Clive Mason *BR* Colin Molyneux **85** ALLSPORT **86** *T* The Independent/Robert Hallam *CL* Colorsport **87** *CR* ALLSPORT/Adrian Murrell *BC* Woodfall Wild Images/John Morrison **88** Reader's Digest/Colin Tatham/Cricket Memorabilia Society **89** ALLSPORT/Graham Chadwick **90** ALLSPORT/Adrian Murrell **91** The Illustrated London News Picture Library **92** Action Plus/Glyn Kirk **93** *TR* Action Plus/Neil Tingle *BC* Colorsport **94** Magnum Photos/Martin Parr **96** ALLSPORT/ Mike Powell **98** The Bridgeman Art Library/Alecto Historical Editions, London

99 *C* Peter Newark's Pictures/Illustration by R. Caton Woodville *BR* Th Bridgeman Art Library/British Library, London **100** *T* Jim Winkley *TL* Jim Winkle **101** By courtesy of the National Portrait Gallery, London **103** *CR* Quake Tapestry Scheme *BL* Nestlé UK Ltd **104** *TL* The Illustrated London News Pictur Library *TR* Dorothy Thelwall **106** E. T. Archive **107** *TR* Images Colour Library Lt *BR* Ross Parry Picture Agency **109** *TL* Collections/Mike Kipling *TR* The Bridgema Art Library/National Maritime Museum, London *CR* Robert Harding Pictur Library/Science Museum **110** Woodfall Wild Images/John Morrison **111** *BL* Bruc Coleman Ltd/Chris James *BR* Collections/John & Liza Forder **112** G.W. Morriso **113** Bruce Coleman Ltd/Allan G. Potts **115** Andy Williams **116** Harry Ramsden' Plc **117** Johnson Consultancy **118** Roger Scruton **119** *C* Donald Innes/A. Marti *CR* Donald Innes **120** Bretts Fish Restaurant **121** T&R Theakston **122** *TL* Reader' Digest/Jon Wyand *C* Roger Scruton/Malton Brewery *CR* Black Sheep Brewer **123** Roger Scruton **124** Wensleydale Creamery **125** Andy Williams **126** *T* Collections/Gary R. Smith *CR* English Heritage/T. Ball *BL* Bibliothèqu Municipale, Dijon **127** Andy Williams **129** British Wool Marketing Board **130** (Collections/Roger Scruton *BR* Collections/Roger Scruton **132** Aspect/Simon Mile **134–5** Martin Peters **136** *CL* Joe Cornish *BL* Collections/Dorothy Burrow *BC* Cephas Picture Library/Nigel Blythe **137** Collections/Richard Whitehead **13** *CL* Reader's Digest/Neil Holmes *BC* Harrogate Museums and Arts **139** *TL* And Williams *TR* Collections/Gary Smith *C* Yorkshire Museum *BR* Reader's Digest Neil Holmes **140** *TL* Woodfall Wild Images/John Morrison *BL* Collections McQuillan & Brown **140–41** Woodfall Wild Images/John Morrison **141** Mich Sharp **142** *TC* York Archaeological Trust *TR* Art Resource, N.Y./The Pierpor Morgan Library *BL* York Archaeological Trust *BR* Brenda Harrison **143** *TR* Roya Armouries *BR* Collections/Dorothy Burrows **144** Collections/Gary Smith **145** *T* W. R. Outhwaite & Son *C* Whitby Museum *BL* Collections/Dorothy Burrow *BR* Collections/Gary R. Smith **146** *TR* Henry Moore Sculpture Trust/Jerr Hardman-Jones/© David Nash 1998 All rights reserved DACS *C* Reader's Digest Neil Holmes **147** *TL* Leeds City Art Galleries *C* Woodfall Wild Images/ Joh Morrison *BR* Calderdale Tourism **148** *TR* Guzelian Photography/Steve Forres *CL* M.R.P. Photography *BL* The Illustrated London News Picture Librar **149** *T* Hogg Design Limited *BR* Woodfall Wild Images/John Morrison **150** *T* Collections/Liz Stares *BR* Collections/Gary R. Smith **151** *TR* English Heritag *CL* E. T. Archive *BR* English Heritage **152** *TL* English Heritage *CR* Collections Gary R. Smith **153** *TR* English Heritage *CL* English Heritage *BL* English Heritag **154** *BL* Andrew Lawson *BR* English Heritage **155** *TL* Robert Harding Pictur Library *TR* By courtesy of The National Portrait Gallery, London **156** *TR* Th National Trust Photo Library/Matthew Antrobus *BL* The National Trust Phot Library/Mark Fiennes **157** *CL* Collections/Roger Scruton *BC* Collections/Roge Scruton **158** *TL* The National Trust Photo Library/Charlie Waite *C* Andre Lawson *CR* Cephas Picture Library/Dorothy Burrows **159** *TR* Ardea, Londo John Mason *CR* Joe Cornish *BR* Collections/Graeme Peacock **160** *TL* Image Colour Library Ltd *TR* Roger Scruton *BL* North York Moors National Par *BR* NHPA/David Woodfall **161** Collections/Gary R. Smith **162** NHPA/ Davi Woodfall **163** *T* Ardea, London/David & Katie Urry *BR* NHPA/Henry Ausloo **164** NHPA/John Buckingham **165** Rex Features Ltd/Nils Jorgensen **166** *TR* Re Features Ltd/Julian Calder *CL* Guzelian Photography/Asadour Guzelian *CR* Gett Images **167** *CL* Rex Features Ltd/Richard McLaren *C* BBC Picture Archives *CR* Th Ronald Grant Archive/ABP **168** *CL* The Anthony Blake Photo Library/G. Buntroc *CR* Woodfall Wild Images/John Morrison **169** Tim Smith

SEPARATIONS Litho Origination Group PLC, London

PAPER Périgord-Condat, France

PRINTING AND BINDING Printer Industria Gráfica SA, Barcelona, Spain

615001-2